MW00576041

Advance Praise for
Damned If You Do

"A revealing insider account of international aid in Myanmar at a time of enormous dynamism, upheaval, hope, and violence. International aid was a big part of both the country's historic success as well as catastrophic failures from 2011 to 2021, with many lessons to be learned not just for Myanmar but for our increasingly fragile world."

—Thant Myint U, renowned historian and author of *The Hidden History of Burma: Race, Capitalism, and Democracy in the 21st Century,* a *New York Times* Critics Top Book of 2019

"In this honest account, Goldstein brilliantly describes her efforts to use foreign aid to promote better treatment for the Rohingya minority in Myanmar. Public opinion, political paralysis, and enormous pressure from within the World Bank conspired against her. Damned If You Do *is essential reading for everyone interested in Myanmar, foreign aid, and the moral dilemmas we face in dealing with an imperfect world."*

—Scot Marciel, former US ambassador to Myanmar and fellow at the Shorenstein Asia-Pacific Research Center at Stanford University

"A must-read for students and practitioners of international development. Goldstein documents in heartbreaking detail how the best of intentions falls short within an obsolete aid paradigm. Damned If You Do *is a clarion call for change in foreign aid to grapple simultaneously with global threats and localized conflicts."*

—Mary P. Callahan, expert author on civil-military relations and foreign aid, and associate professor of international studies at the University of Washington

"Damned If You Do *is a long-overdue perspective on foreign aid in Myanmar. Ellen has written a story that no one else could write—a raw and unabashed narrative about the unwinnable position in which we find ourselves as both foreign and national aid workers in Myanmar."*

—Shwe Kyar, Senior Specialist for the World Bank Group Myanmar

DAMNED IF YOU DO

Foreign Aid and My Struggle to Do Right ***in Myanmar***

ELLEN GOLDSTEIN

Ballast Books, LLC
www.ballastbooks.com

ISBN: 978-1-955026-97-0

Printed in United States of America

Published by Ballast Books
www.ballastbooks.com

For more information, bulk orders, appearances, or speaking requests, please email info@ballastbooks.com or visit www.ellengoldsteinauthor.com.

For the many courageous people fighting for human rights, rule of law, and true democracy in Myanmar.

Author's Note: The World Bank has reviewed this manuscript prior to publication. It is a memoir based on my experiences in Myanmar in 2017–2019 and in the United States thereafter. Names and identifying characteristics have been changed and characters combined to protect friends and colleagues in Myanmar. Episodes are interpretations based on recollections by the author. Others may recall these situations differently. The opinions and characterizations in the manuscript are mine alone and do not represent official positions of the World Bank.

Ellen Goldstein
July 2023

Table of Contents

PROLOGUE

Aung San Suu Kyi Testifies

It is not so much what she says but rather that she shows up at all. She is wearing a somber dark blue jacket and plain blue shawl over her traditional long silk skirt or *longyi,* a reflection of the seriousness of the day. Her hair is adorned with fresh flowers, a circle of pink and yellow roses that seems at odds with the mood of the day. It is a day of testimony at the International Court of Justice against charges of genocide. It is December 2019.

She did not have to go. Aung San Suu Kyi, the leader of Myanmar's civilian government, could have left Myanmar's notoriously brutal and corrupt military, the Tatmadaw, to defend themselves at the court. Instead, a woman who rose up against five decades of a brutally repressive military regime to become the standard-bearer for the country's 1988 democracy movement and who endured decades of house arrest at the hands of the military junta chose to testify at the International Court of Justice at The Hague. A global democracy icon who won the Nobel Peace Prize in 1991 for her nonviolent struggle for democracy and human rights chose to defend the brutal actions of the Tatmadaw.

Yet I am not surprised, only sad and frustrated. I lived and worked in Myanmar as the Director of the World Bank, an international organization devoted to eliminating poverty. And I sat with Aung San Suu Kyi and members of her cabinet to decide how to spend several billion dollars in soft loans to lift families out of poverty. Expand electricity to rural areas? Provide stipends for poor children to attend school? Improve the environment for small businesses? Government defined its priorities to reduce poverty, and the World Bank provided technical and financial support to help get it done. That is the way it works in developing countries throughout the world. I have worked in many of them.

My arrival in Myanmar in mid-2017 was considered by the World Bank to be an upgrade for the country: its first director-level appointment. This reflected the unbridled optimism of the international community in establishing democracy, civilian rule, and an open society after decades of isolation and repression. Aung San Suu Kyi embodied everything we were trying to do there. So it was expected that international organizations like mine would expand their presence on the ground in Myanmar before and after she took power in 2016.

But today's testimony is her nadir. She simply cannot go any lower, cannot fail more in her moral leadership, cannot demonstrate more what the world had initially not understood: she is a child of the military, even beholden to them for her rise to power.

Yet even the limited power that she has been granted by the military has not been used to promote democracy and protect human rights in her country.

I am not in Myanmar on this ignominious day. I am on the sidelines now, stripped of my position there, watching Aung San Suu Kyi's testimony from my new home in the suburbs of Washington, DC. I was forced out by the World Bank—fired, really—although I chose to jump before I was pushed.

Aung San Suu Kyi is eloquent in her testimony. She honors the court and expresses sympathy "for those who have had to flee their homes and are now living in camps in Cox's Bazar," which is over the border in Bangladesh.

She explains the complex history and ethnic relations of Myanmar and affirms that "we shall adhere steadfastly to our commitment to nonviolence, human rights, national reconciliation, and the rule of law. There will be no tolerance of human rights violations in Rakhine or elsewhere in Myanmar."[1]

I no longer believe her.

She says the right things. She always does. Or enough of the right things that diplomats and development workers like me cling to her words in the hope that they are true. In the hope that they will be translated into progress on the ground. But as she speaks, my eyes widen, and I shake my head and cluck my tongue in disbelief. How can I believe her when I have heard these same explanations and promises so many times before? She is repeating excuses I have heard for more than two years—excuses that stand in the way of truth and accountability.

She says that the court and the world had "an incomplete and misleading factual picture of the situation in Rakhine State in Myanmar" and that the world misunderstood the meaning of military "clearance operations." She explains the military was only interested in the Arakan Rohingya Salvation Army (ARSA), a terrorist organization active in Rakhine State.

She tells us that an Independent Commission of Enquiry is investigating, so it would not be appropriate to make any judgment or take any action.

She says that "it cannot be ruled out that disproportionate force was used by members of the Defense Services in some cases in disregard of international humanitarian law, or that they did not distinguish clearly enough between ARSA fighters and civilians."

But then she goes on to say that "these are determinations to be made in the due course of the criminal justice process, not by any individual in the Myanmar government."

---

[1] "Transcript: Aung San Suu Kyi's Speech at the ICJ in Full," *Al Jazeera*, December 12, 2019, https://www.aljazeera.com/news/2019/12/12/transcript-aung-san-suu-kyis-speech-at-the-icj-in-full.

She could add, "And certainly not by me," but this is already well understood by those of us who have worked with her and felt the disappointment of a global democracy icon failing to speak up for those who need it most.

Will anybody ever take accountability for the three-quarters of a million people forced to flee their homes with nothing, wading across the Naf River and seeking refuge in an unwelcoming Bangladesh in August 2017? Will anybody ever take accountability for the hundreds of villages burned to the ground and the thousands of women raped, men killed, and babies thrown into raging fires?

CHAPTER 1

Becoming a Do-Gooder

(1960-2012)

Who am I to ask such troubling questions about Myanmar?

It is important to say what I am not. I am not from Myanmar (formerly known as Burma). I am not a scholar of Myanmar, a historian, or an expert on human rights, ethnicity, or conflict resolution.

I am an international bureaucrat: Director of the World Bank, a specialized agency of the United Nations with nearly two hundred countries as members. The institution was born in 1946 to finance post-World War II reconstruction under the watchful eye of its largest shareholder, the United States. At the time, the other countries of the world—all shareholders—agreed to name an American as World Bank president, a convention that persists to this day. With the success of European reconstruction by the 1960s, the World Bank turned its gaze to development of low- and middle-income countries in Africa, Asia, and Latin America. Its money and technical advice for economic development helped combat global poverty while furthering the values of liberal Western democracies and their market economies.

I joined the World Bank several decades later, in the mid-1980s, after finishing graduate school for global development policy. It was the world's premier development agency, attracting top-flight academics and development thinkers. It felt like I had won the lottery. My dream career.

I became a global foot soldier in the war to eliminate poverty. I was like tens of thousands of foreigners working overseas in the aid business—whether in international organizations like the World Bank, national agencies like USAID, or charitable nongovernmental organizations like Care. And like most such foot soldiers, I took pride in being able to work in some of the world's craziest, most difficult environments, deploying wherever I was sent and hitting the ground running to make good things happen.

I rose slowly through the ranks of a male-dominated organization. I was considered too small and too female to be taken seriously at first, yet simultaneously chided for being too assertive and abrasive. I blamed myself and struggled to smooth the rough edges, rising into the managerial ranks. At one point, I became a whistleblower, exposing a sexual relationship and professional favoritism between my boss and a subordinate. I paid a price for blowing that whistle in terms of career advancement. But after several decades my track record of delivery and sheer persistence paid off: I snagged a series of coveted positions as Country Director, leading the World Bank's operations on the ground for anywhere from one to six countries at a time.

This is how I ended up in Myanmar, one of the World Bank's fastest-growing programs in 2017. My assignment as Country Director also covered Cambodia and Laos. It was just another assignment in a long career moving around the globe—to Macedonia, Burkina Faso, Tunisia, Zambia, and Bangladesh, among other assignments. The destinations were not glamorous, but I loved them. I loved learning about a complex history and culture in each new place. I loved tailoring a development strategy to the unique circumstances of each country. I loved motivating our team to transform our vision into results that changed people's lives. I had purpose in my life. And I loved showing my daughters the diverse ways in which humans inhabit the earth through a childhood lived globally.

I loved each country and its people, and I loved my job, even when grappling with wicked, intractable problems. While Director for the

Bangladesh program, starting in 2010, I initiated a mega-project to build a six-kilometer bridge over the Padma River. This was a truly transformational project that would measurably increase economic growth by linking two halves of the country together. With big projects come big contracts, and with big contracts comes the risk of corruption—of attempts to unduly influence the awarding of multimillion-dollar bids. Corruption was endemic to Bangladesh. The country ranked last in the world on various corruption indicators.

Even before the bridge project began disbursing funds, the World Bank found evidence of corruption reaching up to ministers and members of the prime minister's family. I was under immense pressure from headquarters to be tough on corruption while simultaneously maintaining good relations with the government. It was not possible to strike that balance.

I was excoriated by Bangladesh's government even as I was suspected by World Bank leadership of being soft on corruption. I was criticized in Bangladeshi television and newspaper headlines daily. Military and civilian intelligence officers spied on me regularly, and I feared for the safety of my children until the World Bank removed me unceremoniously from Bangladesh in 2013. It was the low point of my career, yet I left knowing I had done many good things in my four years there, including getting millions of poor children into school and providing clean water and electricity to millions of rural households.

Like other aid workers, I tended to stay for three or four years in each country, trying to do some good. We aid workers are international do-gooders. I am a do-gooder.

I blame my childhood.

My childhood was not particularly traumatic. I had a stable middle-class life in a leafy suburb of Milwaukee. But I remember on the playground, the naughty boys chasing eight-year-old me. One grabbed me and called me a "kike," which I knew was a bad word about being Jewish. My puniness saved me. I squeezed into a cranny where others could not fit. The boys hurled insults my way until they got bored and found another unpopular child to torment. I was a skinny girl with narrow-set brown eyes and frizzy dark curls, wedged between the red bricks and cement blocks of my school. From my safe space, I saw all the blue-eyed, blond kids jumping rope and playing foursquare. Many of them were polite and kind. But I felt different. I felt "other."

We were a reform Jewish family, meaning we stripped away much of the religious ritual, leaving only the guilt behind. I went to Sunday school at Temple Shalom, but halfway through each class I snuck out to buy Twizzlers and Milk Duds at the nearby 7-Eleven. I remember being ten, sitting in class and struggling to unwedge a Milk Dud from my molar when the annual Holocaust lesson began. I do not remember much of what was said, but I saw the pictures of wagons collecting dead bodies inside the Jewish ghettos, grainy films of Nazi troops shoveling, shoveling, shoveling bodies into mass graves, shockingly naked bodies with limbs flopping, shoveled so quickly after death that the corpses did not have time to grow rigid. And later, at the time of liberation, the cameras panning the blank faces of survivors behind concentration camp fences, skin so taut and eyes so empty that they already looked dead, like skeletons propped up in a Halloween display.

This is the loop tape of my childhood: corpses being shoveled into mass graves at Auschwitz or Bergen Belsen or Mauthausen. It did not really matter which camp. The message from my teachers, my rabbi, my parents, and my parents' friends was all the same: six million Jews died, but you are alive. Six million others died too—Catholics, Roma, communists—but you are lucky. You are alive. And if you do not remember this, *it could happen again*. If you do not keep your eyes open during the video, *it could happen again*. If you do not recognize the signs today, *it could happen again*. They lived through it on both sides of the Atlantic, and they wanted to ensure that the children of my generation understood that if you do not work every day for a better world, a more humane world, a more just world, *it could happen again*.

I felt the guilt of being alive mingled with the fear that anybody—any group, any society—could slide down the slippery slope toward fascism, discrimination, and extermination of my people. Or your people. Or anyone, really.

I was a serious girl—a responsible child who studied hard to win approval from the adults around me. I grew up knowing I had a duty to fix the problems I saw, to right the wrongs in society, to fight for justice for those who could not. This was the Jewish duty of *Tikkun olam* translated simply as "repair the world." Anything less would be a disappointment from such a clever girl, such a good girl. Expectations were high. Perhaps I would be a doctor (saving lives!) or a lawyer (demanding justice!), the stereotypes of Jewish families everywhere. Still, I wanted more. I wanted to break from the stereotypes and see a wider world.

And so I became a warrior for a better world. I "fight poverty with passion and professionalism," to quote the World Bank's mission statement.

I joined the army of aid workers who fanned out to the poorer parts of the globe, offering money, advice, and skills to make development happen. I rose through the ranks of the World Bank until I led teams of hundreds of technical specialists on the ground designing projects that would change people's lives, lifting families out of poverty forever. And I watched to see the results of my work: children able to go to school, farmers getting crops to new markets, single mothers starting small businesses, foreign investors creating jobs, governments providing for the poorest of the poor. I loved my job. And the girl who felt like an "other" in Milwaukee got to meet all the "others" out there. From N'djamena to Kathmandu, from Lusaka to Dhaka, from Ouagadougou to Tirana, I got to be a global citizen and a development warrior. A do-gooder, living her dream.

It was no big deal when I was asked to go to Myanmar. In fact, it was a consolation prize, sheepishly offered. My dream was to go to Vietnam. I grew up watching the Vietnam War on television every night. My parents protested it, and my older brother narrowly avoided the draft in its waning years. I watched the nightly newsreels of caskets draped with American flags returning to US soil. I saw the pictures of Vietnamese civilians bombed and shelled, bloody and fleeing along dirt roads and through rice paddies. And I vividly recall the final helicopter lifting off the roof of the US Embassy as Saigon fell to the communist Viet Minh—an iconic Cold War image of America in retreat. It was my fifteenth birthday. I felt sad but also confused. I did not really understand how we reached this point. Politicians in Washington screwed this up. Would we ever be able to fix it? And I carried into adulthood a need to understand what led us into this unsuccessful war, along with a hope that the door to Vietnam would one day reopen and we could do something positive there for a new generation.

Now, forty years later, I had the opportunity to help Vietnam transition to a freer society with a more open economy. The job of World Bank Director in Vietnam was available, and it was time for me to leave my position as Director in the Balkans. I competed hard for the job. I studied the region and the country, its history, its politics, its economy. I practiced my answers. And I aced the interviews.

Normally, I would not know this. The recruitment process is supposed to be confidential. But the day afterward, my phone started to ping.

"You did it! Excited you will be coming to Vietnam!" texted one of the interviewers from the day before.

"Heard you are the next Director for Vietnam! Congrats!" texted another colleague.

Nearly a dozen more congratulatory texts from colleagues followed. Could it really be true?

My boss and I were traveling together in the Balkans. Over coffee he confirmed, "Heard you did great! You should hear good things soon."

And as icing on the cake, I heard from the Vice President of Human Resources the next day: "So I understand I am talking to the next Director for Vietnam!" he said by way of hello.

I could hardly believe it! It was a dream come true!

The next day, I was seated in a conference room when I got a phone call from my future boss, Charlotte, the Vice President for East Asia. My heart leapt. This was it: the phone call offering me my dream job! My current boss gave me a thumbs-up and a wink as I left to take the call.

"Do you know why I am calling?" asked Charlotte.

Well, this is awkward. What am I supposed to say? "Yes, to offer me my dream job," seemed a bit presumptuous. So I stammered, "I am assuming this is about Vietnam..." and trailed off.

"Actually, I am calling about a different job. I thought maybe you would be interested," she responded.

I was confused.

As an afterthought, she added, "Well, um, on Vietnam, I am sorry to say that you did not make the final two candidates. So I thought maybe you would like to consider..."

But I did not hear what she wanted me to consider. My ears were buzzing, and my brain was whirling. I did not make the final two candidates for Vietnam? How was that possible? It went against everything I had been hearing inside the institution.

I stumbled through the call and hung up. I was not interested in her other job. I felt numb.

When I reentered the room, my boss threw me a big smile across the room. I gave a quick shake of my head, and he looked puzzled.

Later, he did research behind the scenes. "She already has a candidate she wants in the position," he told me.

"Then why didn't he compete with the rest of us?" I asked. After thirty years in the institution, I knew the right way to position somebody to win a competitive process. We all knew this. It was a basic survival skill of the bureaucracy.

"She is a new vice president. She made a mistake," my boss said slowly. "Really surprising. But the institution does not want to penalize her too much for this, so they are going to reconvene the interview panel and let the guy interview."

This hastily arranged interview was found by the panel to be "on par" with mine. And, after the fact, this other guy was declared the winner of the competition. My dream job was gone. I was robbed! I was angry and bitter. Why did we even maintain the charade of a competitive process?

In the days to follow, I received a dozen new texts:

"What happened???"

"So sorry."

"Really unfair."

I knew I could make a scene. Competitive recruitment is a long-espoused and cherished principle at the World Bank. We have an internal justice system. I could have fought it. I wanted to fight it.

But even if I had won the battle, I would have lost. It would have confirmed what they said about me. What they said about so many women leaders at the World Bank. The corridor talk that dogged my career since the early days.

"She has sharp elbows."

"She is difficult."

"She is demanding."

"She is aggressive."

"She does not suffer fools gladly." (My favorite, as if that is a bad thing.)

It is strange because my immediate bosses loved me because I always delivered and got results, even under the most challenging circumstances. My staff also loved me because I was passionate, set high standards for myself and others, and always went to bat for them within the bureaucracy.

Still, I was dogged by criticism I could not seem to shake from peers and staff on other teams.

So I sucked it up. I let go of Vietnam without a fuss. And I was rewarded for my *mature* handling of this shitshow several months later when I got a phone call from my boss.

"Do you want to go to Myanmar?" he opened.

"Sure. Why not?" I responded. The World Bank had not offered me any other assignments lately, and this seemed like as good a job as any for a Country Director.

And that is how I became Director for Myanmar at the World Bank in early 2017. No studying, no interviews, no pretense of competitive recruitment. Just a consolation prize for saying nothing.

CHAPTER 2

A Glimpse of the Golden Land

(December 2012)

Years before I worked in Myanmar, I went there as a tourist. I thought I might get only one opportunity in my life to visit such a reclusive place. My assignment as Country Director in neighboring Bangladesh was coming to an end in late 2012, so I searched for a tour company that held the keys to entering the isolated country. I wanted my husband and two teenage daughters to see something that very few people in the world would ever see.

"Try Shalom Myanmar," was the reply from a Facebook friend.

Shalom Myanmar? Initially I thought maybe "shalom" meant something in Burmese, like "tourism" or "scenic." But no, I had stumbled on Myanmar's only Jewish tour company in Yangon (formerly Rangoon), Myanmar's largest city and former capital. It felt quirky and somehow auspicious, so I signed my family up.

Shalom Myanmar was my first clue to a Burmese past largely lost to the outside world. I had always imagined the country as I first heard of it: isolated, mysterious, completely closed to the outside world. This was indeed the case for its history under repressive military rule from 1962 to 2011. But before that dark period was a history of strong and independent Burmese kingdoms dating back centuries, followed by a period as part of British India from 1824 to 1947, after Britain colonized

India and annexed Burma to it. This was followed by a brief time as a newly independent and democratic nation from 1947 until the military coup in 1962.

Now, I am touring historic Yangon and seeing not the recent past of isolation but vestiges of an earlier past as a vibrant and cosmopolitan commercial center.

We walk along a riverfront crowded with decrepit warehouses that reflect the city's past prominence as a port and commercial center for Southeast Asia. Under British India, economic opportunity drew all manner of entrepreneurs and wanderers, creating a diverse and powerful city that made Burma among the richest spots in Asia. This included several thousand Jewish families, drawn from places like Baghdad and Damascus to build their businesses. Their traces are evident in the crumbling but elegant colonial-era buildings, like the Sofaer Building, a commercial headquarters for an Iraqi Jewish family long since departed from Myanmar. Rangoon even had a Jewish mayor at one point. I am fascinated and elated to find traces of my tribe here, where I least expected it.

Indeed, nineteenth-century Burma was a magnet for ambitious immigrants of all types. I can see their places of worship as we explore the historic city center: Saint Mary's Cathedral, Holy Trinity Cathedral, the Emmanuel Baptist Church, the Armenian Apostolic Church, the Surtee Sunni Jumma Mosque, the Sri Kali Hindu Temple, the Musmeah Yeshua Synagogue. Like the Jews, many immigrant groups numbered only in the thousands. But by the 1930s, those of Indian origin—who were only about 7 percent of Burma's total population—were more than half the population of Rangoon and dominated the country's commerce and colonial administration. This did not sit well with the indigenous population.

Their place of worship remains the spiritual center of modern Yangon: Shwedagon Pagoda. This vast Buddhist temple complex sits atop Yangon's highest hill, its massive gold leaf spires visible from afar. It is the largest of the tens of thousands of golden-topped pagodas dotting

Myanmar, giving the country its nickname: The Golden Land. I walk the inner circle of Shwedagon, and it is dazzling. The sun glints off the golden spires, small mosaic temples, and massive golden Buddha figures. The mood is peaceful and reverential as small groups of women in silk longyis and monks in saffron robes stroll past, pausing to pray and offer small gifts to the Buddha. I know that nearly 90 percent of Myanmar's population is Buddhist, but now I learn that this includes the dominant Bamar ethnicity, who gave Burma its name, as well as many other ethnic groups like the Shan, Mon, and Rakhine. Some ethnic groups like the Karen, Kachin, and Chin have sizable Christian populations, whereas groups like the Rohingya, Kaman, and Panthays are largely Muslim. Immigrants were not the only source of diversity in colonial Burma, and this is even more true today.

The next day, we visit the Secretariat, a decrepit colonial administration building with red brick arches and massive teak stairwells. I am looking at an empty room, trying to imagine the bloody scene described by our guide:

> It was 1946, and armed assassins burst in and assassinated General Aung San, military leader and founding father of independent Burma. His daughter, Aung San Suu Kyi, was just two years old when he and half a dozen other leaders of Burma's independence movement were brutally murdered. Six months later, Burma gained independence from Britain and its first democratically elected government.

This is when I learn that Aung San Suu Kyi, world renowned democracy icon, is herself a child of the Burmese military. Sadly, independent Burma also proved to be an intolerant Burma, and it forcefully expelled its immigrants. Hundreds of thousands of immigrants of Indian origin were marched across the border after independence, many killed or dying along the way. It was in keeping with India's own Partition, one of history's largest forced displacements, of Hindus toward India and Muslims to newly established Pakistan. Over time, other immigrant groups were forced out, although small communities remain: the Portuguese, Armenians, Jews, and others.

I realize that I have been told the Burma story before; I have World Bank colleagues whose immigrant grandfathers barely survived the long march out of Burma back to India.

As we walk the grounds of the Secretariat, our guide finishes the story with the Burma I know better. A military coup in March 1962 put an end to democratic government and ushered in five decades of not only repressive authoritarian rule but also severe economic mismanagement. Here I know more than my guide. The military's "Burmese Way to Socialism" proved to be an economic disaster, through not only centralized control of industries but also the corruption and cronyism that accompanied it.

At independence in 1947, Burma was one of the wealthiest countries in Asia, exploiting its jade, rubies, and timber. Fifty years later, at the start of the twenty-first century, it was among the poorest countries in Asia. The East Asian Economic Miracle that propelled its neighbors to prosperity completely bypassed Burma, alone in self-imposed isolation and sanctioned as a pariah state.

I can see all this in the streets of Yangon: the nineteenth-century rise of Burma and its twentieth-century decline. I see it in the elegant colonial-era buildings: riverfront hotels, banks, government offices, and markets. Ornately carved doorways and cornices speak to the heyday of Rangoon as a humming, cosmopolitan commercial center. But it is all crumbling and disappearing under layers of grime, disfigured by open sewers and heaps of trash. Unreplaced by anything more modern. Largely untouched and unchanged by economic development—good or bad—over the past seventy years.

The shops also feel like another era. They are small and dark, selling bulk spices and grains from open sacks. We sit in one of the innumerable tea shops, on colorful plastic chairs from China. Cheap plastic goods from China are everywhere—a sign of both limited income among

Yangon's consumers and the continued presence of this neighboring giant even at the height of Burma's isolation.

We are served piping-hot tea mixed with sweetened milk. No matter how white the mixture, it all tastes too sweet. And the mood is also sweet but sad. I am wistful, seeing Burma's past decaying and disappearing and knowing that the dreams and aspirations of so many generations were snuffed out by decades of repressive military rule.

Following the military coup, the outside world knew little about conditions inside Burma for five decades. When the door was finally cracked open in 2008 following a deadly cyclone, the outside world found a country where nearly two-thirds of the population was in absolute poverty, more than half the children were chronically malnourished, and nearly three-fourths of households lacked basics like electricity and piped water. A SIM card for a cell phone—something hawkers peddled for less than a dollar in neighboring Thailand—would cost several thousand dollars on Yangon's black market. Not the phone. Just the SIM card. Myanmar was a country of widespread poverty, deprivation, and isolation.

Yet even during these dark times, the country remained an unimaginable cultural and archeological treasure. Now here I am in 2012, watching a red-orange sunset atop one of the 2,500 pagodas and stupas in the ancient capital of Bagan. Strolling with saffron-robed monks on the teak spans of the U Bein Bridge in Mandalay. Gliding silently in long wooden boats through the dawn mist on Inle Lake to capture the distinctive foot-rowing style of local fishermen. It is glorious and enchanting. Each morning I stroll the teak walkways of our hotel as mist rises from the lake, feeling the spiritual and calming atmosphere envelop me.

Later I learn that our magical hotel is owned by the family of a notoriously corrupt military leader. I feel betrayed but wiser: a reminder that the tentacles of the Tatmadaw reach into every sphere of life in Myanmar.

We return to Yangon for a final day before our departure and stand awkwardly in front of an unremarkable gray metal gate on University Avenue. We crane our necks to get a glimpse of the house where Aung San Suu Kyi remained under house arrest for most of two decades.

She left her British husband and two young sons in the UK in 1988, returning to Burma temporarily to care for her ailing mother. Her return coincided with a boiling over of public dissatisfaction with a corrupt and ineffective military regime. During six months of student-led protests, she emerged as the standard-bearer of Burma's democracy movement. Ultimately, the military leader of the country, General Ne Win, stepped down in September 1988, only for a reconstituted military leadership to crack down more brutally on the democracy movement.

During this period, Aung San Suu Kyi (or The Lady, as she is known to her followers) founded a political party, the National League for Democracy (NLD), and became the most visible and vocal advocate for democracy and self-determination in Burma. She picked up the mantle of her father as a founder of independent and democratic Burma. Back in the 1940s, the military fought to throw off the yolk of colonialism and establish an independent and democratic Burma. They were the heroes. Over the years, and especially after the 1962 military coup, the Tatmadaw mythologized its role as protector of the nation and its people, protecting even against internal threats like student protesters and ethnic minorities. Many ethnic minorities, realizing that independence meant a Bamar-dominated state rife with discrimination, emerged as democracy advocates and freedom fighters under the military regime, through the establishment of ethnic armed organizations. Meanwhile, the Tatmadaw, once warriors for Burmese independence, became synonymous with authoritarianism and repression.

They also changed the country's English name from Burma, which was a colonial mispronunciation of Bamar, to the local name: Myanmar. This was part of a larger effort to replace colonial names with indigenous names, but because it was done by a military regime deemed illegitimate, the US and UK continued to officially call the country Burma, as did many early democracy activists. The UN formally recognized the country as Myanmar in 1989.

Under international pressure in 1990, the military half-heartedly held general elections in which the NLD won a majority. Unwilling to cede power, the military nullified the election results and placed The Lady under house arrest. The following year, she was awarded the Nobel Peace Prize for advocating for freedom and democracy for the Burmese people. The Nobel committee stated that they wanted "to show support for the many people throughout the world who are striving to attain democracy, human rights and ethnic conciliation by peaceful means." Twenty years passed before she was released from house arrest and could give her acceptance speech in person. She could not even attend her husband's funeral in England in 1999.

As I stand in front of the home that became her prison, I am awed by her persistence and courage. She was denied her family, denied a normal life, yet she never wavered from her devotion to the cause of democracy for her people. As I catch a glimpse of the house, it feels anticlimactic. She is not there today. She was released from house arrest a few years earlier. By 2008, the military junta could no longer ignore Myanmar's long-standing failure to thrive. They adopted a new Constitution that began a slow-motion movement toward democracy and reintegration into the global community. Not a revolution but an evolution—a tightly managed transition to a more democratic state. They promised elections would be held in 2015. Yet the military's Constitution ensures that even with elections in a few years, the Tatmadaw will retain control over the country's defense and internal security, including the Ministries of Defense, Home Affairs, and Border Affairs, as well as granting the military a mandatory 25 percent of seats in Parliament.

We have three years until the promised elections. Still, I am elated by recent progress, and so is the Myanmar public. The Lady is free! She is touring the country to rapturous crowds. She is campaigning hard and will surely triumph in the promised election given her widespread public adoration.

Six months before my visit to this house, she finally traveled to Norway to accept her Nobel Peace Prize. I watched on television as she recalled how she felt hearing the news twenty years earlier:

> What the Nobel Peace Prize did was to draw me once again into the world of other human beings...to restore a sense of reality to me...and what was more important, the Nobel Prize had drawn attention to the struggle for democracy and human rights in Burma.
>
> Over the past year there have been signs that the endeavours of those who believe in democracy and human rights are beginning to bear fruit in Burma. There have been changes in a positive direction; steps toward democratization have been taken...Burma is a country of many ethnic nationalities and faith in its future can be founded only on a true spirit of union.[2]

Now I am visiting this secluded land. The mood of locals I meet is a mixture of relief and disbelief. Of exhilaration and exhaustion. People still speak cautiously—only when we are walking outside in the open—a reflex from years where idle chat was grounds for imprisonment.

After Aung San Suu Kyi's travel to Norway in 2012, the United States eased decades' worth of economic sanctions on Myanmar's military regime. Other countries followed suit. During our visit, the road from the airport is still festooned with flags and billboards heralding a recent and unprecedented event: President Obama visited Burma! He was the first US president to visit the Golden Land—something that would have been unimaginable for the people of Myanmar and for the whole world just a year or two earlier.

---

[2] Aung San Suu Kyi, "Nobel Lecture," The Nobel Prize, June 16, 2012, https://www.nobelprize.org/prizes/peace/1991/kyi/26193-aung-san-suu-kyi-nobel-lecture-english/.

While I still cannot buy a SIM card in Myanmar for less than a thousand dollars in 2012, I can spend five dollars on the latest fashion trend: the ubiquitous *O'Burma* T-shirt to celebrate the historic visit. Who can resist? After all, I imagine I will never come this way again.

CHAPTER 3

Arriving in Myanmar

(June 2017)

I left Myanmar as a tourist in 2012 only to come back as a diplomat in 2017. Not really a diplomat. More of an undiplomatic diplomat. I have full diplomatic status, but I am not an ambassador representing a specific country or foreign policy. I am the face of the World Bank, an international organization owned by all its member countries, including Myanmar.

The World Bank was established after World War II as an apolitical organization, according to its Articles of Agreement. Nonetheless, with voting weighted by financial contribution and a US president by convention, it is easy for outsiders to accuse the World Bank of being an instrument of US foreign policy. Those of us on the inside understand that it is not quite so simple. Decisions require a careful balancing of the interests of all shareholders—not only the US but the European powers, Japan, China, India, Australia, Brazil, Saudi Arabia, and more. Still, at its most fundamental, the World Bank is a product of post-war Western thinking, of neoclassical economic theory and capitalist models to promote market-oriented reforms.

In the 1960s, the World Bank turned its focus toward the developing nations of Latin America, Asia, and Africa. It was a sound Cold War strategy to shore up the edges of the free world, and it brought poverty reduction into focus. Since then, the organization has seen economic growth as necessary but not sufficient: growth needs to be broad-based, with good governance to ensure equal opportunity and redistribute wealth through public infrastructure and services that reach the poor. While never explicitly discussed in this apolitical institution, economic development is assumed to buttress democracy or at least foster democratic tendencies throughout the developing world.

I consider myself an undiplomatic diplomat because of my character. I have no small talk; I cut right to the heart of issues. I speak from to-do lists. I promise only what I can deliver and then deliver what I promise: billions of dollars combined with technical advice to transform ideas into results that improve people's lives. I underwrite policy reforms and national programs that build roads, foster private businesses, improve healthcare, modernize waste management, increase energy efficiency, and achieve a host of other worthy goals.

I work with the highest levels of government: prime ministers, finance ministers, cabinet secretaries. They love me because they can trust me. I do not waste their time. I have no hidden agenda. I deliver. On time. Under budget. I take great pride in these relationships and my ability to deliver for them.

Thirty-plus years into my career in global development, I feel confident that I can do the same in Myanmar as the plane touches down on the tarmac in Yangon in late June of 2017.

I am happy to be flying from one overseas assignment to the next without spending much time in the United States. I feel confident and comfortable moving into a new assignment in a new country, while I am anxious and uncomfortable about what is happening back home. The inauguration of Donald Trump as president of the United States several months earlier seemed like a farce, a bad joke, a clown car of a moment in a liberal democracy like ours.

I remember attending a watch party for Democrats Abroad on election night in Austria, where I was living back in November 2016. I dressed carefully in a white pantsuit to honor America's suffragettes, pinned a red, white, and blue ribbon to my lapel, and stepped out for what I expected to be an historic night: election of the first female president of the United States. But I crawled home to bed at 3:00 a.m. for an early workday with nothing yet decided. The early election returns were disheartening. But I was optimistic. The Democratic strongholds were large urban areas and would report later, I knew.

My husband woke me after a few hours.

"Donald Trump is our president," he said with a lopsided grin.

"Ha ha. Very funny," I said sleepily.

"No, really. Donald Trump is our president."

"You're kidding, right?" My brain was refusing to register. "That's impossible!"

I stood up too fast and dashed dizzily to the living room to see the results for myself. It was true.

I spent the day at my office in a zombie-like state. Some part of my brain wanted to believe this was a nightmare from which I would awake.

But I never woke up from this nightmare. The American people had somehow elected a greedy con man, a grifter, a flim-flam artist who grabbed women by the pussy, mocked disabled people, vilified Muslims, caricatured Jews, and considered white supremacists to be "fine people."

I flew into Washington on inauguration day so that I could join the hundreds of thousands of women and men marching to the National Mall to protest Trump's blatant disrespect for women and minorities. It felt good to do something—anything—to raise our voices, but in the coming months I saw things happening in America I never thought possible. Trump's attempt to ban Muslim immigrants was shocking in its unabashed Islamophobia. His blatant disregard for civil liberties enshrined in America's Constitution and Bill of Rights was dismaying.

I was depressed and anxious about the state of my country. I became hypervigilant, obsessively scanning the news for the latest Trump travesty. I could not sleep. And by June I was feeling that maybe—just maybe—my new assignment in Myanmar would be challenging enough, complex enough, satisfying enough to take my mind off the worst transgressions back home.

It has to be. This will be my survival strategy.

CHAPTER 4

Meeting The Lady

(July 2017)

Just a few days after arriving in Myanmar, I am careening down the center of a vast and empty highway with some new colleagues. We are in Nay Pyi Taw, the capital city built by the military smack in the middle of Myanmar's dense jungle. I am both proud and puzzled. A few short days after my arrival in Myanmar, I have been granted an audience with the newly elected head of government, Aung San Suu Kyi. It speaks to the high regard in which the World Bank is held and in which I, as the newly appointed director, will be held. We can hold our own with any ambassador or foreign dignitary beating a path to the door of global democracy icon and Nobel Peace Prize winner Aung San Suu Kyi. This meeting reassures me that our Myanmar staff—about whom I know almost nothing—have the right connections to the right people to make this happen.

I am puzzled to be the only vehicle on a sixteen-lane highway more appropriate for central Los Angeles than this sparsely populated area. In 2002, Myanmar's former military dictatorship built a new capital in the dead center of the country to exert better control over the conflict-ridden territory. They operated on the "build it and they will come" approach. Their authoritarian control guaranteed that at least long-suffering civil servants would take up post there.

"Did the military really think you would need all sixteen lanes?" I ask Kyi Sin, our local research assistant. "It seems a bit excessive, no?"

He clears his throat. "Ah yes. It is not exactly like that, Ellen." He glances around and lowers his voice as if to prevent eavesdroppers. "It was built to allow a jet to land and take off here if the military leaders ever needed to escape."

He nods at my raised eyebrows. Now I understand the highway, and I understand the paranoia of the Tatmadaw.

We arrive at a ministerial building that looks identical to every other in Nay Pyi Taw, uniformity being the hallmark of the military mind. Protocol officers lead us to a large reception room with chairs along either side and two sofas at the head for the state counsellor and her honored guest. After ten minutes, the state counsellor herself enters from a side door, looking lovely and fragile. As always, she is wearing a longyi with a matching silk jacket, a shawl wound over one arm, flat sandals, and sprigs of fresh jasmine in her upswept hair.

With her straight spine and impassive expression, Aung San Suu Kyi looks every bit the part of the daughter of a freedom fighter for independent Burma, the leader of the 1988 democracy movement, and a decades-long prisoner of a repressive military regime. I feel coarse and Western in my business suit and clunky shoes as I shake her delicate hand. The high-backed, carved wooden chairs and overstuffed upholstery in her reception room make her seem smaller, like a songbird in an ornate cage.

As flashbulbs from the official photographers die away, she welcomes us and signals for me to begin.

"State Counsellor, it is indeed an honor to meet with you today," I venture. "I have just arrived to take up my position as the first World Bank Director in Myanmar. This is an upgrade of our presence in Myanmar to reflect the importance we attach to the country's progress in political and economic transition."

"Let me extend a warm welcome to our country," says Aung San Suu Kyi, smiling attentively. It is difficult to know if she recognizes the

World Bank or distinguishes us from other international organizations, but this is not surprising in a country only recently awash in aid agencies and aid workers.

"I would be grateful to learn more about your highest priorities for Myanmar in the next two years," I say.

"Peace," is her unhesitating answer. "We must pursue the peace process. We cannot progress without unity among our people, without ending the bloodshed." She speaks at length of the need to forge a sustainable peace with the dozens of ethnic armed organizations and the communities they represent after decades of conflict.

"And what do you consider most important in terms of economic development?" I ask, posing a question more in line with the World Bank's mandate to eliminate poverty.

"Development must support the peace process," she says, not wavering from her theme.

And I warm to her theme as well.

"The World Bank can help generate a peace dividend by creating economic opportunities in areas of the country that are committed to peace," I say.

She responds enthusiastically to this idea, leading me to ask, "In your view, State Counsellor, what do households in these areas need most?"

She hesitates as if searching for an answer and then finally replies, "Electricity and roads. That is most important: electricity and roads."

It is not an elaborate answer, but in a country where only 30 percent of the population has access to electricity, it is certainly not wrong.

The ethnic organizations operate in largely rural areas, so I broach the topic of agriculture and livestock development.

She pauses for a moment and then asks, "Do you think children can develop properly without milk?"

Well, this is unexpected. I cock an eyebrow a fraction of an inch in bemusement but swiftly shift gears. We are here to talk about priorities for economic reform and allocation of millions of dollars in aid money.

But to deepen our relationship, my deputy and I engage The Lady in a lively discussion of veganism and milk alternatives. And then our time is up.

As I rise to leave, I realize that the state counsellor has articulated no clear vision for the economic transformation of her country. Although disappointing, this is not uncommon among political leaders with no prior experience in government. I have seen it before—for example, in countries emerging from the dissolution of Yugoslavia in the early 1990s. Indeed, this is the *raison d'etre* of the World Bank: to support new leaders such as Aung San Suu Kyi in defining a vision of inclusive development that will allow them to reverse decades of economic mismanagement and bring millions out of poverty.

It will be a privilege and an honor to help her grow into her power as a leader.

The photographers capture our parting handshakes. The photos are posted on the state counsellor's Facebook page and then on mine later that evening.

My older daughter, Isabel—not one to boast on social media about her parents—also posts the photo, saying, "Just an everyday picture of my favorite lady boss Ellen Goldstein meeting a Nobel Laureate!"

I feel proud of the example I am setting for my daughters.

I also feel proud and increasingly excited to work with a leader who has such a singular focus on peace in Myanmar. I am learning that the country has been wracked with conflict not just for decades but for centuries. After this first meeting with Aung San Suu Kyi, I think back to what she said five years earlier to the Nobel committee:

> Everywhere there are negative forces eating away at the foundations of peace...I am thinking of prisoners and refugees, of migrant workers and victims of human trafficking, of that great mass of the uprooted of the earth who have been torn away from their homes, parted from families and friends, forced to live out their lives among strangers who are not

> always welcoming...ultimately our aim should be to create a world free from the displaced, the homeless and the hopeless, a world in which each and every corner is a true sanctuary where the inhabitants will have the freedom and the capacity to live in peace.[3]

So inspirational! And spoken with such moral authority borne of her own suffering under decades of house arrest.

That night, I reflect on my first official meeting in Myanmar. I cannot imagine a more exciting job in a country moving rapidly to embrace both democracy and development. To think that I stumbled accidentally into this job! I feel so lucky. I have been granted a golden opportunity in the Golden Land.

---

[3] Aung San Suu Kyi, "Nobel Lecture."

CHAPTER 5

Visiting the Hluttaw

(August 2017)

My introductory meetings with government officials continue for a few weeks. This means waking up at four in the morning and wrapping myself in a traditional floor-length longyi, which—I am assured by our local staff—is much appreciated by the government. Then with mincing steps, I make my way to the airport for the six o'clock flight to Nay Pyi Taw.

The alternative is to fly up the night before and spend the night in one of the dozen or so complexes that make up an isolated "hotel zone." All hotels are identical, oversized complexes built before the country opened to the outside world. They are now managed by chains like Hilton and Sofitel, who do their best to put their brand on a complex that looks just like the one across the street. And down the block. And across the next street.

I avoid staying the night at one of these vast and empty complexes, but when I cannot get a morning flight, I am forced to go up the evening before and stay at a hotel.

"Enjoy your evening, madam!" cry the staff, who are lovely and solicitous, as I step out of a largely empty dining hall and head toward my room in an outbuilding.

"You want a ride, madam?" they ask, pointing out a waiting golf cart.

But I wave no thanks and mince along to my building as I look forward to *finally* unwrapping my longyi. I step hesitantly through long, dimly lit corridors in a deserted building. It is ominous and vaguely depressing. Much better to take the early morning flight from Yangon—catching the "local bus" as it is called by the diplomats and development workers I greet as we shuffle onboard.

Having met The Lady, one of my next important meetings is with the Speaker of the Parliament. The Parliament complex, or *Hluttaw* in Burmese. Like most buildings in Nay Pyi Taw, the Hluttaw is grandiose and oversized, a thirty-one-building pagoda complex meant to represent the thirty-one planes of existence in Buddhist cosmology.

"Please come this way," says one of four protocol officers who greet me, my deputy Levon, and Kyi Sin, ushering us into a cavernous lobby.

"Look here. Myanmar traditional clothes," says another officer, leading us to a crowd of brightly costumed mannequins.

I notice that traditional outfits vary a lot by ethnicity: from the embroidered woolen jackets of the mountain areas near the Chinese border to the diaphanous silk shawls of the delta region.

Ever the undiplomatic diplomat, I blurt out, "Why are all the mannequins Caucasian?" and immediately cringe. But they are the mannequin equivalent of modern Vikings: a group of super-sized blond Barbies and Kens ill-suited to represent Myanmar's ethnic diversity.

Thankfully, nobody acknowledges my tactlessness, and we continue to admire the display.

"Please come to the resting room," says a protocol officer.

We are led to a waiting room, an enormous traditional hall with beautifully painted wooden beams. I feel small as we perch on overstuffed sofas with a dozen uniformed guards standing nearby.

The traditional hall has been modernized with a state-of-the-art flat-screen television of gigantic proportions bolted inelegantly to the wall. Clearly a source of pride for today's Myanmar: no longer cut off from the outside world, parliamentarians can stay abreast of world events by tuning in to CNN International or BBC World or... *Saturday Night Live*? Levon and I exchange bemused looks watching Alec Baldwin impersonate Donald Trump. The television audience laughs. The guards remain stone-faced. Undoubtedly drawn from elite soldiers, the parliamentary guards would nonetheless have had little exposure to Western television shows, particularly a highbrow comedy like *SNL*. Do these guards and the parliamentarians know that this is not, in fact, the US president, Donald Trump? Somehow I doubt it, but I am tickled to be watching *SNL* in the antechamber of the Myanmar Parliament.

It speaks to an almost unimaginable digital transformation in Myanmar in just a few short years. Indeed, as I learn about all the good things the World Bank is doing in Myanmar, the most stunning—the most transformative—has been the opening of the telecommunications sector. Controlling information flow was one of the military regime's top priorities. The country was closed to mobile phone and internet providers until the transitional military government took office in 2011.

In 2012 and beyond, the World Bank provided much of the technical advice needed to open the country to modern technology. The SIM card that cost nearly a thousand dollars when I visited in 2012 had dropped to a couple of dollars now in 2017, not much different than the rest of Southeast Asia.

The transition government had been persuaded to undertake this radical reform because they trusted the World Bank to provide neutral advice. Our staff are perceived as freer of the geopolitical and commercial motives often ascribed to consultants from specific countries.

On our telecoms team for Myanmar, the most trusted advisor of all was a dynamo named Dolkar. It was unusual to meet a female telecoms specialist anywhere, but downright astonishing to meet one from Southeast Asia, particularly from the tiny mountain Kingdom of Bhutan. Soon after my arrival, she dropped by to brief me on the latest reforms.

"She was my babysitter, you know," says Dolkar. "The Lady. Aung San Suu Kyi. Her husband came from the UK to Bhutan in the 1960s to tutor our king. She came with him. She did not have much to do, so she babysat for some of the families."

"Does she recognize you now?" I ask incredulously.

"Yes. I usually visit her when I am here. Just informally." She reflects for a moment. "I think she is quite isolated now. If you can, talk to her frequently, Ellen, about anything, not just work."

"Well, I know who to call if I get in trouble!" I tease. But I marvel at this unlikely connection.

These improbable connections exist everywhere I go in the world, and they play a big part in building trust. This is especially true in a country and society as historically isolated and distrusting of outsiders as Myanmar.

I remind myself how quickly the country opened, and how alien it is for Myanmar's residents to have access to information within the country and from the outside world. Less than a decade earlier, it was nearly impossible for the outside world to learn anything about life inside Myanmar.

When cyclone Nargis made landfall in the delta region of Myanmar in 2008, the immediate impact was dire and evident from satellite images. When the military refused to request humanitarian aid and allow relief workers to enter the country, the consequences became cataclysmic, with over 140,000 dead and millions homeless and at risk of starvation and disease.

As the death toll mounted, the military generals cracked the door open to a small number of international relief workers. And Mya Mya—my executive assistant, my meeting wrangler, my cultural interpreter—was there to help them.

"I was hired by Doctors without Borders. They were the first ones to come," she explains. "I can never forget it. Everywhere was flooded, so we had to take boats to where the villages had been to search for hurt and hungry people."

And now she tears up in the telling. "Families were stuck in trees for days or floating on homemade rafts. And everywhere there were bodies floating by. They were swollen and rotting, but nobody could pick them up. We did what we could for survivors, but it was not much."

It is a gruesome scene and grueling for those brave enough to go.

I am in awe of Mya Mya's courage and the untold stories that she—and probably many of our local staff—can share to truly understand the history and collective psyche of this country.

"The government—the military—would not let us bring cameras or phones in the boats. I mean, almost nobody had a phone back then except the foreigners, but the Tatmadaw would not let us bring them. They did not want the world to see what happened. To see how bad it really was," she finishes.

She is talking about 2008, less than a decade ago. From then until my arrival now in 2017, the share of people in Myanmar with a cell phone rose from less than 3 percent to 94 percent with the opening of the telecoms market. It is a meteoric rise unequaled in any other country on earth, and it speaks to the desperation of a population starved for information and connection.

Now I am sitting in the Parliament feeling overjoyed that the World Bank has played a part in this stunning transformation. Our technical advice and investments are helping people in Myanmar connect to the outside world and to each other. And this digital revolution supports a freer press and people's right to information in a more democratic society. At this point, Facebook has become the preeminent source of news and information exchange for the population. Even the military generals post daily to their pages. And parliamentarians watch *Saturday Night Live,* it seems.

Suddenly, a man wrapped in a men's longyi with a traditional white jacket and Burmese headwrap bustles into the waiting room toward a neighboring sofa.

"They are Caucasian because that is all that is available from Bangkok at a reasonable price," he explains in flawless, British-accented English.

I cringe again thinking of the mannequins. A lesson for me: what gets said gets reported.

"That's so interesting, and the costumes are so beautiful," I stammer.

"I organized the costume exhibit to bring some life into the lobby," he explains. Then he says with evident pride, "My English is self-taught because...well, nobody went abroad to study back then."

"You speak wonderfully," I say, attempting to atone for my earlier tactlessness.

"I am a senior advisor here at the Hluttaw," he continues. "Many of the parliamentarians elected in late 2015 have never held public office. They know nothing about legislative procedures, so I just try to help them with the basics."

Then he bounces up and is gone. I will never see him again. We are summoned to our meeting with the Speaker of the Parliament. As we file out, *Saturday Night Live* moves to the weekly musical act.

CHAPTER 6

Ministry of Foreign Affairs

(August 2017)

We continue our rounds of introductory meetings, Levon and I, supported by our local research analyst, Kyi Sin. He is indispensable in ensuring that things we say are truly understood by our government interlocutors, and that we correctly interpret and understand what is being said to us. It is not a translation issue—we have translators when needed—this is cultural, political, social, and historic analyses to make sense of what we hear. Throughout my career, I have made a point of bringing local staff to all government meetings, not only for my benefit, but to ensure that governments see their own people working for the World Bank, working to reduce poverty and inequity within their own country. For most governments, it is an immense source of pride.

We make the rounds of all relevant ministries including health, education, energy, and transport—ministries we worked with to finance national projects. As an organization devoted to economic development, our accountability and daily association is with the Ministry of Planning and Finance. In contrast, embassies and most other UN agencies are accountable to the Ministry of Foreign Affairs.

Nonetheless, paying an introductory call to the Ministry of Foreign Affairs is particularly important in Myanmar. State Counsellor

Aung San Suu Kyi herself serves as Foreign Minister, an unusual arrangement for a head of government. It is an arrangement that ensures—after decades of imprisonment within Myanmar—that she can travel abroad and represent the country and her people in international arenas.

Best then for us to pay an introductory visit. Not to see the state counsellor, whom we have already met, but to see the Deputy Minister of Foreign Affairs, U Kyaw Tin. He is a career foreign service officer who served through the previous military regime and now handles the day-to-day business of the ministry. Letters are sent with photocopies of our UN *laissez passers* for me and Levon, as well as a national identity card for Kyi Sin. After several weeks a meeting is secured.

On the appointed day, we fly to Nay Pyi Taw and are ushered into a waiting room at the ministry. Kyi Sin looks particularly resplendent in his wraparound silk longyi tied at his waist topped by his formal white jacket.

We wait a long time in a windowless room. We peruse a marketing pamphlet trumpeting Myanmar's modernism with grainy photos of concrete flyovers and commercial shopping malls.

A woman enters the waiting room and beckons us to follow. We stand and shuffle toward her.

"No, only you," she says, waving at me and Levon.

"Uh, no, he is with us," I say, signaling to Kyi Sin to come closer.

"We sent in three names, and he was approved..." adds Levon.

"No, no, no...no Myanmar, no Myanmar," she struggles to explain in English.

"But he is an expert on our team. He has been approved by the ministry," I explain, thinking maybe they are mistaking him for an interpreter they feel is not needed.

"Only you. Only foreigner."

"We can't...we don't...that's not acceptable..." I splutter.

Kyi Sin sidles up to me. "You go. You get me? You go anyway...it's important," he whispers.

Levon and I exchange uncomfortable glances. It goes against everything we believe in. But we are new here and Kyi Sin's eyes are boring into us, willing us to go on without him, willing us not to make a scene right here and now.

So we go without him.

The meeting itself is unremarkable. We explain what the World Bank is (an international organization and specialized agency of the United Nations), how we are governed (by government shareholders including Myanmar), and what we do (focus on economic development and reducing poverty). The deputy minister welcomes us and talks about the government's priorities for peace, development, and integration in the world economy. All standard stuff.

"We look forward to working with you and seeing you again in the future," says the deputy minister as the meeting draws to a close.

"We also look forward to close collaboration," I say politely. "Next time, we would like to bring a member of our Myanmar staff with us. They are the ones most responsible for advancing our program. We cannot operate here without them." I smile broadly.

But the deputy minister just smiles back, shakes our hands, and says nothing more as we file out.

We find Kyi Sin sitting uncomfortably in the waiting room. Waiting for us. Eyes downcast.

"What the hell was that?" I say when we are safely locked in our vehicle and hurtling toward the airport.

"Unacceptable! Fucking unbelievable! We cannot tolerate that," growls Levon.

"It's just the way they think," explains Kyi Sin, but I see the anger in his eyes. "Very narrow. Ministry of Foreign Affairs is a ministry to talk to foreigners."

"...to talk to foreigners? You mean a Ministry for Foreigners?" I muse.

"Exactly. A Ministry for Foreigners."

I start to comprehend their logic, however twisted.

Since arriving in Myanmar about a month earlier, I had begun to see how pervasive the mistrust of foreigners was in a country stoked by decades of isolationist military propaganda. The Ministry of Foreign Affairs sees itself as a defensive bulwark against foreigners—a way to vet foreigners and protect the nation from their dangerous ideas. A ministry to ward off foreigners, not a ministry to implement foreign policy.

The flip side is a ministry with blatant and utter disregard for its own people. What value could a local person—even a local expert—bring to a discussion with foreigners and their ideas? Indeed, they must be shielded from the risks!

This way of thinking is a holdover from decades of repressive military rule and its xenophobic propaganda. I knew that it was still prevalent in military-run ministries like defense and border affairs, but this is my first encounter in a ministry controlled by Aung San Suu Kyi's civilian government.

The internal contradiction chafes at me: a civilian government fighting for democracy—fighting, as Lincoln said, for *government of the people, by the people, for the people*—unwilling to allow them in a meeting about their own country's development. It is the antithesis of everything we are working toward.

Later, I write a letter to our accountable ministry, the Ministry of Planning and Finance, expressing our disappointment. The letter states our intention to include local staff in all meetings with government. Beyond the letter, we vow never to proceed with a meeting where local staff are excluded.

But we do not need to. No other ministry ever forbids local staff to participate. It seems that the "Ministry for Foreigners" was reflexively adhering to an authoritarian past which will inevitably give way to a more democratic approach as the country opens gradually to the outside world.

I cannot see it going any other way.

CHAPTER 7

Doing Good

(2017-2018)

I quickly settle into my job. As Director for Myanmar, I am responsible for our relationship with the government, collaboration with diplomats and development partners on the ground, outreach to the public, definition of our strategy and program, and management of the local team. I am accountable for everything the World Bank does in Myanmar, so I spend considerable time visiting and understanding the projects we finance. In the course of the two years I am in Myanmar, I am frequently reminded of the many good things that we are doing to create a modern and prosperous country.

Shortly after my arrival, I witness nothing short of a miracle while at Inya Lake for a two-day workshop with the Ministry of Planning and Finance to assess their progress in public financial management.

One by one, the ministry's directors—mostly women—stand up to present how they are transforming Myanmar's public finance systems from rigid, archaic, and handwritten to flexible, modern, and automated. Most had limited English skills a few years ago and are now speaking confidently about their action plans to enhance Myanmar's weak revenue generation, improve budgeting processes, and monitor public expenditures.

The Director of Revenue announces, "Our medium-term goal to introduce the value-added tax is...achieved!"

The Director of Public Expenditure Management is next with her assessment of progress: "Our goal to release budget allocations on time...is 87 percent achieved!"

Our World Bank public finance specialist is part technical expert, part cheerleader. "What do we say?" he shouts after each presentation.

"Collect more! Spend better!" the ministry team responds gleefully.

Maybe I should print T-shirts for them.

I am bursting with pride although I had little to do with this miracle.

The World Bank reengaged in Myanmar soon after the 2011 political transition began. My predecessors invested heavily in modernizing public finance policies and systems. It felt like a familiar challenge for those of us who worked in the former Soviet Union and Eastern Europe after the Berlin Wall fell in 1989. I had years of experience helping young governments in places like Albania, Serbia, and Bulgaria implement changes to move from centrally planned economies to more globally integrated and market-oriented economies. Most World Bank staff had been drawn into that historic transition, and after several decades of effort, we knew roughly how to do it.

All the familiar challenges of a classic economic transition now applied to Myanmar: deregulating prices and markets, modernizing financial markets, privatizing and regulating industries, building efficient government systems, upgrading infrastructure, and enhancing accessibility and quality of public services. It was all about good policies, capable institutions, and investments in people and basic infrastructure.

I have done this before, I remind myself. *I know what I am doing.*

And tonight, on the shore of Inya Lake, we are celebrating some of the early victories in Myanmar's economic transition. And there is no better way to celebrate in Southeast Asia than with karaoke.

Who knew about the Burmese-language version of the John Denver classic "Take Me Home, Country Roads"? But the Deputy Minister of Finance U Myo Myint Aung is wrapping up a surprisingly tuneful rendition and handing the microphone to me to continue in English. This is karaoke relationship building, and I am game.

I follow along, warbling something about my heavenly West Virginia home. It is not pretty, but it is the best I can do.

We follow with a Burmese/English rendition of "Top of the World" by the Carpenters. And truth be told, I am feeling on top of the world this evening. Clearly the World Bank has done the right thing to invest in public finance systems in Myanmar. The team spent a hefty amount of money to do an analysis where each chapter became a master class in public finance management for the government. The team conducted training so that ministry directors and staff could do their own analyses and define their own reform paths. It was brilliantly conceived, and after a few years, the progress is phenomenal.

And we are rewarding that progress. A few months before going to Myanmar, I met with my predecessor, the previous director for the Myanmar program, based in Bangkok. He explained that they put in place two alternating series of development policy loans (DPLs) over six years, one for public sector reforms and one for the private sector. The DPLs would put hundreds of millions of dollars directly into Myanmar's budget each year as a reward for adopting good policies to modernize public finance and liberate a constrained private sector. It is a bold strategy, reflecting the optimism of the international community that Myanmar finally has a government that cares about its people—a government that will do the right things.

These two series of DPLs will channel more than a billion dollars directly into Myanmar's fledgling government over six years, to be used for adopting the right policies and spending money on the right things, like basic healthcare and education.

The first such chunk of money—$200 million—has already been approved to reward this laudable progress in public finance (*Collect more! Spend better!*). It will flow into the Myanmar budget within a few months—September or October, depending on the speed of Myanmar's legislative process.

At least, that is my plan.

In the meantime, I take trips around the country to see firsthand what else we are financing. Our team sets me up to cut ribbons, release balloons, and make congratulatory remarks in remote villages where men and women are celebrating building a rural road, a classroom, or a community center—all financed by the World Bank through the National Community Driven Development Project. It is a chance for me to talk to villagers about progress they are seeing in their lives. I am never happier.

One of the most memorable trips is to Myeik, the commercial capital of the Tanintharyi Region. This region is a long finger of land in southern Myanmar bordering the Andaman Sea on the west and Thailand's hill country on the east. The Myeik Archipelago is a spattering of islands off the coast in the Andaman Sea.

Five members of our team accompany me to attend the government's inauguration of a solar power mini grid on a remote island: Htein and Silvana (our engineers), Shwe Zin (our program assistant), Alex (our environmental specialist), and Mya Mya (my executive assistant). The mini grid was financed by the World Bank under a rural electrification project.

"Let's get to the boat," says Shwe Zin as we walk across the tarmac of a tiny airport.

"Whoa, that's a speed boat—I mean, it's a racing boat!" I exclaim when we reach the port.

"Yeah, this is a new thing since last year. It takes only two hours to get to our camp—it would be much longer with the regular boats," she explains as I climb aboard. Soon we are bouncing across the water with two enormous engines cranking at full throttle.

"This is unreal. It's gorgeous!" I yell to the team as we cut through expanses of turquoise water, passing forested islands with pristine white sand beaches below cloudless blue skies.

"Nobody has seen this, Ellen," explains Htein. "The Tatmadaw controlled this whole area in the past. They kind of still control it today."

"It's a tourism paradise. I can't believe it!" I exclaim.

"They didn't allow any development here. There are no hotels. We're staying in the only place they've allowed: a camp with tents on the beach," he continues.

Sometimes our work has unexpected rewards. It is more beautiful than I can imagine. We are overnighting here to make it to the mini-grid site on time tomorrow morning.

We have a few hours before sunset, so we snorkel out to shallow coral reefs. World-class snorkeling in a tropical paradise seen only by a privileged few. And I am now one of them.

I sit with the team after dark at a rough wooden table off the beach.

"Dinner looks very good, very fresh," says Mya Mya after touring the various grills. Our hosts bring platters with a whole fish, large prawns, massive lobsters, and something that resembles crayfish, fresh from the sea, grilled up with a bit of salt and spices. Every morsel is delicious.

"That's probably the freshest seafood you'll ever eat," says Alex.

I nod, fully sated and content to listen to the slapping of the waves on the beach. With no lights nearby, the stars burn intensely.

Eventually I crawl into a tent set on top of thick foam mattresses resting on a wooden platform just off the beach. This tent tower makes me laugh. It reminds me of the story of *The Princess and the Pea,* except that I fall into a deep and untroubled sleep.

"We need to hurry," says Shwe Zin the next morning. The boat races across the water again, but this time we are on a deadline. We pull into a dock, and a local official leads us past a crowd of curious children.

"Please put your clothes on here," he says, bringing us to his own home—a traditional teak house on stilts—to change into our longyis for the impending ceremony.

"These solar mini grids are pretty amazing," I say to Silvana as we pull on our traditional outfits.

"They are the perfect solution for these islands," she responds. "They are efficient and cost-effective in a lot of places in Myanmar that are too remote to expand the national grid. And now they can be transported in a single shipping container."

"Really? That's incredible. How many households does this one serve?" I ask.

"Four villages on this island...so probably about five thousand families," she responds.

I am ecstatic that the $400 million the World Bank provided to Myanmar for rural electrification is producing results like this. I have seen how electricity transforms lives, allowing children to study at night, nurses to keep vaccines cool, farmers to irrigate crops, restaurants to open at night, and every family to charge a cell phone. Here in Myanmar, that allows access to information inconceivable under five decades of military dictatorship.

For the inauguration ceremony, a brightly colored tent has been erected, with Buddhist flags fluttering and musicians playing flutes and drums nearby. I walk over and find Mya Mya engaged in a rapid-fire Burmese conversation with officials from the Ministry of Electricity and Energy.

"They have no translation," she says, pulling me off to the side. "They want you to speak without it."

"That's too bad. I've come a long way to have nobody understand me," I reply sadly.

Mya Mya is determined. She returns to the officials for another animated conversation.

"Okay. They're worried the translation will take too long, but it's okay. I told them you'll be short."

"It's okay? Who will do it?"

"I'll do it. They have nobody else."

It is probably the first time most of the villagers in the audience have heard a foreigner in translation. It is a big hit. Mya Mya translates my jokes so I hear delayed ripples of laughter from the crowd. She does brilliantly. Even the time-pressed officials are delighted when I praise the efforts of the ministry to expand electricity to remote areas like this. Afterward, the audience crowds around to greet me and nod approvingly at my longyi.

"Come see the water dancers!" says Mya Mya, always finding opportunities to share Myanmar's diverse culture with me.

A dance troupe of women—girls, really—in bright yellow longyis and deep red lipstick balances clay pots filled with water on their heads as they dance. The younger girls of eleven or twelve may balance only a pot or two, but the most skilled dancers balance four pots on their heads in a precarious vertical tower.

"Oh my god! How do they do that?" I say aloud.

I am feeling dazed by the heat and mesmerized by the bright costumes and graceful swaying of the dancers. A young girl bobbles momentarily off balance, and water streams down her face, but she continues to dance. I learn they traveled from the regional capital of Dawei for a full day by bus and by boat to be here. They are celebrating electricity: a life-changing development that few in these villages expected after years of broken government promises.

The mini-grid facilities are clean and bright. I step into the field of new solar panels, and one of our team snaps my photo as I jokingly twirl around. I look afterward at the photos and am horrified. My hands are swept out like a professional model at a new car show, displaying the solar panels as if I were personally responsible for them being here. It is embarrassing. I will not let the team publish them on our Facebook page.

Nonetheless, I am proud that in just a few short years, access to electricity in Myanmar has risen from less than a third of the population to more than half. That is about eleven million more people out of the country's fifty-four million who are charging cell phones, pumping fresh water, and studying at night. Yes, we are making a difference.

Cell phones. Electricity. Education. So many good things are happening! Although I had wanted other jobs more, now that I am in Myanmar, I cannot imagine a more exciting and challenging job than here, in a country moving decisively down the path toward democracy and development after years of repression and isolation.

CHAPTER 8

A Fragile and Conflict-Affected Country

(January-July 2017)

I am not naïve, of course. I know that Myanmar is officially classified in the international community as a "fragile, conflict- and violence-affected country." And I have earlier experience in pursuing economic transition amid ethnic and religious conflict.

I worked for nearly a decade in the Balkans after the violent dissolution of Yugoslavia in 1989. Ethnic and religious identity were a source of conflict or added fuel to the fire of other grievances that first tore Yugoslavia apart and then continued to destabilize many of its successor states. My job was to help the Macedonian government implement social and economic reforms as they struggled to find compromises between the majority Slavic population and the ethnic Albanian minority.[4] Keeping Macedonia calm was particularly critical as nearby Bosnia exploded into war along ethnic and religious lines from 1992 to 1995 and grappled with an uneasy peace and frozen conflict thereafter. I remember writing about "ethnic cleansing" of Bosnian Muslims and

[4] I lived in the former Yugoslav Republic of Macedonia, today known as Northern Macedonia.

being overruled by my boss on the grounds that the phrase was "too sensitive." *Too sensitive for whom?* I wondered, experiencing for the first time a level of risk aversion at the World Bank that seemed...offensive? Immoral?

A few years later, I had to evacuate my daughters—ages one and three—to the US as Macedonia became the staging ground for NATO bombing of Serbia. This was in response to conflict between ethnic Serbs and Albanians that ultimately led to Kosovo becoming an independent nation. I stayed behind to evacuate my team if necessary and help stabilize Macedonia. As a young mother, I felt the guilt of risking my children's safety and then abandoning them with friends thousands of miles away for several months to do my job. But it was the right thing to do, working with a government in Macedonia that chose to stay on a peaceful, democratic, and tolerant path while others around them collapsed into war and crimes against humanity.

I heard my share of individual stories—intimate stories—about the brutality of war and about crimes committed against innocent civilians. The saddest meeting I ever attended was with local staff in Rwanda in 1995 as the World Bank reopened its office following the 1994 genocide.

I was considering moving to Rwanda to complete the reopening and engage with the new government, which was eager for help to reduce poverty and ease social tensions. I went for a visit and was greeted at the airport by a driver in a tired-looking car with a World Bank flag clumsily lashed to one side. As we drove past police checkpoints en route to the hotel, a white Toyota Landcruiser crossed us at an intersection.

"That's our car," said my driver.

"Oh? Another World Bank car?" I asked.

"No, the only car. But we don't have it anymore."

"What do you mean? We sold it?"

"No. It was stolen during the events. They don't give it back."

"How are you sure it is ours?"

"I know our car. And it still has the plate."

As we turned at the intersection to follow the vehicle, I saw that they had not even bothered to remove the diplomatic license plate from the car looted during the chaos, in the deadly violence that locals now refer to euphemistically as "the events."

Typically, on arrival in a new country, I would meet with the local team to get a firsthand account of the development challenges, the priorities of the current government, and the contours of the World Bank program. Before arriving at the office in Rwanda, I assumed today would be no different than in other countries.

But sitting with a dozen staff surrounding me, I reflected on the stolen car. And then I threw out my usual playbook and said, "I know this is difficult, but what happened to you—and what happened to the office—during 'the events'?"

It felt as if a light switch flipped. Eyes opened wide. People glanced at each other. I heard murmuring.

"After our resident representative was evacuated, we were here alone. We destroyed confidential documents, put the car up on blocks, and locked up the office. Like we were told to do by headquarters," said a local economist.

"And then what happened?"

"We are fortunate. Only two of us were lost. The rest..."

"Two were lost?"

"Yes, only two staff were killed, but the rest of us managed to escape."

"Killed? How horrible. And you escaped? How?"

"However we could. We went to different borders. By car or bus. Or we walked," answered the executive assistant.

Eyes bulged and hands clutched at throats as troubling memories poured forth.

"It was dangerous. Fires were burning everywhere. And bodies were lying on the road, hacked to pieces," added an assistant.

"How did the World Bank help you?" I asked.

"There is no policy to help local staff escape."

Now my eyes widened. Staff rushed to reassure me.

"Most of us were lucky. The resident representative in Burundi decided on her own to send local staff in cars to find us at their border, in the refugee camps. Then they took us home with them."

"We lived with them until we could come back here. Then the World Bank helped us by reopening the office so we could work. But we still don't have our homes," said an agriculture specialist.

"What do you mean?"

"Our apartments and houses were occupied during the fighting. We're trying to get them back, but we don't know who to talk to."

"Where are you living?"

"Wherever we can. Some with family, some in temporary rooms. It's crowded."

"But really we're just lucky to be alive," concluded one.

"Yes. We're alive," said another. And I heard it being repeated around the room like a mantra.

After the meeting, I asked the executive assistant, "What do people at headquarters say when you tell them what happened here?"

"You're the first one to ask," she replied.

I just gaped at her in disbelief.

I was so angry that on the plane home, I wrote like a fury, preparing a memo to senior management telling them the life-threatening story of our Rwandan staff. At that time, the World Bank followed UN policy to leave local staff sheltering in place during conflicts. The rationale was that this was safer than uprooting staff and their families to become refugees with no homes and no work. I pointed out the fallacy in this logic if the risks of sheltering in place were death, torture, or imprisonment. Particularly if World Bank staff were targeted.

Later I was congratulated on this memo by senior managers, with one telling me, "This needed to be said."

In the next few years, as the world acknowledged the tragedy in Rwanda and officially declared genocide, the World Bank changed its policies to protect local staff in life-threatening situations. Leaders on the ground—leaders like me—were given the right to decide if evacuation of local staff was warranted. Staff and their families could be evacuated to nearby locations and absorbed temporarily into other offices to keep staff working and earning to support their families in times of upheaval.

I like to think that my memo helped bring about a change to recognize the high human costs of conflict and to value all World Bank staff equally.

It was this experience of working in countries shaped by ethnic conflict that gave me confidence that I could do the same in Myanmar even before I began my assignment.

While still at headquarters, I reviewed World Bank documents on the country. Each one mentioned ethnic conflict and the ongoing peace process in the introductory paragraphs as part of the context in which we work. How it changed what we were doing in Myanmar was less clear.

Most articles in the global press discussed recent violence against the Rohingya people, a Muslim community of roughly 1.3 million people in Rakhine State, on the western coast of the country, bordering the Bay of Bengal and Bangladesh. According to the articles, in late 2016, the Myanmar military and security forces fired indiscriminately at Rohingya villages from helicopters, killed civilians, raped women and girls, set houses on fire, and detained hundreds of men in unknown locations on unknown charges.[5] Satellite photos show more than 1,200 homes torched.[6]

---

[5] "Myanmar: Security Forces Target Rohingya during Vicious Rakhine Scorched-Earth Campaign," Amnesty International, December 19, 2016, https://www.amnesty.org/en/latest/press-release/2016/12/myanmar-security-forces-target-rohingya-viscious-scorched-earth-campaign/.

[6] Amnesty International, "Myanmar."

One article stated that "some of the Rohingya were gunned down as they tried to cross the Naaf River that separates Myanmar and Bangladesh, while others arriving by boat were pushed away by Bangladeshi border guards and may be stranded at sea."[7]

An estimated 25,000 to 30,000 Rohingya fled from Myanmar to Bangladesh, joining several hundred thousand others who arrived from Myanmar in successive waves of violence dating back to the 1940s.

The military confirmed ninety dead since October 2016, but denied any human rights violations, maintaining that Rohingya militants were responsible for burning down their own houses.

The Ministry of Foreign Affairs said it was a "misinformation campaign" by a "violent group based in Rakhine. They are using our country, our region, as a base...with the intention of disrupting the area, causing unrest, chaos in the area. They are doing this to get international attention, to pressure Myanmar."[8]

This denial by the Ministry of Foreign Affairs raised my eyebrows. In late 2016, the ministry was headed by State Counsellor Aung San Suu Kyi herself, serving as minister.

So after only seven months in power, her government came under fire in the international press, highlighting a "deepening frustration and impatience at the way Myanmar's de facto leader, the democracy activist Aung San Suu Kyi, has brushed off mounting evidence of military atrocities and allowed international agencies insufficient access to the area."[9]

---

[7] Serajul Quadir and Wa Lone, "Hundreds of Rohingya Flee Myanmar Army Crackdown to Bangladesh," Reuters, November 16, 2016, https://www.reuters.com/article/cnews-us-myanmar-rohingya-idCAKBN13B1IO.

[8] Quadir and Lone, "Hundreds of Rohingya Flee."

[9] Nick Cumming-Bruce, "Myanmar 'Callous' toward Anti-Rohingya Violence, UN Says," *New York Times*, December 16, 2016, https://www.nytimes.com/2016/12/16/world/asia/myanmar-rohingya-violence-united-nations.html.

I turned to the previous director for Myanmar, based in Bangkok, and asked, "What do our shareholders think of the recent violence against the Rohingya? What about the United States, our largest shareholder? The Europeans, our strongest champions of human rights? The Chinese, Myanmar's most dominant influence? What do they say?"

"Everybody is concerned," he acknowledged. "But the most important thing is to support and strengthen the civilian government to gain the upper hand after decades of military abuse."

He argued convincingly that things were moving in the right direction. The civilian government was committed to investing in its people and had put its money where its mouth was, with big increases in spending on basic education and health services for long-term development. With our support, they were slowly producing a populace that would demand more from the government and hold the government—including the military—accountable for its actions. Once I reach Myanmar in July 2017, I ask my "brain trust" about this past violence against the Rohingya.

Here I am, a neophyte, in front of three people who have studied Myanmar's history, politics, and culture for well over one hundred years combined. Rachel, on the ground in Myanmar for over twenty-five years, is an expert on ethnic conflicts, including in Rakhine State, the home of the Rohingya. Colin is an Australian academic who dissected the Myanmar military decades before the democratic transition began. Phone Naing is a renown Burmese political analyst who spent years on the Thai border monitoring the repressive regime. I feel extraordinarily lucky to benefit from their counsel so I can begin to understand Myanmar's complex social fabric, military history, and political prospects.

It is complex. I learn that colonial Britain felt compelled to classify Burma's ethnic groups and gave up counting around 135. This does not include the Rohingya, most of whom immigrated to Rakhine State in the nineteenth and early twentieth centuries. They are not recognized as a legitimate ethnic group. The United Nations considers them among the largest groups of stateless individuals in the world.

The two dozen or so major ethnic armed organizations in Myanmar represent communities who fought for decades against authoritarianism and for self-determination and democracy in Burma. Rachel, Colin, and Phone Naing push me to take a more informed look at the map of Myanmar, pointing out the ring of mountainous border areas dominated by ethnic minorities.

"The Tatmadaw has never gained full territorial control in many of these areas," says Rachel.

These are the "conflict-affected areas," to use our international development jargon. Not tiny pockets of conflict but a wide ring of land around the center of the country containing as much as one-third of the population. Close to twenty million people—larger than many countries. They protect themselves from the Tatmadaw in the dense jungles and high altitudes of the border zones.

"Military cleansing operations are a regular occurrence," Colin explains. "The Tatmadaw resorted to them over the past five decades to try to pacify border areas like in Kachin and Shan States."

He tells me that the military justified these operations to root out insurgents within communities, but their actions were indiscriminate: razing whole villages; killing, raping, and torturing civilians; and forcibly displacing families from their homes and fields. Sometimes families were pushed across borders into Thailand, China, or other neighboring countries. The Tatmadaw engaged repeatedly in a counter-insurgency strategy known as the Four Cuts, which aimed to cut off food, funds, information flow, and popular support for armed groups fighting for self-determination.

Between 1948 and 2003, Burmese governments carried out at least thirteen major military operations against the Rohingya.[10] Under the military dictatorship, this included operations in 1975,

[10] Andrew Selth, "Myanmar's Armed Forces and the Rohingya Crisis," United States Institute of Peace, August 17, 2018, https://www.usip.org/publications/2018/08/myanmars-armed-forces-and-rohingya-crisis.

1978, 1989, 1991, and 2002. The only difference in late 2016 was that Myanmar's newfound openness to the world meant that the usual Tatmadaw response—with all its violence and abuses—made global headlines.

"So…" I ask hesitatingly. "What if I told Aung San Suu Kyi that the World Bank would not provide any more money to Myanmar unless the military stopped its violence against the Rohingya?"

Colin chuckles appreciatively.

Phone Naing smiles. "That would be a very noble but not very useful thing to do," he says finally. "The Lady has no authority over the military. It is not like heads of state in most Western democracies. The civilian government has no oversight of the military, and the Tatmadaw has constitutionally mandated authority for all matters of defense, internal security, and border affairs."

I discover that even the military budget is nonnegotiable. The civilian government receives a residual budget to do the things the military wants them to do, which is manage the economy and catch up to rapidly growing Asian countries—the famous Asian Tigers—that left Burma in the dust decades ago.

I am starting to see the full picture. The military retains much power. Civilian power is limited. And Myanmar is a land accustomed to operating in isolation. The majority population—subject to five decades of military propaganda—believes that outsiders are intent on destroying an independent Myanmar.

Foreign aid, now flooding in, remains a small fraction of the economy. Funding from the World Bank—which, at half a billion dollars a year, is among the largest economic aid programs in the world—is less than 5 percent of the government's budget and less than 1 percent of the Myanmar economy. Just a drop in the bucket!

People in Myanmar are just getting used to foreigners arriving, just starting to trust us. If we withhold our aid, they either will not notice at all or will be confirmed in their earlier suspicions that we mean them no good. This includes Aung San Suu Kyi.

Rachel, Colin, and Phone Naing are right. The most important thing we can do is support the gradual opening of this inward-looking society. We need to raise awareness of modern concepts of development and human rights and slowly change public opinion. The key is to strengthen the civilian government to the point where it can exert real control over an unchecked military.

The importance of this historic transition cannot be overstated. Myanmar is gradually opening after five decades lost to the world. After decades of abuse and economic mismanagement, it is important to do what we can within the mandate of the World Bank to reduce poverty. Sometimes those trite sayings hold true: Rome was not built in a day. We cannot let the perfect be the enemy of the good. So we do what we can to lay a foundation for better governance over the long run.

It would be hubris to think we could do anything else.

CHAPTER 9

Are We All Complicit?

(August 2017)

My first month on the job has gone well. I have done the most important introductory meetings. I have begun to build the key relationships that will determine how useful the World Bank will be in the country for the next few years. I have begun to build trust.

I take advantage of the August slowdown in Washington to take a family holiday to Vietnam with my husband and daughters, now ages twenty-two and nineteen. We go from South to North, from bustling Ho Chi Minh City (which I still think of by its pre-communist name, Saigon) to today's capital, Hanoi.

We have a beautiful trip, taking boats up the Mekong River, visiting the magnificent imperial capital in Hue, and relaxing on white sand beaches near Da Nang.

We visit the Military History Museum in central Hanoi for a Vietnamese perspective on the war that dominated my childhood. The Vietnam War—or the War of American Aggression, as it is known here—looms large in my psyche. My childhood was pierced by the anti-war movement, the military draft and its dodgers, the steady stream of American casualties, the Pulitzer Prize–winning photos of villages strafed and naked children running from the firefight. My daughters are learning history today.

It is a disturbing museum, with its displays of American skulls and photos of dismembered and disabled children, victims of American bombing in Vietnam as well as Cambodia and Laos.

Afterward, we sit in a café, drained from this sobering experience, and have a disjointed conversation.

My older daughter, Isabel, asks, "How much should we US citizens feel guilt or responsibility for what happened in Vietnam? Don't we have a moral obligation to do something? Like pay reparations?"

She majored in justice and peace studies at university. Good to see that education is paying off. But my neural pathways lead straight to the Holocaust, so I counter, "Well, to what extent should Germans today feel guilt and responsibility for Nazi atrocities?"

"I mean, were the eighteen-year-olds who were drafted to fight in Vietnam back then responsible for these deaths? Can they really be blamed?" adds my younger daughter, Danielle.

My husband, Eric, weighs in, "Rank-and-file soldiers do not bear responsibility. I mean, some, but not full responsibility."

Isabel needles her father, who is French, "What about French women who had affairs with Nazi soldiers?"

"Their heads were shaved, and they were humiliated, but they cannot be held responsible for Nazi crimes," he insists.

"But they were complicit," Isabel answers angrily.

"I think each individual has moral responsibility for his or her choices," I interject, trying to find middle ground. I am too exhausted from looking at gruesome images to really dig into this argument.

"In some respects, we're all complicit," Isabel persists. "Like Mom working with the government in Myanmar when they are killing Rohingya. She is complicit."

"No, it is not that simple! I'm trying to stop military abuses by strengthening the civilian government."

She knows this but cannot resist skewering me with her righteous sword.

"Sure, but in the meantime, you are complicit in genocide," she says flatly.

Her comment slaps me across the face. I feel stung and sick to my stomach. I have been called many things by many people, but this hurts most.

Complicit in genocide! Knowingly and willfully turning a blind eye to atrocities. Nothing could hurt me more—a Jewish child raised on Holocaust morality tales. I was told just one thing as a child: if you do not say something, if you do not do something, it could happen again.

But no, that is not me. I know what I am doing. It is a complicated situation in Myanmar. I am engaging on the side of greater good versus a known evil. Not engaging—not trying—would be the real crime. Losing this opportunity to strengthen democracy and civilian rule in Myanmar after decades of brutal military repression would be a tragedy.

The slap still stings. My stomach is nauseated. I feel...angry? Sad? Guilty? I am not sure.

I leave my family to their sightseeing. I want to be alone.

It is not as if I have ignored the question. *But is she right? Am I complicit in genocide?* I wonder.

I will ask myself this question many more times as my story in Myanmar unfolds.

CHAPTER 10

What Do We Call Them?

(August 2017)

"What do we call them officially?" I ask Kyi Sin, my resident explainer-in-chief in Myanmar.

He raises an eyebrow in a now-familiar gesture of "it's complicated."

Levon has already done his homework. "The UN calls them *those who self-identify as Rohingya*. With an asterisk."

"An asterisk?"

"Hereinafter referred to as *Rohingya*."

"So we follow the UN? I mean, we're a UN specialized agency," I say.

"I guess so."

"Kinda awkward, huh?"

They call themselves Rohingya. The government, ethnic Rakhine people, and most of the Myanmar public call them Bengalis. This is pejorative, like using the N-word to discuss race in America.

People in Myanmar cannot even quite explain it, but eventually I learn. Rohingya means "from Rakhine" in the Rohingya language. And therein lies the problem for many in Myanmar. The name itself suggests legitimacy, belonging in Rakhine State.

Most of the Rohingya came to Rakhine State after the first Anglo-Burmese War brought the area into British India in 1824. Their immigration was encouraged to support a thriving fishing and commercial hub. The Rohingya population grew rapidly through the 1930s, stabilizing at about one-third of the population of Rakhine State.[11] They are mostly concentrated in three townships of northern Rakhine: Maungdaw, Rathedaung, and Buthidaung, bordering what is today Bangladesh. They are Muslim, although not the only Muslims in Myanmar or even in Rakhine State.

"Some documents just refer to them as *the Muslim community in Rakhine State,*" continues Levon.

"But this confuses them with the Kaman, who are also Muslim and live in Rakhine. But a recognized ethnicity of Myanmar, unlike the Rohingya," explains Kyi Sin.

What the fuck? I think. Out loud, I say, "Let's go with the UN for now. But check with Legal."

The Rohingya speak a dialect of Bengali, the seventh most-spoken language in the world. But calling them Bengalis in Myanmar is a way of saying they belong in Bangladesh. Or India. Not Rakhine State. Not Myanmar. And through the years, their identification documents have been watered down, taken away. They are a people rendered stateless by a country that does not want them.

But the plot thickens because the Rakhine people who gave the state its name and are in the majority there are not sure they want to be part of Myanmar!

Dreams of the glorious Arakan Kingdom persist. It was a Buddhist realm separated from covetous Burmese kings by a protective mountain range. They had extensive trade and relations to the West, toward India. Not toward Burma and China to the East.

It is not so glorious now. Rakhine State is one of the two poorest states in Myanmar. The two major ethnic groups, Rakhine and

---

[11] Advisory Commission on Rakhine State, *Towards a Peaceful, Fair and Prosperous Future for the People of Rakhine: Final Report of the Advisory Commission on Rakhine State,* August 2017, https://www.rakhinecommission.org/app/uploads/2017/08/FinalReport_Eng.pdf.

Rohingya, as well as a few smaller groups, are deprived in many ways: lack of access to electricity, education, piped water, and jobs. The poorest state in a poor country.

As a World Banker, I am always looking for data. What does the data tell us? Do we even have data?

Not much, I learn. The military dictatorship did not want data on social welfare; they did not want to know how the population suffered. Now as the country transitions toward democracy, the first household surveys are being done, with technical support from the World Bank.

"So how bad is it for the Rohingya exactly?" I ask Devi, one of our poverty specialists.

"We can't really say," she answers. "The government will not label them as Rohingya, of course."

"Of course."

"But do we really want data collected by ethnic identity anyway?" she continues.

"I suppose not," I reply. This would perpetuate use of ethnic identity to overshadow and negate national identity.

"That's the whole damn problem, isn't it?" I conclude. But I am frustrated we cannot clearly see the effects of discrimination on the Rohingya. We have anecdotes but no hard data.

A few days later, the poverty team bursts into my office. "We have it, Ellen!" says Devi.

"What? What is it?" I say, seeing their excitement.

"The Rohingya. Foreign language speakers," she says in a rush.

I am confused, so she continues.

"Government asks what language is spoken by each household in the survey. The majority are labeled native Rakhine speakers. The Rohingya are labeled foreign language speakers."

Of course they are. This is ethnic identity in Myanmar taken to its logical conclusion. If you are considered a foreigner, then you speak a foreign language. And there are almost no true foreigners hanging about in Rakhine State, only the Rohingya.

"So here it is," Devi says, unfurling a spider graph comparing "native Rakhine speakers" to "foreign language speakers" in Rakhine State.

"Oh my god." I am aghast. The foreign language speakers fall short on every dimension of social welfare. They are severely deprived in every way imaginable. Less likely to access education, less likely to be well nourished, less likely to own land, less likely to be employed, less likely to have access to credit, and it goes on and on and on. Few in Rakhine are rich, but the Rohingya are the poorest of the poor. It is disadvantage born of discrimination I am only beginning to understand.

From then on, I use this single graph to shut down those who argue that everybody is poor in Rakhine State, with the ethnic Rakhine just as deprived as the Rohingya. It is demonstrably untrue. I have the data.

An opportunity to learn more about Rakhine State presents itself two months after my arrival in Myanmar. It is August 24, and I have decided to attend a press conference of the Advisory Commission on Rakhine State.

The commission was created by Aung San Suu Kyi "to propose concrete measures for improving the welfare of all people in Rakhine State."[12] It is headed by former UN Secretary General Kofi Annan and has three international members and six Myanmar members, including one eminent Muslim. Their role is to *advise*, not to *investigate* like some of the UN-sponsored representatives and commissions.

Today, they are presenting their final report and recommendations to the public after nearly a year of consultations.

I am accompanied by our press officer. When we arrive at the hotel, he is immediately embarrassed. I am the only diplomat among throngs of local journalists. The commission probably briefed the diplomats

---

[12] "Advisory Commission on Rakhine State," Kofi Annan Foundation, accessed March 13, 2023, https://www.kofiannanfoundation.org/our-work/initiative-advisory-commission-rakhine-state/.

somewhere else, but I am too new to have gotten myself on that list. I do not care. I am here to learn. This will do fine.

I peruse the final report while waiting for the commission to arrive.

> Nomenclature: In line with the request of the State Counsellor, the Commission uses neither the term "Bengali" nor "Rohingya" who are referred to as "Muslims" or "the Muslim community in Rakhine." This does not include the Kaman Muslims, who will simply be referred to as "Kaman."

Interesting. A former UN Secretary General is not strictly following UN protocol on terminology for the Rohingya.

The report has eighty-eight recommendations. Some are uncontroversial, even banal, like "Government should carry out labor market assessments" and "Government should expand extension services to farmers." Others make clear the extent of discrimination faced by the Rohingya: lack of citizenship, less-than-full citizenship, lack of identity papers, movement restrictions, forced displacement, restricted access to the labor market, lack of representation. About 120,000 Rohingya are forcibly held in camps for internally displaced persons as victims of violence by security forces and militias in 2012.

Finally, Annan speaks, choosing his words carefully.

"Our recommendations speak to the frustrations of the Muslim population, which feels especially vulnerable because it is deprived of documentation and freedom of movement. This is why we have presented ambitious steps on the central questions of citizenship verification, documentation, rights, and equality before the law."

But he concludes with a warning.

"We are well aware that our recommendations on citizenship and freedom of movement touch on profound concerns of the Rakhine population. Nevertheless, the Commission has chosen to squarely face these sensitive issues because we believe that if left to fester, the future of Rakhine State—and indeed of Myanmar as a whole—will be irretrievably jeopardized."[13]

The recommendations sound reasonable and incremental: things like speeding up the citizenship verification process, revising the citizenship law, and ensuring freedom of movement. Things the civilian government can do over time if they are truly committed to righting the wrongs of decades of discrimination and abuse.

Rome was not built in a day, the commission reminds us. Wrongs can be righted gradually in Rakhine State.

The press conference ends.

The killing begins.

[13] Kofi Annan, "Remarks by Kofi Annan, Chairman of the Advisory Commission on Rakhine State: Press Conference," Advisory Commission on Rakhine State, August 24, 2017, https://www.rakhinecommission.org/app/uploads/2017/08/final_report_20170823-KA-remarks-Press-Conference.pdf.

CHAPTER 11

The Killing Begins

(August and September 2017)

I only learn of it when I reach the office the next morning. Staff are crowded around the television in our lobby, hoping for more information from Rakhine State.

The Arakan Rohingya Salvation Army (ARSA), a militant Rohingya organization, attacked twenty or thirty border posts and an army base in Rakhine at dawn, killing twelve security officers. At least fifty-nine insurgents have been killed by security forces in response to the attacks.

It is another attack like in October 2016, timed to coincide with the release of the Annan Commission's report. While the Tatmadaw has had skirmishes in other border areas of Myanmar since my arrival two months earlier, this is the most serious conflict so far.

I am pulled into my office by Myine, a transport specialist and a Burmese national raised overseas in a diplomatic family. She often helps me understand what I am seeing and hearing in Myanmar.

"Staff are upset. This is serious. I feel I should warn you," she says, looking devastated.

"Yes, it's terrible. The killing," I say. "Warn me about what?"

"Staff feel conflicted about it," she says. "Honestly, many do not care much about the Rohingya. They see the Rohingya as inferior—almost subhuman—and foreign. This was the propaganda of the military regime for many years. But now this conflict makes Myanmar look bad to the rest of the world. It's not supposed to be this way with a democracy."

"Got it. What do you think I should do?" I ask.

"Talk about it, I guess—maybe in a staff meeting. But be careful because many staff won't feel comfortable talking about this in front of others."

I close the door behind me when she leaves and send a quick message titled "Worrisome Development" to my boss in Washington.

Over the next twenty-four hours, it appears the Tatmadaw is responding in its usual fashion, with brutal cleansing operations aimed at rooting out insurgents among peaceful civilians. We do not really know what is happening because the Tatmadaw has sealed off northern Rakhine from journalists, relief workers, and even the civilian government on security grounds. But we can count refugees straggling into Bangladesh on foot or by sea.

A few days later, on August 28, the UN Secretary General issues a statement of deep concern at reports of civilians being killed by security forces in Myanmar's Rakhine State. He stresses that the Myanmar government is responsible for providing security and assistance to those in need and urges the Bangladesh government to continue allowing the Rohingya to seek safety in Bangladesh.

The UN High Commission on Refugees (UNHCR) reports several thousand new arrivals in Bangladesh at this point, but I watch with disbelief as the number soars in days to come. By September 5, the number reaches 125,000. Three days later, it is 270,000. Four days after that, it reaches 370,000.

My Worrisome Development is now a Full-Blown Crisis.

Families flee without gathering anything, arriving on foot or splashing ashore from fishing boats or makeshift rafts crossing the Naf River into Bangladesh.

The pit in my stomach intensifies as the numbers rise. If refugees are streaming out of Rakhine, the military must be killing them there.

Bits of information float around. Men shot. Women raped. Houses burned. Live babies thrown into fires. Civilians scattering as areas are "cleansed." My mind sees corpses being shoveled into the mass graves of Auschwitz. I feel sick.

We can get no photos from northern Rakhine, but photos of exhausted refugees arriving in Bangladesh are everywhere. The world is reacting. Journalists write devastating articles in the *New York Times, Le Monde, Der Spiegel,* and more.

The diplomatic world issues statements, not only from the UN Secretary General, but from Western nations, from the European Union and others. Deeply concerned. Condemning violence. Encouraging the civilian government to do the right things. They call for the most immediate things: restoring security, allowing access by humanitarian organizations, and putting in place the "conditions for safe, dignified, and voluntary refugee return to their places of origin." This is the global standard for repatriation defined by UNHCR. Safe. Dignified. Voluntary. To their places of origin.

"Ellen, the president wants to issue a statement on the situation in Rakhine. Could you please draft something and give it to his comms team?" says my boss.

"Yes, of course, but...are we sure this is a good idea?" I ask. "Maybe behind-the-scenes discussions would be more effective?"

I feel conflicted. Ten-year-old me knows that if you do not say anything, *it could happen again.* We have a moral obligation to speak out when we see atrocities—human rights abuses, extrajudicial killings, ethnic cleansing, genocide. But grown-up me also knows we should be as strategic as possible to improve the chances that a weak civilian government will do the right things.

It may burnish our reputation to join the chorus of deeply concerned statements, but does it help us help Aung San Suu Kyi and her government gain control over the Tatmadaw? If everybody from Desmond Tutu to the Dalai Lama is speaking out, does a carefully worded statement from the World Bank president even matter?

"You may be right, Ellen," says my boss. "Why don't you prepare a draft just in case, and I will discuss it with the president's office."

On September 14, with close to 400,000 refugees now crowded into Bangladesh, the World Bank issues an internally negotiated statement. In it, we are "deeply troubled" (which won out narrowly over "deeply concerned"). We also "call on the authorities to ensure the protection of all people residing in Myanmar and to work with all actors to mount an immediate humanitarian response to the crisis in Rakhine State." Finally, we offer to "immediately reallocate available resources from our existing Myanmar portfolio to support an integrated humanitarian and development response."

The president's communications team initially proposed "protection of all citizens residing in Myanmar," which makes my team slap their foreheads in frustration. *They just do not get it in Washington, do they*? If they all were citizens and had the rights of citizens, this problem would be moot.

And of course, we offer our help. Because that is what we do. My marching orders are clear: help the civilian government—the democratic government—mount a response and be a force for good against the evil Tatmadaw.

Five days later, on September 19, with the number of refugees at 415,000 and rising, democracy icon Aung San Suu Kyi finally breaks her silence.

World leaders have descended on New York City for the 2017 UN General Assembly, but unlike the previous year, The Lady does not feel comfortable leaving her country right now. She has been allowed into power by the military. They could always take it away during a crisis.

Instead, she will give a speech from Nay Pyi Taw. In English. To ensure that she is heard worldwide, foreign journalists and diplomats based in Myanmar are invited. I scramble madly for a seat on the early-morning flight to Nay Pyi Taw but lose out in the rush. Grumbling, I head up the night before for a dreary night in the hotel zone.

The next morning, the hall is packed. Top government officials are in attendance—even the three ministers from the military (Defense, Internal Affairs, and Border Protection)—along with throngs of diplomats and journalists. An enormous stage is set with rows of Myanmar flags, flower garlands, and a single lectern.

Aung San Suu Kyi steps out alone to speak—a solitary figure on this vast stage. The TV cameras zoom in so that the newscasts that evening do not give the same sense I had of a lonely figure overpowered by her surroundings.

But now I am sitting in the hall listening to her words. Hoping and praying that she will rise to the occasion, condemn the military, and defend the rights of all people in Myanmar. Hoping she will give a speech befitting a global democracy icon.

She begins by giving the world a history lesson about the conflicts and complexities of ethnic relations in Myanmar, including in Rakhine. Everything she says is true.

Then she turns to the violence and forced displacement in Rakhine State.

> We would like to understand why this exodus is happening. We want to talk to those who fled as well as those who have stayed. More than 50 percent of the villages of Muslims are intact, and we would like to know why. This is what we have to look toward. Look at the areas where there are no problems. Why have we been able to avoid these problems in those areas?[14]

It sounds like she is minimizing the death and displacement that have occurred and that still seem to be happening in Rakhine. I cringe

[14] Aung San Suu Kyi, "We Condemn All Human Rights Violations" (speech), September 19, 2017, Naypyitaw, Myanmar, Al Jazeera English, YouTube video, 29:24, https://www.youtube.com/watch?v=NJkg2_72uUo.

inwardly, trying to control my body language, especially when she says things that are easily disprovable.

"Since the fifth of September there have been no armed clashes and no clearance operations," she says, and later adds that "all people living in Rakhine State have access to education and healthcare services without discrimination."

These are demonstrably untrue.

But she also says some encouraging things—things we diplomats and development partners will discuss and parse afterward.

> We condemn all human rights violations and unlawful violence. We are committed to the restoration of peace, stability, and the rule of law throughout the state. We are determined to implement the recommendations of the commission. Those recommendations that will bring speedy improvement to the situation in a short frame of time will be given priority. Other recommendations we will have to take time over, but every single recommendation that will benefit peace, stability, and harmony in Rakhine State will be implemented in the shortest possible time.

She expresses willingness to repatriate the Rohingya refugees:

> I can confirm now that we are ready to start the verification process at any time and those who are verified as refugees will be allowed to return without any problems and with full assurance of their security and access to humanitarian aid.

This sounds somewhat promising. Something to work with. She even gives some cautious sense of accountability:

> Action will be taken against all peoples, regardless of religion, race, or political position, who go against the laws of the land

> and who violate human rights as accepted by our international community.

In ending her speech, Aung San Suu Kyi appeals to all of us—the diplomats and development partners—to support her young government:

> Join us in a positive and constructive way to find new paths toward peace and stability, towards harmony...go with us to the problem areas, see for yourself what is happening, think for yourself, what can we do to remove these problems? We need to remove ills and promote the positive. And we want to do this together with you.

Okay, it is not a game-changing speech. Certainly not a ringing defense of universal human rights. But not hopeless. It commits to implementing the recommendations of the Annan Commission report and repatriating the refugees. It is a start. She wants us to work with the government to solve difficult problems. That's what we do at the World Bank.

The global press is not kind. They focus on what she does not say: explain exactly what happened in Rakhine, acknowledge the severity of the situation, hold the Tatmadaw accountable for the violence, call on the Myanmar public to reject intolerance, call the Rohingya by their name.

"It is not the intention of the Myanmar government to apportion blame or to abnegate responsibility," she says.

Afterward the diplomats drink sweetened tea and avoid the dry cake. The press flocks around looking for sound bites. The diplomats strike just the right tone.

"A good first step. We encourage strong action by the government," they say.

I say nothing.

I feel reassured afterward, chatting with the ambassadors, because we all seem to agree on the necessary course of action. It is essential to strengthen the hand of Aung San Suu Kyi and her government to counteract the wrongs of the Tatmadaw and local militias. We need to help her government implement the difficult recommendations of the Annan Commission and—now that the crisis has unfolded—do what is in their power to restore basic security, allow humanitarian relief into Rakhine, and bring back the refugees. Repatriation that is safe, dignified, and voluntary. Repatriation to their places of origin.

It is a tall order, but I do not shrink from it.

I am the leader of the World Bank team in Myanmar. It is my responsibility to figure out how we can help this fledgling democracy in a time of crisis and how we can right at least some of the wrongs.

What kind of a leader—what kind of a person—would I be if I did not at least try?

CHAPTER 12

First Moves

(September 2017)

The month of September is a frenzied blur for me and my team as we prepare daily briefings on the evolution of the Rohingya crisis for headquarters, coordinate regularly with diplomats and other development partners on the international response, and reach out to the civilian government to encourage a vigorous response and offer our financial and technical support to move in the right direction.

Late in the month, my boss asks me to set up a phone call between Aung San Suu Kyi and the president of the World Bank, Jim Yong Kim. They met a year and a half ago, before she was in power, when he visited Myanmar for the first time.

While a phone call between The Lady and the president of the World Bank could reinforce our concern over the Rohingya crisis and our willingness to help resolve it, I feel like my boss is going a bit too far. A phone call like this implies that the World Bank carries sufficient political and financial weight in Myanmar to shape the government's response to a deeply entrenched ethnic conflict. This organizational hubris is frequent and irritating to me. Better to assess our weight and influence first at lower levels—me or even Charlotte—before calling in the big guns.

"I can try," I answer cautiously.

"It would set the right tone for all development partners, don't you think?" she adds.

"Yeah, I suppose."

I am dubious but mostly nervous. After only two tumultuous months in the country, do I have the access and clout needed to arrange a phone call with the head of government at the drop of a hat?

The president's office gives us a time slot less than twenty-four hours away. Morning in Washington, early evening in Yangon.

For those of us sent out specifically to have a relationship with the government, this is a gut-wrenching test of our effectiveness. Diplomats and heads of development agencies are on the ground to nurture relationships, maintain access, and maximize influence. But this takes time. I have been in the country a scant two months during an unprecedented crisis. Can I pull off such a high-level request in less than a day?

I have my doubts. Our administrative staff do not schedule meetings on Monday in Myanmar because they need that day to send official request letters by fax and then follow up with frantic phone calls to get confirmation. Even after the confirmation, they phone the day of the meeting, finding a diplomatic way to ask, "Will they show up for sure?"

So I am not confident that we can schedule a phone call with Aung San Suu Kyi in less than twenty-four hours.

Many ministries in Myanmar do not yet have official government email addresses. And most government officials do not respond to more modern and now widely available ways of communicating: email, text, WhatsApp, etc. So Mya Mya cranks up the official machinery to fax an urgent letter requesting a phone call with the state counsellor at the time when the World Bank president is available.

When no official response is forthcoming within several hours (have they even picked the fax up off the machine?), I turn to our Myanmar staff.

"Does anybody know anybody? How can I get through?" I ask.

In my career spanning nearly forty years in at least a dozen different countries, this has never failed me. Somebody went to school with somebody. Somebody's cousin married somebody. Somebody's electrician works for somebody.

It does not fail me now. We are just five hours away from the appointed time, and I break all the usual rules by sending a personal email to Aung San Suu Kyi's chief of staff, who was a childhood classmate of one of our staff members.

He replies within minutes! He promises to consult The Lady and get back to me.

Twenty minutes later, my cell phone rings.

"Yes, the state counsellor will adjust her schedule to be available for the phone call later today," he says.

"My deepest thanks for your kind help!" I say, in diplomatic hyperdrive. "We are honored that the state counsellor will grant us this time for our president's call."

Holy shit. I managed it. I managed to arrange a phone call at the highest levels of government and the World Bank in just a few hours. I am exhausted, relieved, and proud of our kick-ass team. And everybody at headquarters will see that I have hit the ground running, forging the most important relationships.

They are all sleeping in Washington, so I race to prepare talking points for our president. My boss has me send them directly to our president, who is in New York at the UN General Assembly. He will have his talking points upon waking. I feel like such a star!

One hour before the scheduled call, my boss calls me. That morning, a *New York Times* story recounted the Rohingya tragedy and criticized Aung San Suu Kyi's recent speech.

"The president read it this morning and said, 'Why on earth would I want to talk to this woman?' Ellen, you must cancel the call."

Fuck. It. All. They cannot be serious! I am reeling with disbelief and anger. A phone call between a head of state and the World Bank president is a rare thing. I have arranged perhaps half a dozen in a career spanning nearly forty years, always in unusual and important circumstances. Most of the time, a head of state agrees to meet our president when he is in the country on an official visit planned months in advance. For us to request an urgent phone call and then refuse to take it is both nonsensical and highly disrespectful. It is a slap in the face for Aung San Suu Kyi, Myanmar's elected leader.

But minutes are ticking away, and this is a diplomatic disaster.

I call the chief of staff and make something up.

"My deepest apologies but the president's schedule in New York keeps shifting and, um, it turns out that he must give a keynote address at a UN event in just a few minutes—exactly when we'd scheduled the call. I deeply apologize for this unexpected shift that will force us to postpone the call."

I'm sure the chief of staff is not fooled. Global opinion of The Lady has plummeted with recent news coverage of the Rohingya crisis. Still, he plays along.

"It's unfortunate that we must postpone, but I understand. Please do not hesitate to contact me when the next opportunity arises."

We both know the opportunity will not arise. And my future access to the state counsellor just took a brutal beating. Now is the time I need to have the strongest possible relationship with her if I am to influence her government's response to the Rohingya crisis. I suspect I will pay dearly for this.

I am angry at my bosses for pulling the rug out from under me and disheartened by the likely consequences. And I know that they will nonetheless expect me to have easy access to the state counsellor whenever they need it in the future.

CHAPTER 13

Freezing Funds

(October 2017)

The Rohingya refugee numbers continue to rise, reaching 500,000 as September turns to October. They will reach 700,000 by December 2017, creating the largest refugee camp in the world in southern Bangladesh.

"Jim wants us to send a strong signal that the continuing violence and displacement in Rakhine is unacceptable," says my boss. "If we demonstrate moral leadership, other international partners will likely follow."

"Then let's freeze the budget support," I answer, knowing this will be controversial. My idea is to indefinitely postpone the $200 million already teed up to flow into the government's budget.

To outsiders, it seems the most logical thing to do. How could we reward the Myanmar government for its misdeeds by pouring $200 million into their budget to spend as they like—perhaps even to fund more violence and human rights abuses?

The team that prepared the budget support voices all the counterarguments.

"The government implemented all the reforms we asked them to before the Rohingya crisis exploded, and our board approved it already," the team leader reminds me. "Government already took all the administrative measures necessary to receive the funds. On what grounds could we now change our minds? It would be a breach of contract!"

A breach of contract is something the World Bank preaches against in countries where rule of law is weak. In short, this is an unacceptable—and unauthorized—thing to do.

Even if we can legally justify it, I ponder, *Is it the right thing to do?*

It would punch a hole in the budget of the civilian government without constraining the military. The civilian and military branches of government are administratively separate. The risk of money flowing from the civilian budget to the military budget would be extremely low. More likely, freezing this money would undermine civilian programs, including the emerging relief effort in Rakhine State and efforts to create conditions for refugee return.

And it would undermine the government's trust in the World Bank, another blow to our ability to influence the response in Rakhine. As if the aborted phone call to the state counsellor were not enough.

Yet our president has both a laudable concern for human rights and a wary eye on unflattering headlines for the World Bank. He speaks of our work to reduce poverty in glorious terms as "bending the arc of history" and our decisions as "being on the right side of history."

I want to be on the right side of history too. And it may generate a positive headline in the *New York Times*, which Jim would like.

Interestingly, the UN Secretary General, whose organization has greater experience than the World Bank in working with Myanmar, urges the World Bank's president to show restraint given the military-civilian power balance. Whatever we do, we do not want to undermine the civilian government in its struggle to exert power and influence over the military, nor do we want to send Myanmar back into isolation, military dictatorship, or the powerful embrace of China.

In the end, I choose to freeze the funds. We simply cannot be seen releasing millions of dollars to the government even before they restore basic security and allow humanitarian relief into Rakhine. It would look bad. Really bad.

My hierarchy readily agrees.

Legally justifying the freeze calls for some clever storytelling. But this is not my first rodeo.

"I need you to show how the economic framework on which we based the budget support could be affected by the Rakhine crisis," I tell our economic team. And they oblige with a story that the crisis may destabilize the economy by reducing tourism revenues and discouraging foreign investment.

In the year to come, it turns out to be half true. Tourism revenues fall substantially due to the Rakhine crisis, but foreign investment—largely from China and other Asian neighbors—remains strong.

For now, though, I have my story: the economic conditions on which the flow of funds was predicated can no longer be assumed, so *we have no choice but to wait and see*. It is not a robust story, but it is good enough to legally halt this flow of money for a while.

"Because of changes in economic conditions due to the Rakhine crisis, the World Bank has taken a decision to postpone the budget support," I explain to my karaoke partner, the Deputy Minister of Planning and Finance.

He and his team are the only people in Myanmar who understand how this budget support works. They are the only ones who really care. My predecessors taught them the advantages of budget support linked to economic reforms and showed them the policy matrix that outlined all the things they had to do to get the money. And we promised that when these things were completed, we would write a check.

Now they are proud to have completed all the actions in their matrix. But I am telling them that we cannot write the check. More actions are needed. They look puzzled; I'm sure they are confused by my changing rules after decades of immutable rules.

After a long pause, the deputy minister asks, "When will you bring us the new matrix?"

"The new...matrix?" I stammer. But I am thinking, *Oh my god, we trained them too well.* I feel a rush of pride and almost motherly love toward this team, which is ready to take on new actions to get the money released.

I sigh and explain, "Unlike the earlier actions, the actions needed now are not within the control of your ministry. They are related to the crisis in Rakhine State and include stopping the violence, restoring personal security, allowing humanitarian relief, and creating conditions for refugee return."

These actions are political and controversial. They involve decisions by the weak civilian government, but also by the powerful and recalcitrant Tatmadaw.

The deputy minister is a calm man. A bureaucratic survivor who spent years inside an authoritarian regime. "We cannot do these things," he says sadly. "But we will try."

I believe I made the right choice to freeze the money. Nonetheless, I am left feeling uneasy and deflated. I am undermining economic progress in Myanmar. I am slowing the transformation of the state. And I am eroding trust in the World Bank.

Is it possible that we are overreacting to one horrific conflict in an historically conflict-ridden country? I do not know.

But I have another reason for freezing the budget support, one I cannot talk about with the government, my diplomatic partners, or even my team in Myanmar. I freeze the budget support to avoid a more drastic and more damaging decision by our president.

I am feeling strong pressure to do something highly visible to express our outrage. And in his moments of frustration, our president spins out ideas like freezing our entire $2 billion portfolio or stopping all new projects.

I shudder at the thought of everything we worked for grinding to a halt, collapsing around me. It would halt the progress we have made in empowering rural communities and expanding basic education, healthcare, clean water, and electricity, as well as modernizing infrastructure and the investment climate. Everything we are doing to support Myanmar's historic political and economic transition would stop cold.

Better to rip the bandage off quickly and be done than to have our hands tied in the future as we try to help the civilian government respond to the Rohingya crisis. Better to freeze the $200 million now than lose the use of nearly $4 billion in existing and future aid.

Especially because the government said that they would do the right things. Aung San Suu Kyi said it in her speech: they would implement the Annan Commission recommendations, work toward peace and stability in Rakhine, and repatriate the refugees.

The World Bank's shareholders—from the US to the Europeans to the Australians to the Japanese—want us to do this. They believe we must help the state counsellor and her government or risk losing democracy and civilian leadership in Myanmar after decades of military dictatorship. Even neighboring China, one of our largest shareholders, wants stability in Rakhine State and encourages us to help the government implement a credible response to the crisis.

It has been a crazy, tumultuous five weeks since the initial attacks in August 2017, but those of us in Yangon—the diplomats and development partners—believe we have some chance of success in addressing the Rohingya crisis if we come together, knuckle down, and work with the government to develop a clear roadmap going forward. I am ready.

CHAPTER 14

What Are We Doing in Rakhine?

(October 2017)

"All right, what are we actually doing in Rakhine?" I ask, gazing around our cramped conference room.

Myanmar is the fastest-growing program in the World Bank—or at least it was until the Rohingya crisis began—so now we have around seventy staff playing musical chairs in a charming but decrepit villa meant for a staff of only twenty.

Today, everybody is piled into the dingy conference room—some standing halfway out the doors—to figure out what we are going to do to keep our promises to our board: help all communities in Rakhine and focus more on inclusion in the conflict areas of Myanmar.

"Let's start with what we're actually doing in Rakhine," I repeat.

I need to know if projects supported by the World Bank are reaching Rohingya families. But I am careful with my language even with my own team: we say we want to reach "all communities in Rakhine," including "Muslim communities."

This has been the downfall of my brother and sister UN agencies. Those with long histories of working in Rakhine—like World Food Program and UNDP—stand accused of helping only the Rohingya, caring only about the Rohingya, at the expense of ethnic Rakhine and other communities there. Since the crisis began, the military and the

Rakhine State government have prevented these agencies from entering Rakhine for humanitarian purposes.

The World Bank is not burdened with this accusation—we have only been in Myanmar for five years. We are considered more technical, neutral, and apolitical. We can still get authorizations to visit parts of Rakhine. We must protect this if we are to keep our promise to our board.

"Are we doing anything in Rakhine?" My eyebrows rise in dismay as I struggle to keep my tone even.

Slowly the team offers some morsels of hope. Some villages have been electrified. Some rural roads have been paved. It becomes clear that answering this question is harder than I imagined. Although the projects we finance include Rakhine, we often do not know exactly what communities are served there. Yet this is the first question now being asked in Washington and other world capitals. So we need to look systematically at every project we finance in our $2 billion portfolio.

We discover we can lump those projects into four categories:

1. Those that build institutions that benefit the whole country, not specific to Rakhine
2. Those that take advantage of specific locations to spur economic growth, like hydropower plants on certain rivers, and none of which are in Rakhine
3. Those that have nationwide coverage, so every school or health clinic benefits, including all those in Rakhine
4. Those that operate in only some townships in every state and region, including Rakhine

In the end, I have a decent story to tell Washington.

"The national health project we finance provides grants to all health centers and hospitals in Rakhine and even provides mobile health clinics to reach displaced people—mostly Rohingya—in camps," I explain.

"The national education project we finance reaches all 3,200 public schools in the seventeen townships of Rakhine and provides stipends for poor students in Rakhine, distributed by villages themselves, including Rohingya villages. The nationwide community-driven development project operates in three townships in Rakhine, including two Muslim-majority townships, mostly Rohingya. And the rural electrification project reaches all seventeen townships in Rakhine, reaching 450 villages—including Rohingya villages—with grid and off-grid electricity. These projects use innovative digital technology to track locations and beneficiaries, so we know exactly who we reach."

I am grateful that we finance some activities that benefit Myanmar's most disadvantaged people.

It is not as bad as I feared, but also not as good as it could be.

We can do so much more in Rakhine. It is a priority now to respond to the crisis. If we can convince the government, we can do amazingly creative things to reach all communities and even help the refugees in Bangladesh until they can return home safely and voluntarily.

CHAPTER 15

Talking to the Board

(October 2017)

It is October 5, and I am back in Washington to help my vice president brief the World Bank board on the Rohingya crisis unfolding in Myanmar.

It is the second time in only two weeks that we have briefed the board. This is highly unusual and reflects the deep level of global concern over the violence and alleged human rights abuses in Myanmar. We are also atoning for our sins: some executive directors were unhappy that our president issued a public statement about the crisis without consulting them.

When we brief the board, we must choose our words carefully. As an apolitical organization, according to its Articles of Agreement, the World Bank tends not to talk directly about human rights—or the lack thereof—in its member countries. Instead, we talk about social inclusion, nondiscrimination, and equal opportunity, all appropriate goals within our mandate to eliminate poverty. And all essential for the long-suffering Rohingya.

Now, the night before our board meeting, I hurriedly draft opening remarks for my boss to deliver. I'm in a jet-lagged daze after thirty hours of fly time but this is important. I must get it right.

"Ellen and our team in Myanmar are working closely with the diplomatic and development community in a call for immediate de-escalation of violence, reestablishment of law and order, access to northern Rakhine State for humanitarian purposes, and a return of internally displaced populations and refugees," I write, echoing the UN Secretary General's statements.

Then I try to strike a delicate balance: "Our response needs to be vigorous and principled, carefully coordinated across the international community and calibrated to support Myanmar's continued progress toward peace, democracy, and civilian rule after decades of civil war, isolation, and authoritarian military rule."

Calibrated is the right word. Strong enough to respond to the Rohingya nightmare without blowing Myanmar off its path toward democracy.

Last time we briefed the board, we had deep concerns but no specifics for executive directors. Now, in early October, we are starting to have a plan. We are freezing the budget support. And we will have "an enhanced focus on the recovery and development needs of all populations in Rakhine State."

This is a neutral way to say we will try to protect the estimated 500,000 remaining Rohingya and bring back the refugees. And we will launch "a systematic and sustained effort to enhance our focus on social inclusion...in conflict-affected states and regions." We will up our game, not only for the Rohingya but for all ethnic minorities who are disadvantaged and discriminated against in Myanmar.

I think it's a pretty good speech. Good enough.

The next day, as executive directors drift into the boardroom, I punch my employee identification number into the keypad in front of me, and my name lights up on a jumbo screen, showing who has a seat at the table.

I always feel important in the boardroom, with its soaring ceiling, flags of member states ringing the walls, and enormous horseshoe-shaped table. Seats around the table are assigned to executive directors representing different governments. But today I am not important. I am only here to take notes so my vice president and I can remember what each government wants us to do about the Rohingya crisis.

I take nearly verbatim notes, identifying executive directors and their countries, so we remember who supports our strategy and why. This is critical because what gets said inside the boardroom is confidential. The discussions are deliberative and therefore private, with only an anodyne summary of the board decision made public.

I am prohibited from sharing my notes publicly to avoid identifying specific countries and their views. Afterward, I recall that my boss does a great job with the opening remarks, sounding warm and approachable. She delivers our main message: the need for a carefully calibrated approach that both responds to the Rohingya crisis and safeguards Myanmar's transition to democracy.

I walk out of the boardroom feeling energized. Powerful. Proud that we have defined a response to the Rohingya crisis that is widely supported by our shareholder countries.

My interpretation of what was said falls into three broad categories. Board members from many Muslim-majority countries emphasize that a Muslim population is being killed and forced to flee in massive numbers. So it cannot be business as usual. But we should stay in business! That is their message. Walking away from Myanmar or failing to act would look bad for the World Bank and do nothing to help the Rohingya.

Western democracies also urge us to stay engaged in Myanmar. They support our plan to enhance social inclusion for all populations. And they caution against strong public statements that would risk our access to the government. Instead, they suggest we use our leverage to crack the door open for greater change. We must work quietly to influence actors, not inflame them, and avoid undermining agents of change, including the civilian government.

Several Asian countries note that it is counterproductive to issue public statements. Public criticism risks causing Myanmar's insular society to turn inward again, back toward isolation and Big Brother China.

Two outcomes are evident. First, our executive directors delivered a collective slap to our president for joining the frenzy of public statements without consulting them. Second, they offered strong support to stay engaged in Myanmar and figure out how to best help the Rohingya and serve all communities that face discrimination, exclusion, and conflict.

I realize that words I quickly scribbled the night before in a jet-lagged daze will become our new mantra for Myanmar: "stay engaged with a greater focus on social inclusion in conflict areas." In fact, this will become the cornerstone of everything we do in the months and years to come.

I am relieved to have the support of our board. But I am exhausted from the past five weeks of frenzied crisis response and shuttling between Yangon and Washington.

As I walk away from the boardroom, one executive director catches up with me. His country has a dominant role in delivering aid throughout Asia and a nuanced understanding of Myanmar's decades-long ethnic strife and human rights abuses in Rakhine.

"Rough ride?" he asks amiably.

"I thought it went okay. What do you think?" I respond.

"We, the board, asked the World Bank to be more engaged in fragile and conflict-affected countries. This is what we signed up for."

CHAPTER 16

Learning about Conflict and Exclusion

(November and December 2017)

United Wa State Army. Chin National Front. Shan State Army. Kachin Independence Organization. New Mon State Party. I am trying to get my head around a few of the ethnic armed organizations, or EAOs, who fought for decades for democracy and self-determination along the borders of Burma. They often spilled over into neighboring countries with ethnic affinities—for example, the Wa in China and the Karen in Thailand. It seems there are over two dozen major organizations and many minor ones, sometimes splintering and forming new groups with confusingly similar names. How does the Karenni National Progressive Party differ from the Karen National Union or the Karen National Liberation Army?

I squint to locate them all on the map of Myanmar, and I see the ring of border states, dominated by ethnic minorities, around the central regions, which are dominated by ethnic Bamar. The outer ring is mostly remote and mountainous. This is the ring of conflict, where thousands have been killed and hundreds of thousands displaced over decades in armed clashes with the Tatmadaw or between ethnic groups.

Conflicts are about rights, land, and control of precious resources like timber and jade.

The Tatmadaw considers its military actions essential to pacify the country. In the outer ring, the EAOs maintain small armies, control territory, and provide services like healthcare and education to their people. It is a completely different world from Yangon and Nay Pyi Taw. And it is not a marginal world: about one-third of Myanmar's population lives in this outer ring.

I am shocked to discover that one in every three townships in Myanmar, mostly within the outer ring, has suffered from armed conflict in the past few years.[15] And out of Myanmar's estimated fifty-four million inhabitants, eleven million of them lack identification documents or full citizenship rights.[16] This figure does not even include the estimated 1.2 million Rohingya who were in Rakhine before the refugees fled.

This means that every fifth person in Myanmar lacks full rights and faces legalized discrimination. They cannot enroll in certain universities, join the civil service or army, move easily around the country, or participate fully in the labor market.

While the Rohingya face the most severe constraints and abuses, they are not the only ones facing discrimination and exclusion. The more I learn, the more daunting my new mantra to "stay engaged with a greater focus on social inclusion in conflict areas" is becoming.

Sometimes I feel stupid not to have known all this earlier on. But I am not alone, it seems. Among the World Bank team living or working in Myanmar, the uninformed fall into two distinct categories.

First are foreign staff, often excellent technical specialists—people who understand how to construct a suspension bridge or change the course of a river anywhere in the world. Most have not read a single

---

[15] Adam Burke et al., *The Contested Areas of Myanmar: Subnational Conflict, Aid, and Development* (San Francisco: The Asia Foundation, 2017).

[16] "The 2014 Myanmar Population and Housing Census," Myanmar Information Management Unit, accessed March 13, 2023, http://themimu.info/census-data.

book about Myanmar's history. It seems incredible at first, yet upon reflection it is understandable: they move to a new assignment in a new country on a few months' notice. They are immediately overwhelmed by the unending workload and twenty-four-hour email demands while they get their families settled into new houses and new schools.

Because they lack knowledge of Myanmar's cultural complexity, they sometimes make dangerous mistakes. We have one such person on our telecommunications team. He is part of the amazing team that opened Myanmar to modern communications, but he does not understand the conflicts and resulting fragility in Myanmar.

"Ellen, good news: the government wants to use savings in the telecoms project to extend the pilot on spectrum monitoring, which has been really successful," he says.

Sounds reasonable to me. Honestly, with Rohingya dying and fleeing, I am in crisis mode, so our successful telecommunications work is a low priority for me right now. But always looking to understand our portfolio better, I ask idly, "By the way, what is spectrum monitoring?"

He explains it to me in terms I can understand. Governments throughout the world digitally monitor cell phone operators to make sure they are registered and legitimate and that they pay taxes and do not engage in illicit activities. If the governments find intruders, they can block these intruders out of the spectrum. This is a normal regulatory function. As part of our efforts to develop modern regulatory functions in Myanmar, we have helped the government pilot spectrum monitoring in the two cities of Yangon and Nay Pyi Taw.

"Now they want to use project savings to extend to Wa State," he concludes.

"Wa State? Did you say Wa State?" I ask. The Wa live in a highly autonomous region on the Chinese border. The Wa State Army is Myanmar's most armed ethnic armed organization, supported heavily by China, and Wa telecommunications are provided only by Chinese operators.

"Yeah, Wa State," he says, checking his notes.

In my head, I am screaming, *Are you out of your goddamn mind?* But instead I say, "Do you know you could start a fucking war by cutting off cell phone service to Wa State?"

Silence from his side.

I decide that we will not use project savings to expand spectrum monitoring to Wa State just now. But I also decide that international staff need some kind of training on Myanmar's troubled history.

The other category of uninformed staff is misinformed. Many of our Myanmar staff suffer long-term effects of authoritarian and isolationist rule. The military regime destroyed Burma's once-enviable education system and exacerbated colonial-era ethnic identities. The Tatmadaw instigated an "us versus them" strategy to promote a kind of national unity—in this case the majority Buddhists against Muslim "others" (including the Rohingya), who they have been told are bent on destroying an independent Myanmar.[17] The Tatmadaw insists that only the military can defend the nation from this evil "other."

Today, extremist Buddhist leaders also hold sway over Myanmar's population to root out Muslim "insurgents" in their midst. I am bowled over by images of Buddhist monks in saffron robes beating up those labeled "insurgents" and "enemies" in the name of a peaceful Buddhist Myanmar. Public opinion in Myanmar overwhelmingly sees the Rohingya as outsiders, inferior beings, and an existential threat to Myanmar's existence.

Phone Naing, my political advisor, puts it in an even broader historical context.

"The people of Burma have been in extreme isolation since the early 1960s," he reminds me. "They missed some of the world's great social and political movements, including decolonization in Africa, the Civil Rights Movement in the United States, the dissolution of the Soviet Union, and the end of apartheid in South Africa."

---

[17] Francis Wade, *Myanmar's Enemy Within: Buddhist Violence and the Making of a Muslim "Other"* (London: Zed Books, 2017).

He is spot on. Concepts of democracy, self-determination, and human and civil rights were never taught and rarely learned in authoritarian Myanmar. This past isolation and incomplete education contribute mightily to today's widespread distrust and discrimination in Myanmar, particularly against Muslims. Our Myanmar staff are no exception.

So I decide that we need human rights training.

Initially I think Myanmar history training will be for foreign staff like me to overcome our abysmal ignorance of the country's complex story. Hopefully, we will stop embarrassing our Myanmar staff. But Myanmar staff come to talk to me.

"We know what the Tatmadaw taught us, but we want to hear our history the way you hear it."

And they are so right. During the training, they share their knowledge and personal experiences with the foreign staff while absorbing new information along the way.

In contrast, I decide to do the human rights training in Burmese by a local human rights activist—effectively barring most foreign staff. The reaction of Myanmar staff afterward is like an answer to my prayers.

"We always thought human rights was something made up by the West," says a procurement analyst.

"Now we see that human rights are rooted in Buddhist thought," says an administrative assistant.

"We read a historic Burmese poem that shows how our culture is built around human rights," says one of our program assistants.

I am so pleased with the result that I tell several ambassadors, who mount their own human rights training for embassy staff. This is how we crack open the door to leverage greater change. This is what our board wants me to do.

A month after our presentation to the board, I am in a hurry to keep our promise to the executive directors to focus more on social inclusion in the conflict areas of Myanmar. Basically, I want to chant our new mantra until everybody starts chanting it too. So I organize a team workshop to motivate staff to figure out what we can do differently.

The uninformed categories of staff—myself included—are blessedly counterbalanced by a group of staff with profound professional and personal knowledge of Myanmar's conflict-ridden history and current situation. It is almost a miracle that this group of people is assembled here, in 2017, at this critical moment.

We have foreign staff like Hannah, who was a diplomatic baby in Burma years earlier and is now an expert on its rural development. And Dieter, half Austrian, half Burmese, who came to Myanmar in the early days of the transition and has a fine-grained understanding of ethnic relations and the peace process. We have Myine, fully Burmese but raised in the UK, whose unparalleled emotional intelligence helps interpret Myanmar culture and society for us foreigners. We have Htein, fully Burmese, who left his family and job in Sydney to return to Myanmar to bring electricity to the population once the political transition began.

And we have staff with profound insight and experience who were raised in Myanmar and never left. We have Shwe Kyar, daughter of a high-ranking military leader from a Buddhist ethnic minority, whose intellect is so keen that she was able to learn independently and go beyond the false narratives taught in school about the dangers of the wider world and the indispensable force of the Tatmadaw to maintain a peaceful and independent Myanmar. And Wai Htun, one of our few Muslim staff members, who patrols his Yangon neighborhood at night to ward off violence against his community. And my assistant, Mya Mya, who speaks up and speaks truth even when it is uncomfortable. And in discussing ethnicity, exclusion, and conflict in Myanmar, it is so often uncomfortable.

At the workshop, our research assistant, Kyi Sin, joins a panel to discuss conflict and human rights in Myanmar. He is a rare commodity in Myanmar: he understands the meaning of human rights, appreciates Myanmar's ethnic diversity, and is committed to building a diverse and tolerant society.

Where did he come from? How did Myanmar produce him? I wonder.

"Oxfam," he responds simply when I ask about his background, meaning that he worked for the human-rights-based organization before joining the World Bank.

Soon thereafter, I ask Kyi Sin how we might contact a small—I would even say obscure—ethnic armed organization in a remote township.

"Yes, I know the guy," says Kyi Sin, and I burst out laughing.

"What do you mean you 'know the guy'? Do you know every guy in every ethnic armed organization in a country of fifty-four million people?" I ask.

"Ellen, it's like this," he says wearily. "When I was a student in 1998, I listened to the shortwave radio and heard countries like America saying they supported democracy in Burma. So I joined the democracy movement with Aung San Suu Kyi leading us. And we were naïve. We thought America and France and other countries would come and help us, but of course they did not. So I was arrested and sent to prison—to Inn Sein prison here in Yangon, which is a famous one for torture."

"I'm so sorry—" I interject, but he is not finished.

"I was eighteen, so my parents went to whomever they could—to any officials they knew—and begged and bribed them to move me to a better prison. I was sent to a far prison in Shan State near the border. And all the ethnic armed organizations were in jail there too. I spent four years with the leaders of most ethnic groups. So, yeah, I know the guy."

Now I am speechless.

A few days later, I find Kyi Sin at work near midnight.

"Why are you here so late?" I ask with a smile.

"I'm studying for my exams," he says. "You know I didn't finish my education because I went to prison. So now I'm getting a master's degree in finance."

"That's wonderful, Kyi Sin!" I reply, feeling happy that he can finally have the education he wants.

But I reflect on how lucky we are to have Kyi Sin on our team. I can find a thousand guys to read a balance sheet but only one who can explain the difference between the Karenni National Progressive Party, the Karen National Union, and the Karen National Liberation Army. Not only can Kyi Sin explain the difference, but he knows the right guy to see every time.

CHAPTER 17

Hope for Harvesters

(November 2017)

Crops are starting to rot in the fields in northern Rakhine. It is late November, and the fields of Rohingya farmers are ripe, golden, and ready for harvest. But the farmers are all gone. As are the fishermen and the small shopkeepers and the tea stand owners. Those who survived fled to Bangladesh.

The UN launches a global appeal for donations so the refugees in Bangladesh do not starve. Several miles away, the food they planted stands ready in the fields.

"Well, that's just fucked up," I say to my colleagues at our monthly happy hour in the office.

"Especially because our emergency flood project bought twenty-six brand-new harvesters for the government in Rakhine about a year ago," says one of our project coordinators.

"Seriously?"

"Yeah, they are just standing in Sittwe," he says. Sittwe is the capital of Rakhine State.

"You can see the individual fields perfectly in satellite photos," says Levon. Human Rights Watch had recently released satellite photos showing over two hundred villages that had been burned to the ground since August. In most cases, the fields were left untouched nearby.

"Umm, do we know whose field is whose?" I ask.

"Yeah, the government has village records, and now that Bangladesh is registering the refugees, we could theoretically match them," says James, our lead social development specialist.

What better way for Aung San Suu Kyi to demonstrate her government's commitment to bringing the refugees back than to support them right now, even while in Bangladesh? We financed harvesters. The Myanmar government can harvest the grain and truck it across the border or sell it in the local market, transferring the money directly into the hands of the owners—the farmers in the refugee camps—so they can buy food in Bangladesh.

I feel a little adrenaline rush thinking about it. It is innovative and insanely ambitious. But what if it worked? *It would be so cool.* And it would demonstrate to the refugees that the civilian government is working to help them return.

I am so jazzed that I go back to my office instead of heading home after the happy hour. I write up a one-pager about this new project idea and send it to my boss.

"Great that you are thinking outside the box to help resolve the crisis," she replies. She also likes a regional approach that reaches across the border between Myanmar and Bangladesh. It would be a great "quick win," she adds.

With crops rotting, this has a short fuse. We take the flight to Nay Pyi Taw as soon as possible to see the Minister of Agriculture, Livestock, and Irrigation.

"The state counsellor has asked each minister to define a plan to assist in relief and recovery in Rakhine," he explains. "And we're concerned about the crops in the fields."

So far, so good. We carefully tell him about the harvesters, the satellite images, and the potential to match fields to refugees in Bangladesh.

He looks pleased to be reminded of the twenty-six new harvesters already in Rakhine that the government could use to help harvest the fields.

"We will consider your idea and contact you soon," he concludes.

We are chuffed! *What if we really could pull this off?*

The ministry keeps us waiting a few days but eventually they call us back.

"Yes, we'll harvest the fields using the harvesters in Sittwe," says the minister. "And to answer our state counsellor's request to support the relief effort, we'll use the grain for humanitarian aid or sell it to finance humanitarian aid in Rakhine."

I cringe a bit as he continues.

"In this way, we feed all the suffering people, including the remaining Bengalis," he says proudly.

I cast a sidelong glance at my colleagues and shift uncomfortably in my big chair near the minister.

"It's wonderful that you will harvest the crops, Mr. Minister," I begin. "If you sell the grain, we can arrange for you to pay the farmers who grew the grain, who are now in the refugee camps in Bangladesh." I avoid saying "Rohingya" to sidestep the name controversy.

But he insists on the government's plan to use the crops directly for relief aid. They are proud of their compassionate idea—it is exactly what the state counsellor would want to show the international community. A proper relief program in Rakhine for the approximately 500,000 remaining Rohingya and all the other poor communities.

I try to explain gently. "The grain belongs to the farmers, wherever they are. If you do not pay them for what they produced, then the World Bank cannot allow you to use the new harvesters to collect the grain."

On this point, I am clear and firm. Not paying the farmers would constitute expropriation of their crops by the government without proper compensation. We cannot be party to that.

The minister looks confused. First the World Bank comes to offer new harvesters to harvest the grain. Now the World Bank is telling them they cannot use the new equipment?

But the minister cannot be persuaded to change the government's plan.

After multiple discussions, the ministry team assures us they will not use the harvesters we financed. They will find other equipment in other states. Our harvesters stand shiny and new in Sittwe while the grain is harvested for relief aid in Rakhine.

"It was a brilliant idea," I console our team. "Perhaps too ambitious given sensitivities."

I am frustrated at missing this opportunity to be innovative across borders. The failed harvester idea underscores the need to work more systematically with the government to develop a proper plan for relief and recovery in Rakhine. They need a plan that will pass international muster in respecting human rights and social safeguards, as well as creating the proper environment for refugees to come home.

I turn my attention to a more systemic solution.

CHAPTER 18

The Conundrum

(December 2017)

All international aid donors are struggling to figure out a response to the Rohingya crisis. We are all being pushed by our bosses and our constituencies to do the right thing, to help the poor and those affected by conflicts, especially the Rohingya remaining in Rakhine State.

"Are you working in conflict areas?" I ask every ambassador or head of aid agency that I meet.

"It's a bit ironic, but our aid policy until now has been explicitly to avoid conflict zones in Myanmar," says one ambassador. And he is not alone in his response.

I get it. The number-one rule for aid organizations working in conflict areas is do no harm. Do not let your attempt to do good things make the situation worse: exacerbating tensions, reinforcing discrimination, inflaming communities.

And it is admittedly hard to get results in areas wracked by violence. Ambitions must be reduced. Expectations must be lowered among taxpayers footing the bill. And often it is dangerous for aid workers. Getting your citizens kidnapped or killed while delivering foreign aid is an ambassador's nightmare.

So if I can do good somewhere else in the country and get better value for money, *why wouldn't I?*

My job at the World Bank—our mission—is to reduce poverty. And Myanmar has poor people everywhere.

Does it matter where I reduce poverty? If I can lift five thousand families out of poverty in a peaceful location, is that better than lifting five hundred families out of poverty in a conflict zone? Is there a trade-off between reducing poverty and promoting peace in Myanmar?

Our poverty specialists help the government measure who is poor. Now I go to them for help thinking through this conundrum.

"There are many more poor people in the center of the country. Fewer in the minority border zones, but they are poorer," says Bianca, a young poverty specialist.

"So we could have a strategy of working only in peaceful areas for the next five to ten years and probably reduce poverty in the country much faster?"

"Yes. You got it."

"And we would be heroes back in Washington for driving down poverty?"

She hesitates. "Yeah, probably...as long as the country doesn't go up in flames."

"There is that, of course."

Bianca and her team come back to me with a wonky map they produced with the government entitled the "Multidimensional Disadvantage Index."[18] It shows deprivation in education, employment, healthcare, water supply, sanitation, and housing using fourteen different indicators.

"See the bright red areas?" she asks me. "Those are the most deprived townships where the average person suffers from five to seven disadvantages out of the fourteen," she explains.

"Jeez, it looks just like the map of conflict areas," I blurt out.

---

[18] "Multidimensional Welfare in Myanmar," World Bank, December 3, 2018, https://www.worldbank.org/en/country/myanmar/publication/multidimensional-welfare-in-myanmar.

And it does. It is a ring of red all around the borders of Myanmar. Those in the remote mountain areas, mostly ethnic minorities who have lived with conflict for decades, are deprived in many, many ways, from unemployment to unsafe water to lack of shelter.

Everybody in Myanmar knows this. But now, for the first time, we can see it in bold colors. We have solid data. We cannot escape it. And we can tailor our strategies to address it.

I shake my head to see so clearly the toll of discrimination and underdevelopment on minorities in Myanmar. But it also makes me more determined than before to change our strategy.

We can do many good things in the center of the country to reduce poverty significantly. But if we do nothing to fix the misery of the minorities on the periphery, simmering conflicts are likely to explode in the future and wipe away any progress. And with one-third of Myanmar's population in the periphery, excluding them from economic opportunities will slow down growth not just for them but for everybody.

Everybody—whether ethnic minority or Bamar majority—will pay the economic price in the long run.

The country already missed out on the Asian Economic Miracle that brought neighboring countries prosperity in past decades. Playing catchup with the rest of Asia will require everybody on the team to be in the game. That has never been the case, as the Rohingya crisis makes abundantly clear.

So the World Bank strategy to support Myanmar's economic transition needs to change. Social inclusion must be among the highest priorities if economic growth, poverty reduction, and prosperity are our long-term goals.

We reengaged in Myanmar five years earlier to support a transition from a centrally planned to a market economy. We did it before in the former Soviet Union and Eastern Europe after the fall of the Berlin Wall. It is something we know how to do.

And parts of that strategy worked well for Myanmar. But I see now that it is not enough.

We need a strategy that also recognizes how Myanmar's not--quite-there democracy and widespread conflicts impact economic development. And vice versa. Because it goes in both directions.

Do not get me wrong. My predecessors were not naïve. They understood the challenges of democracy and peace in Myanmar and wrote about them frequently to explain the country's political context. But as far as I can tell, the fragility of democracy and peace did not seem to shape or drive our strategy for economic development.

But maybe I am being unfair. After all, it was my predecessors, not me, who financed rural electrification and community empowerment in every state and region. They were the ones to send money to every school and health center in Myanmar.

But they did not tilt our aid specifically toward the country's conflict-ridden periphery.

Now we will. As we close out 2017, the new mantra is fast becoming an imperative for me and my team: we must enhance our focus on social inclusion in conflict areas. We must tilt our aid specifically toward those most in need, toward ethnic minorities in the more remote border areas of Myanmar.

Headquarters asks us to reduce poverty. Aung San Suu Kyi asks us to promote peace. We need to find the path to do both, including in Rakhine.

CHAPTER 19

Slaughter at Inn Din

(December 2017)

Today I am lingering on my patio rather than rushing for an early morning flight to Nay Pyi Taw. This feels luxurious. It is mid-December, and Myanmar's weather is at its finest. Brilliantly sunny and dry after the long and dreary rainy season. The tropical flowers are blooming, and the vines create lush green walls around me.

Susie brings me my morning breakfast.

"Your tea, madam!" she sings cheerfully.

I have given up asking her to call me "Ellen" and my husband "Eric." It will be the colonial-era "Madam" and "Boss" to the end of our days, it seems.

Susie and her husband, Nay Moo, came with the house. The owner of the house trusted them and recommended we hire them. They are ethnic Karen, part of a long-standing tradition in Burma of the ethnic Karen working as domestic staff in the homes of foreigners. The British trusted the Karen, who are mostly Christian, to serve in the military and in their homes. The Karen fought with the British in World War II. In contrast, the Burmese, including Aung San Suu Kyi's father, initially sided with Japan, switching to the winning side only late in the war.

I did not know when we hired Susie and Nay Moo that they were among the lucky ones: they have official identification documents and full citizenship. Many of their friends do not.

Nay Moo is using a machete somewhere to wage war on the bamboo in the yard. The hacking sound stops, and a moment later he places the English-language paper, *The Myanmar Times,* on the table next to me.

Two local journalists working for Reuters have been arrested. I exhale in exasperation. So much for Myanmar's much-vaunted press freedom since the political transition began in 2011. It feels like one step forward and two steps back sometimes.

Journalists Wa Lone and Kyaw Soe Oo were arrested for accepting confidential documents about what happened in Rakhine. In the days to come it emerges that the military entrapped them by luring them to dinner with a promise of confidential documents, giving them the documents, and then arresting them for violating the Official Secrets Act.

The fate of the two journalists is unclear. But what they were reporting on is crystal clear. The sick feeling rises in my throat. I remember photos from Nazi concentration camps. Soldiers standing behind a row of men kneeling in terror. Collapsed bodies, shot from behind, being kicked into a mass grave.

Except now the photos are in the village of Inn Din in northern Rakhine. On the morning of September 2, the military police ordered Buddhist villagers to dig a shallow grave. Ten Rohingya men—a fisherman, a teacher, some shopkeepers, a farmer, and even two high school students—were roped together, kneeling and waiting for the shots from behind. It is all there: the kneeling "before" photo, the bodies in the grave "after" photo, and the presence of the military police. We even have testimony on what happened from respected Buddhist elders and retired military men.

They say two victims were hacked to death by Buddhist villagers, but the rest were shot two or three times each by military and paramilitary police. This is the first powerful evidence of gross human rights abuses by the Tatmadaw. Ethnic cleansing. Some say genocide.

This evidence is desperately needed to counter the denial that is everywhere in Myanmar:

"Because the world does not understand our complex history."

"Because the Rohingya are terrorists who attacked us first."

"Because Islamic terrorists must be rooted out."

"Because the killing has been done by vigilante groups who cannot be controlled by our security forces."

"Because the Rohingya burned their own homes before fleeing."

"Because they don't really belong here anyway."

The excuses and rationalization are everywhere. This is the strongest evidence to emerge thus far that the Tatmadaw is guilty and must be held accountable.

I am left wondering if our efforts to strengthen the civilian government can ever chip away at the dominance and destruction of the Tatmadaw. And can Aung San Suu Kyi's national government really exert influence within a state dominated by ethnic Rakhine leaders?

Do we have any other choice but to try?

The World Bank will try to help Aung San Suu Kyi's government do the things demanded by the international community: restore law and order, allow humanitarian relief operations, and create the conditions for safe and voluntary refugee return to Myanmar. And we will help them do what we do best: create economic opportunities for all communities to reduce poverty in the longer run.

Public opinion in Myanmar is overwhelmingly against refugee return. Our Myanmar staff tell me honestly, "We understand this strategy. Most of us even agree with it. But we cannot discuss it with our families and our friends. They just don't understand."

CHAPTER 20

A Powerful Ally

(January 2018)

Rohingya are still fleeing Rakhine State, and no plan exists to move beyond this. Aung San Suu Kyi has committed to relief, recovery, and development in Rakhine in her statements, but her government is struggling to figure out what to do. Our strategy at the World Bank is to try to bring together all parts of the government to define a solid plan for relief, recovery, and—eventually—development in Rakhine State.

We can help. We are experts at defining plans—national development plans, sector strategies, action plans, any kind of plan, really. We are big believers in defining a clear plan and then implementing it.

Also, the government trusts us. We are perceived as relative newcomers and neutral technocrats in Myanmar unlike others who have flamed out. Especially the United Nations. The United Nations Development Program (UNDP)—also big believers in plans—spent much of the year before the crisis trying to help the government define a "socioeconomic development plan for Rakhine State." It was never finished. A consultants' draft exists, I am told, but I cannot get my hands on it.

The perception is pervasive here that UN agencies are biased and working only with Rohingya at the expense of the ethnic Rakhine. As a result, they are now locked out of Rakhine. Even agencies like the UN High Commission for Refugees (UNHCR), which are most qualified to address the Rohingya crisis, are cooling their heels in Yangon. Waiting. Frustrated.

I go to see a few of the most important ambassadors.

"If the World Bank has access, you should give it a try," says one.

"If you can crack the door open, why not?" says another.

"If you can create an entry point, you should do it," says the third.

Nobody has any better ideas.

We may be in a position to do what other UN agencies cannot. And most importantly, we can provide cover to other UN agencies to work with us. We need them desperately. We need people who know refugees and humanitarian relief and food aid. Because we do not.

"It'll be difficult, but let's try to help the government define a Relief-to-Recovery-to-Development Plan for Rakhine State," I explain in a staff meeting. "We can call it R2R2D for short."

"Wasn't that the droid in Star Wars?" jokes James, our lead social development specialist. And for his cheek, I give him the dubious honor of organizing this task.

But before we can organize, we must persuade.

Back in Nay Pyi Taw, we meet with the Minister of Social Welfare, Relief and Resettlement, Dr. Thein Aung Win. A physician by training, he is a former UN official and more progressive than most other ministers. We have worked closely and productively with him and his team to strengthen health services for displaced populations and to combat childhood malnutrition.

Now he has been charged by Aung San Suu Kyi to lead her government's response to the crisis in Rakhine State.

"We're calling it a Relief-to-Recovery-to-Development Plan for now," I explain to the minister. "But you can call it whatever you want. It'll be your plan—your government's plan—so that everybody is on the same page and working to achieve the state counsellor's goals in Rakhine."

"Yes, it must be led by the government. This can be useful. Let's have a workshop to begin," the minister concludes.

Afterward, I am elated as we race to the airport for our evening flight to Yangon.

"Well, that felt hopeful," James says. "They seem to want to respond to the crisis in line with Aung San Suu Kyi's speech."

"Man, if we can pull this off, it'll be good for all development partners working here, good for Myanmar, good for the remaining Rohingya and eventually even returning refugees," I add.

I breathe a sigh of relief. Maybe we can start to turn this shitshow around. Better late than never.

We leave no stone unturned in trying to build political support for R2R2D. Who can influence Aung San Suu Kyi the most? Who can influence the military the most?

One possible answer to influence Aung San Suu Kyi is something called the advisory board. She has established a ten-member board to advise on implementing the recommendations from the earlier Annan Commission. This is one of many commissions, boards, committees, and entities established by the state counsellor under pressure to act on Rakhine. Half its members are international public figures, including the chairman, who is a former deputy prime minister of Thailand, as well as Bill Richardson, who is the former governor of New Mexico, a former Clinton Administration bigwig, and a veteran US diplomat.

Richardson now works for himself as a roving mediator, negotiating sensitive deals in places like North Korea. As a champion of Aung San Suu Kyi's early struggle for democracy, Richardson's long-standing friendship with the state counsellor is just what we need to persuade her to develop an R2R2D Plan for Rakhine.

In January 2018, the advisory board prepares to visit Myanmar.

"Damn it to hell. I can't get a meeting with Bill Richardson!" I complain.

The advisory board is programmed from dawn to midnight. I cannot get an opening in the flurry of meetings with ministers, generals, and ambassadors. I am angry to be brushed aside.

But maybe there is a way. I make some phone calls and land an email address for Richardson's chief of staff. We are the only organization to have done economic surveys in Rakhine, and this might give me an advantage.

"If Governor Richardson would like, I can provide an economic update on the situation in Myanmar and in Rakhine State. The World Bank has recently completed a special *Rakhine Economic Report*," I offer.

The lure is strong enough. I get a meeting!

But it is in Bangkok. Tonight. Before he flies to Myanmar tomorrow.

I race to the airport for a hopper flight to Bangkok and arrive at his hotel about four hours later.

It is early evening, and he is jet-lagged, but Bill Richardson is sitting across from me in an elegant hotel dining room.

"Rakhine normally contributes less than 4 percent to Myanmar's national income," I explain. "The collapse of the economy there due to the Rohingya crisis has had little direct impact on the larger Myanmar economy."

I offer a well-rehearsed story on the economic situation and wait for his questions.

"What about the Reuters journalists? What do you know about their condition?" he asks.

"I only know what I hear in the international and local press," I say. I tell him what I've heard and then steer back to my own agenda.

"Let me highlight one priority for you, Governor. Despite saying the right words, the civilian government seems to be spinning its wheels rather than making progress in Rakhine," I say. "It's not so much ill will as lack of capacity."

"What do you recommend?" he asks.

"We are proposing a Relief-to-Recovery-to-Development Plan for Rakhine State defined by the government with support from the World Bank and other partners, including UNDP and UNHCR," I respond. "And we need support from the highest levels of government—from Aung San Suu Kyi in particular—if it is ever going to happen."

Bill agrees to use his influence to promote an R2R2D plan for Rakhine State. He will be a powerful ally for us with The Lady. Just what we need.

I am so pleased that I treat myself to ice cream at the airport before catching the last flight back to Yangon that evening.

It was a long and crazy day for me, but I have high hopes that with Bill's help, we can build a solid coalition for the R2R2D plan.

CHAPTER 21

Richardson Quits

(January 2018)

Twenty-four hours after returning from Bangkok, I receive a terse email from Richardson's chief of staff. "Bill is resigning. En route to airport. More later."

I am distraught. This cannot be!

But it can be.

In record time, Richardson concluded that the advisory board is "a pro-government cheerleading squad...and I don't want to be part of a whitewash."[19]

The more salacious story is that he started arguing with Aung San Suu Kyi as early as the opening dinner. He requested the release of the Reuters journalists, which, according to Richardson, left the state counsellor "furious" and "quivering."

While waiting in Tokyo for a connecting flight to the US, Bill speaks to stringers for the *New York Times*: "She's in a classic situation that politicians and leaders get themselves in when they don't want to listen to bad news and they have sycophants around them who don't want

---

[19] Hannah Beech and Rick Gladstone, "Citing 'Whitewash,' Bill Richardson Quits Rohingya Post," *New York Times*, January 24, 2018, https://www.nytimes.com/2018/01/24/world/asia/bill-richardson-myanmar-rohingya.html.

to tell them the real situation. I hope this will be a wake-up call for her, but I sort of doubt it. I think she has added me to her enemy list, which includes the United Nations, the international media, human rights groups, and Nobel laureates. I'm afraid it's a very long list."

I am frustrated by my wasted effort, but I thank Richardson's chief of staff for letting me know right away.

By the next morning, Myanmar's state-sponsored press is spinning the story in the government's favor, claiming Richardson made a personal attack on the state counsellor. In response, they claim, the government decided to terminate his participation on the board.

I meet with one of the government ministers the next day to prepare for our workshop. He tells me in reproachful tones that Richardson "drank too much at dinner," as if this invalidates the message.

A government spokesman is also quoted in the *New York Times*: "He needs to understand clearly that he is supposed to give advice only about the Rakhine issue, not everything about Myanmar. He cannot say whatever he wants to say."

At least the spokesman is honest about that.

It feels like a complete loss for me because my means of influencing the ever-more-isolated state counsellor are shrinking. We still have a green light from the minister to go ahead with an initial R2R2D workshop, so at least that is something.

And in the end, Bill Richardson does one thing for me.

The next morning, he places an opinion piece in the *Washington Post* entitled "Three Steps Myanmar Should Take to Turn the Rohingya Disaster Around."[20] First, he recommends that Aung San Suu Kyi establish moral leadership on the Rakhine issue.

Not likely, I think cynically.

---

[20] Bill Richardson, "Three Steps Myanmar Should Take to Turn the Rohingya Disaster Around," *Washington Post*, January 26, 2018, https://www.washingtonpost.com/news/democracy-post/wp/2018/01/26/three-steps-myanmar-should-take-to-turn-the-rohingya-disaster-around/.

Second, he recommends that the country establish accountability mechanisms for the perpetrators of violence.

Yes indeed, but *not something the World Bank can do.*

Finally, Bill writes, "Myanmar must develop a strategy to deal with Rakhine that appropriately prioritizes and sequences among the recommendations of the Rakhine Advisory Commission...to ensure that key challenges such as freedom of movement, citizenship and closure of internally displaced persons camps are addressed effectively...the Myanmar government should work closely with international partners to develop clear and public plans that lay out the step-by-step process by which these issues will be addressed and benchmarks met."

He advocated for R2R2D in the only way he could. This softens the blow for me.

My bosses will see it in the *Washington Post.* When they ask me what the World Bank is doing to act on Bill Richardson's recommendations, I will be ready.

Richardson closes by saying, "Myanmar must immediately correct course and recognize that the international community wants to help it to do so."

They have their chance in just a few days at the R2R2D workshop.

CHAPTER 22

A Scoping Mission

(January 2018)

To prepare for the R2R2D workshop, I send a technical team to northern Rakhine. We go about it quietly, taking advantage of our neutral reputation. I cannot go—my position would attract the kind of attention we do not want. We submit a request for travel authorization through bureaucratic channels without fanfare, and it is granted.

This becomes the first unsupervised and unescorted visit by an international partner into northern Rakhine.

And it is devastating.

Afterward, Kyi Sin; our lead economist, Per; and our conflict advisor, Mac, file into my office, looking shell-shocked.

Per explains that they drove through two townships that had majority Rohingya populations before the crisis and then returned by boat.

"Look," says Mac, holding out his cell phone. "Rohingya villages totally decimated. Rakhine villages standing untouched nearby." He shows me photo after photo of charred ruins in the foreground with intact villages of thatched huts in the background.

"Crops have rotted in the fields. But local markets are resuming cautiously, along with some local services like healthcare and education," says Per.

"Well, that's something, I guess," I say, unable to drag myself away from the photos.

"But really, everybody we spoke to—villagers of all ethnicities—fears more violence," says Mac. "And we spoke to many Rohingya who say they are facing both official and unofficial restrictions on their movements. More restrictions than before the crisis."

"They can't go out to search for work or food, but they haven't received humanitarian aid," adds Per. "The Red Cross and recently the World Food Program have begun to distribute food, but it is just not enough."

"And how did they react to the World Bank getting involved?" I ask.

"They begged us to stay engaged in Rakhine," says Kyi Sin sadly. "They don't want the international community to forget them."

The team also saw evidence of Myanmar's largest construction firms at work on the ground, sent out by the Union Enterprise for Humanitarian Assistance, Resettlement and Development (UEHRD), an entity established by the state counsellor to coordinate response to the crisis in Rakhine. Their efforts are portrayed as a patriotic duty, but the companies stepping forward are cronies of the military eager to curry favor and win lucrative contracts from the government.

These companies are already at work on road and housing construction to prepare for large-scale refugee resettlement. Neither the refugees themselves nor the remaining Rohingya in Rakhine have been consulted. This is not unusual for companies that have been working with the Tatmadaw for decades. It would never occur to them to consult with affected populations in line with international standards.

"We saw some of the new housing," says Mac. "Families are already occupying it."

Kyi Sin lowers his voice. "They were ethnic Rakhine. Do you understand?"

I do understand. They are land-grabbers, most likely migrants from southern Rakhine taking advantage of abandoned Rohingya land in the north—land that has been promised to the refugees when they return to Myanmar.

I crumple over my desk in frustration. Rumors have circulated about land-grabbing, but this is proof. It will be difficult to reverse whenever the refugees return.

"But at least the Rakhine government has agreed that our idea of a sequenced plan would be helpful," Per adds.

"So they've agreed to attend the R2R2D workshop?" I ask.

"They said they would," says Mac.

This is one positive sign amid much disturbing information.

We agree that this is an important opportunity to introduce international standards for the repatriation and resettlement of refugees. It is a chance for the government to clean up its act.

CHAPTER 23

Relief-to-Recovery-to-Development Workshop

(February 2018)

Today is the day. R2R2D Day.

It is the first time since the killing and fleeing began in August of last year that we will see how Aung San Suu Kyi's government is thinking about fixing the mess. How they will restore law and order, expand humanitarian assistance, repatriate the refugees, and promote economic recovery. It has taken longer than we hoped, but we are here at last.

I explain to my boss back in Washington, "We want to jump-start a six-month process to define, validate, and finalize a plan to address short- and longer-term needs in Rakhine State. This will include both the remaining Rohingya and returning refugees."

"Six months? Isn't that a long time just to develop a plan..." she trails off.

"We've already gone six months without a plan and with almost no progress," I respond. "Realistically, things move slowly in Myanmar, especially if we're serious about getting everybody on board: central government, Rakhine government, and all ethnic communities. It's going to be painfully slow."

"What is the latest on numbers?" I ask Mya Mya a few hours before the workshop begins.

"Everybody is coming. Almost all ambassadors and heads of agencies. Close to fifty," she replies.

I sigh in resignation. All diplomats and development partners want to attend, but it risks overwhelming a notoriously inward-looking government. I am irritated by the crowding in, but I also recognize the pressure they are under. Each ambassador or head of agency desperately wants to report back home that something—anything—is progressing to alleviate the Rohingya crisis.

Some of us feel we have specific reasons to be in the room. The World Bank, the European Union, and the United Nations have a worldwide partnership to help countries recover from conflict and to promote peacebuilding. For the workshop, each of us brings a representative from another country in conflict, such as Ukraine, Nepal, and Colombia, to talk about their experience. This will be most useful to Myanmar. The UN High Commission on Refugees (UNHCR), the World Food Program (WFP), and the International Red Cross, which are engaged in the humanitarian response already or need to be involved in refugee repatriation, must attend to explain international norms and practices.

A few hours later, I am surrounded by fifty ambassadors and heads of agencies and a greater number of government officials from nineteen ministries and agencies, sitting at round tables listening to the opening session. A huge backdrop behind the stage announces the "Launch Workshop for a Relief-to-Recovery-to-Development Plan for Rakhine State."

The various ethnic communities of Rakhine State are not in the room. That was a step too far for the government in this initial session. We are tiptoeing forward gingerly.

At this moment, I am grateful to have insisted that no ambassadors or heads of agencies speak at the opening ceremony because that would never have ended. Only government officials are speaking, reviewing progress to date and reiterating the state counsellor's promise to implement the recommendations of the Annan Commission.

We are putting the government firmly in the driver's seat. This is essential if we want full buy-in to this process.

I am immediately disappointed because the man who approved this workshop, the soft-spoken Minister of Social Welfare, Relief and Resettlement, does not show up to the opening ceremony.

I wonder if I miscalculated. Maybe he saw that no ambassadors or heads of agency were speaking, so he delegated it to a lower level. Or maybe he does not want to be too closely associated with this high-risk undertaking. His absence sends the wrong signal to the rest of the government about the importance of this Relief-to-Recovery-to-Development Plan.

Instead, the Director of Disaster Management opens by reviewing the government's progress in responding to the Rakhine crisis. I twist the earbuds to better catch the translation.

He talks about last year's effort to prepare a socioeconomic development plan for Rakhine State, which was never finalized.

"We also attended a seminar with UNHCR to learn about repatriation and resettlement policies, and we signed an agreement with Bangladesh on refugee repatriation," he concludes. We all know that this accord was signed in November 2017 and falls far short of international standards for voluntary, safe, and dignified refugee return.

The Director of Disaster Management then turns it over to Doctor Myint Lwin Aung, Coordinator of UEHRD, on behalf of the state counsellor.

Doctor Myint Lwin Aung is an energetic and optimistic fellow with whom I have already shared a few cups of tea to better understand UEHRD. He is fluent in English and has past experiences working with the foreign aid organizations.

His slideshow on the government's response to the Rohingya crisis highlights single words like "equity" and "transparency" without elaboration.

"We have created nine task forces across the three pillars: humanitarian assistance, resettlement, and development for Rakhine State," he explains. "We have made substantial progress in preparing reception centers, transit camps, new roads, and housing for returning refugees." He flashes photos of new infrastructure—lots of new infrastructure.

When he is finished, we take a group photo for the ministry's Facebook page, and then the ambassadors and heads of agency withdraw to file their reports.

Now the government gets down to work. I am particularly impressed to see representatives from military-controlled ministries like Home Affairs and Border Affairs, as well as the Myanmar Police. About ten foreigners remain—mostly organizers and experts on relief and resettlement. A half dozen Myanmar staff from my office also stay. They have been critical in conceptualizing and organizing the workshop and are currently facilitating small groups at each table.

I listen as each group summarizes their initial ideas to strengthen the government's response to the Rohingya crisis.

"We can hire more minority teachers and teaching assistants to reassure minority students and parents," says the representative from the Ministry of Education, reading off her group's flipchart.

"We can eliminate movement restrictions and have a special team to guarantee mobility," says the officer from the police.

This feels...positive. I am witnessing what feels like a miracle.

Civil servants are suggesting how to strengthen security, how to reach all communities in Rakhine, how to rebuild trust, how to ease movement restrictions, and how to ensure access to health and education.

Granted, it will not immediately solve deep-seated problems of discrimination and lack of citizenship for the Rohingya, but the ideas coming forward are more progressive than I imagined. They are practical and positive. If we continue like this, in six months we will have a detailed and well-sequenced plan that might even help resolve some of the more intractable problems in Rakhine State.

I glance at my colleagues, and they feel it too: that flicker of hope. That whiff of possibility. That pride at being part of the solution rather than part of the problem. Doing the right thing, no matter how hard. There are no easy solutions, but we might be able to make real progress in the long run. I smile at James. He made this happen.

I hear a commotion behind me and swivel in my chair.

"What is this? What is happening? We said no internationals! No internationals!"

It is the Deputy Minister of Social Welfare, Relief and Resettlement, and he is livid that foreign organizers and experts are listening to the small groups.

No, he is not livid. He is afraid. Deeply afraid. We must be making a liar out of him: he must have told his superiors that no foreigners would attend the working sessions.

"You can't be here!" he repeats in agitation.

"Deputy Minister, we're so sorry if there was a misunderstanding," I say.

But our Myanmar staff jump in to explain in Burmese that all foreign dignitaries have left. Only a smattering of foreign organizers and experts remain, which was agreed to in advance to facilitate the workshop.

They calm him down, and finally he agrees that we can listen to the reporting at the end—but all foreigners must leave during the working sessions.

"What about our Myanmar staff, Deputy Minister?" I ask cautiously. I do not want the World Bank's presence to derail the whole workshop.

"It's okay," he says quickly, waving his hands as if to say, *What could it possibly matter?*

Then he hustles out of the conference hall.

The deputy minister's panic reflects a deep-seated fear among many in Myanmar, including both civilian and military officials. It is a tendency not only to see foreigners as an existential threat to the nation, but to see their own people as inconsequential, irrelevant. And in this, they fail to comprehend the democracy toward which they have chosen to move, with its defining shift in power toward the people.

That is it in a nutshell, I think as I cool my heels outside the conference room.

Despite the foreigner flap, the workshop proves productive. I listen to the final reporting and am more hopeful that incremental progress could be made.

"Cautiously optimistic," I say in my report to headquarters. "Tentative initial steps toward a clear plan."

"Congratulations. This is an important step forward," they reply.

"Congratulations" is a word I will hear a lot in the next few weeks. I am praised by local ambassadors and development partners for nudging the government along the right path. It feels possible to us all that the government could define a plan over the next six months that would meet immediate relief needs, set the stage for internationally acceptable repatriation of the refugees, and implement the recommendations of the Annan Commission for a more peaceful and prosperous Rakhine.

The World Bank team maps out our next steps.

We want to have a workshop in Rakhine State with representatives from all communities, including the Rohingya. Community participation is essential in defining the path forward. Then we want to have a joint mission to Rakhine—the World Bank and other UN agencies together with the central government—to begin scoping out the R2R2D Plan.

The minister forwards a report of the workshop to the state counsellor's office. I assume he also forwards a copy to the military. He assures me they are ready to proceed with the next steps as soon as they get a green light from above.

We are on track to have the R2R2D plan by the middle of 2018. I can see a dim light at the end of a long tunnel.

CHAPTER 24

I Visit Rakhine

(February 2018)

I close my eyes and doze in the passenger seat. I flew back from Nay Pyi Taw last night after the R2R2D workshop and am heading back to the airport before dawn the next day. I startle awake when our driver, Si Thu, opens the window and shouts something in Burmese. He is negotiating something with military guards—we are not at the usual drop-off at the departure terminal. "What...what is happening?" I rouse myself.

"Madam, we must wait at special VIP," he explains.

He drops me in the dark at the VIP building, and my anxiety rises as I watch him pull away. I am hustled through a security check of my passport, diplomatic card, and invitation letter from the government. Then I am led to a VIP waiting room to wait until we fly. I perch on an uncomfortable velvet sofa in the VIP lounge and fiddle with a tiny teacup as fellow ambassadors and heads of agencies file in.

This is my second attempt to join a government-sponsored visit for diplomats and development partners to northern Rakhine. The last time I waited four hours before the military canceled the visit due to heavy fog.

The government wants to show us the progress they are making with humanitarian relief and preparing for refugee return. I do not expect a balanced and realistic picture of the situation, but we all feel obligated to take the government up on their offer to visit prohibited areas.

We talk in hushed little groups. Western ambassadors raise their eyebrows over a recent visit from the Japanese foreign minister, who committed $23 million in aid money to support refugee repatriation without setting any conditions on how to do it right. All agree that Japan's soft approach reflects their deeper worry: China's dominant influence in Myanmar.

"How did the workshop turn out yesterday, Ellen?" asks one ambassador.

"Better than expected. Government officials had surprisingly useful and pragmatic suggestions," I say, and then I give a quick overview of the results.

"It's a step in the right direction, for sure," says the ambassador.

"Congrats, Ellen. It would be something if we can bring a little order to the government's efforts," says another.

"Let's see where it goes," says a third. "And let's see what today's visit brings."

The skies are clear, and we are loaded into military cargo planes and helicopters for the visit. My plane includes Bob Rae, former prime minister and now special envoy on Rakhine from the Canadian government, and Claudette, deputy at UNHCR and a woman I admire for her fierce integrity and deep knowledge of Myanmar's citizenship laws and identity documents. Several ambassadors from Western and ASEAN states are also with us, as well as one of the many secretaries of the Japanese Embassy in Yangon and two or three Myanmar security officers.

We fly to Sittwe, the capital of Rakhine State, and then up the coast to northern Rakhine. It is too noisy to talk. I enjoy flying this way, with warm air blowing around our faces from the open windows. I lean out of a porthole to enjoy the aerial view and get a strong blast of wind on my face.

I fish out my phone and hold it perilously out the window to capture some images on the ground. I need a better camera with a powerful zoom lens, but this will have to do today.

Below I see a soft green and sandy coastline. *Click.* I snap pictures of boats, little crescent-shaped boats lying on the sandy beach like a splay of dead fish. They are painted bright white and easy to spot lying in the sand where they were abandoned months ago. They look forlorn. Wooden pirogues left to bleach in the sun when their Rohingya fishermen fled.

We touch down for our first visit at a reception center for returning refugees. This is Taung Pyo Letwe, right across the border from Bangladesh. Long white buildings with blue roofs look fresh and ready—the construction progress is impressive. But I am dismayed by the barbed wire and electric fences surrounding the rows of barrack-like buildings. It will not be a warm reception for refugees when they return.

"Here. Come here," calls a military officer, ushering us into a building labeled Biometric Registration.

"Here we'll register the refugees with biometric data to identify them. And we begin the National Verification Process (NVP)," says the commander.

Young officers in jaunty slouch hats are positioned eagerly behind computers and cameras to show how the biometric registration will occur.

"Can you show us how it will work?" I ask.

"Today, no," says the commander. "We have no power—a power outage today—so we can't show it on the computer."

I am guessing they have many power outages.

The eager young officers do a pantomime of the process instead.

Claudette offers me more information than our hosts. "All returning refugees—regardless of their prior citizenship status—are required to go through the National Verification Process," she explains. "And they'll have to turn over existing citizenship documents, so it is regarded with deep suspicion by the Rohingya community."

"Why would any of them do it?"

"In theory, if they accept the NVP card, they'll finally be free to move around northern Rakhine. To go to work. To go to school. But in reality..." She looks doubtful.

We are told that the security forces are preparing to receive refugees on foot or by water.

I walk to the pedestrian entry.

"Taungbro Bridge," says a young male guard. I look at the old wooden structure and see a cement signpost labeled "Bangladesh-Myanmar Friendship Bridge."

The bridge was inaugurated in a different time, when the two countries were not gripped in an intractable conflict over nearly a million Rohingya without a home. Not much friendship displayed now, but the irony appears lost on my Myanmar hosts.

I can see across the buffer zone into Bangladesh, where I spent four years earlier in my career. Recently some desperate refugees from Myanmar made it into the buffer zone only to be refused entry to Bangladesh. Now they are squatting in the buffer zone, where they will be flooded out when the rains begin in a few months: stateless people living in a no-man's land.

A wave of anger and sadness washes over me as I watch them. I turn away from the end of the bridge as if I were a refugee stepping back into Myanmar. I am greeted by four giggling young women in smart military uniforms.

"What do you do here?" I ask in English.

They smile with incomprehension. The guard explains, "The lady soldiers search lady refugees." Now I notice the curtained hut in which the body searches will be conducted as the refugees return to Myanmar. Welcome home.[21]

We then fly to a so-called transit center at Hla Pho Kaung. It looks like a concentration camp from the air, with long, low barracks and high barbed-wire fences. My anxiety rises as I step inside the fences.

Initially, government officials called this a transit camp, which conjured up disturbing images for foreigners, so now it is called a transit center for up to 25,000 refugees at a time.

---

[21] See my photos from Chittagong on February 9, 2018.

"How long will returnees stay here?" asks special envoy Bob Rae. He and the rest of the diplomatic community are leery about creating a temporary camp for displaced persons after seeing others become permanent prisons for people chased from their homes.

"Up to six months," says our military guide.

"Six months?" says Bob, making sure he heard correctly.

"I mean, only three months," amends the guide.

"Really just one month," says his commander. "Well, it will depend on things."

One month? Three months? More or less. We hear different answers.

I leave the gaggle of concerned ambassadors and walk beyond the barracks. Rows of trucks, construction equipment, piles of wooden boxes.

Wait. Are those...tents? Our tents? Holy crap!

Yes, the wooden boxes are clearly labeled "24 m2 Rectangular Tent" with the logo of UNOPS, the United Nations Office for Project Services.

The World Bank financed these tents as part of the government's emergency flood response project several years earlier. UNOPS was contracted to procure and deliver the tents. They are not our tents. They belong to the government. But they were purchased using a World Bank credit for a certain purpose: to respond to natural disasters like cyclones and flooding.

Could these tents be used for a manmade disaster such as the Rohingya crisis? Could they be used to house returning refugees for a month or three months or six months?

I know the answer: only if the government meets the UN conditions for safe, voluntary, and dignified return of the refugees to their places of origin. And they are currently far, far away from that.

We explained all this to the government already. They agreed not to use the tents until the conditions were met. Yet here they are, ready to be erected at a moment's notice.

Damn it! Maybe the military is blatantly disregarding our concerns. Maybe the civilian government did not understand. Either way, it makes me look bad. Like I do not care about the conditions for refugee return. Like I do not care about human rights.

Click. Click. I snap photos for proof and return to the group. Later, back in my office, I will draft another sternly worded letter to the government about the stringent conditions for tent use. And I will likely receive a letter back assuring me that goods purchased under the World Bank loan will not be used unless we agree that the conditions are met. While I still have hope these tents might someday support safe, voluntary, and dignified refugee return, my hopes are fading fast.

In the meantime, our government-sponsored visit to northern Rakhine continues.

"Now we'll visit a peaceful Rohingya village with model housing," says our guide.

Aung San Suu Kyi had asked us to find out why some villages are peaceful, and why some Muslims coexist without conflict with their Buddhist neighbors. Well, here we go.

Male villagers are lined up to greet us. The ambassadors spring forward to shake hands, taking advantage of the opportunity to have a candid word with the few Rohingya we will meet on this day. I follow suit.

The Danish ambassador next to me says, "We want to help you. We are here for you. Have hope," as he moves down the line.

One or two villagers have enough English to say quickly, "We are afraid. We want to leave." Then the receiving line is over, and we are ushered to wooden benches to learn about this peaceful village.

A government official explains the model housing project financed by China and points to several houses under construction nearby. A village administrator, who is Rohingya, is standing by to answer questions, shifting uncomfortably from foot to foot.

The EU ambassador wastes no time trying to debunk some of the government's far-fetched assertions. "Did you burn down your own houses?" he asks the village administrator.

The man looks like he might faint. "Well..." he stammers. "We don't know what happened." And that is all we ever get from him.

I peel off from the crowd and go looking for the women. I had assumed they were not considered important enough to greet us, but I am wrong. There are no women in the village. Only men and boys. Now I understand that these men and boys were brought here for this visit. A completely staged Potemkin village for the diplomats.

They stand awkwardly on the porches of the unfinished model homes. *Click. Click.* I snap photos of them, and nobody smiles. Later I look back at their sullen faces and sunken eyes and feel like crying.

This day already feels interminable, but it is not over yet.

We are taken to a government building for tea and cake and a speech on the government's progress in responding to the crisis.

I am struck by the genuine pride of the ministry officials in everything they have built—reception center, transit center, new roads, model houses. It is like a house cat bringing a dead bird home to its humans, unaware they are recoiling from the gift. Nobody acknowledges a need to consult with the Rohingya or with any communities involved, including those who ran away.

Flying back in the cargo plane, I lean uncomfortably out the porthole, gripping my phone. I have read every news report and seen the satellite data of hundreds of villages destroyed or damaged. But I have not seen it up close until now.

Click. Click. Click. I snap photos of the ground as fast as I can. Empty fields in neat rectangles clearly demarcated. *Click.* Lush trees in green rings around the settlements. *Click. Click.* Inside the trees, burned-out settlements. I snap furiously. *Click. Click. Click.* Charred wreckage of house after house. Walls burned and crumbling. Blackened stumps of young trees with a few mangled branches remaining. *Click. Click.* Household detritus—clothes, pots, buckets—strewn on the ground.

I feel shocked and nauseated but compelled to keep snapping away. I must document for myself people's homes lying in ruin, their lives upended. And I hear the voices of my childhood in my head: *If we forget, it could happen again.*

And then I see it. Among the dark splotches of charred buildings, I see clean, sand-colored areas. At first, I cannot tell what they are. Then I look closer and see big sweeping motions in the sand, like a vacuum cleaner on a deep rug. Bulldozers. Many bulldozers. Clearing away the wreckage, plowing under the charred remains of people's lives. *Click. Click. Click. Click.*

I snap as fast as possible to document what is there before it is gone. I know that satellites have documented the changes far better than my grainy photos, but I click and burn it into my brain anyway. *Because if we forget, it could happen again.*

I lean as far out the window as possible for as long as possible, taking in the carnage and the coverup.

When we finally touch down in Yangon, I walk toward our waiting vehicles with the young secretary from the Japanese Embassy. He was sent on reconnaissance for the $23 million his government just pledged for Rakhine State. He looks shaken.

"It's really bad, isn't it?" he asks before driving off.

CHAPTER 25

Changing the Way We Do Business

(March and April 2018)

I report back to headquarters on my visit to northern Rakhine, using words like "disturbing" and "deeply troubling." I also find it shocking, depressing, and abhorrent. It is not right. Not even close.

Can it be fixed? Fixed enough to pass international muster? *Fixed enough to let me sleep?*

The military commander, Senior General Min Aung Hlaing, uses Facebook to announce the findings of the military investigation into Inn Din. The Tatmadaw acknowledges that military and security forces killed the "Bengali terrorists." In a post on April 10, 2018, the senior general announces that seven soldiers have been convicted of murder at Inn Din and sentenced to ten years in prison. It is the first time the Tatmadaw has acknowledged responsibility for extrajudicial killings. Is this a sign of greater accountability to come, perhaps?

I cling to any signs of accountability and progress.

In these early months of 2018, we get a lot of practice telling our story about the progress the government is making in responding to the Rohingya crisis. It is a good story. And a bad story. Depending on how you tell it.

"The security situation has improved but the remaining Rohingya live in fear," I say. "And the government is carrying out its own relief efforts but still prohibits most humanitarian organizations from assisting and is unable to keep pace with needs."

And on and on it goes, every bit of progress somehow less than it first appears. Government has eliminated some formal movement restrictions, but local vigilante groups and village administrators still enforce their own restrictions.

Government has signed a Memorandum of Understanding with Bangladesh on refugee return but without committing to proper international standards. Government is preparing for refugee return, but largely through construction of ominous facilities and camps. Government has agreed to close camps for internally displaced Rohingya but is moving them to restricted villages, not to their places of origin. Government is building new housing for refugee return but is also bulldozing evidence of atrocities and allowing land-grabbing to occur. Government has a process in place to assess citizenship, but minorities mistrust a process that has stripped them of past documents and rights. Government is implementing many of the Annan Commission recommendations, but not the most fundamental ones related to citizenship, civil rights, and discrimination. The Tatmadaw is showing some accountability for killings, but the journalists who uncovered it are still detained.

Is it two steps forward and one step back or vice versa? Sometimes it is hard to tell.

But my bosses and shareholders are counting on me and my team to accelerate the forward progress and limit the backsliding as much as possible.

What other option do we have? Keeping Myanmar on a path toward democracy and reintegration with the world is just too important, and China's influence is still too dominant to give up.

While it will not solve the biggest problems, I know that we can at least change the way we design the projects funded by the World Bank.

What if primary schools could receive extra funding for showing that minority children were attending every day? What if we prioritized investments in the border states instead of nationwide for off-grid electricity? What if we linked small community investments—like feeder roads—to trust-building exercises between ethnic communities?

"Can you come up with a tool that will help our teams ask the right questions about conflict and exclusion? A kind of peace and inclusion filter?" I ask our Social Development team. I am thinking especially about the power engineers and transport specialists whose minds are more on turbines and asphalt than on the social dynamics of Myanmar.

A few weeks later they send me a prototype.

"Why is it thirty pages long?" I ask, wielding my red pen. "And why is it now called Inclusion and Peace Lens?"

The team hesitates. Finally, the team leader says, "Our team handles inclusion. The post-conflict team handles peace. We wanted to come first."

I strike out most of the text, and we succeed in creating a short tool with just twelve questions to help teams design social inclusion and conflict resolution into their projects. And it makes a difference.

"Initially it felt like a purely bureaucratic exercise imposed by you," says one project leader.

"In the end, though, it changed our design, both where and how we operate."

In fact, the Inclusion and Peace Lens wins an innovation prize at the World Bank about a year later as I am preparing to leave Myanmar.

But for now, I am just happy that we are cooking on all burners to change the way we do business—just as we promised our executive board.

CHAPTER 26

Spring Meetings

(April-June 2018)

Mya Mya frowns as she reads a letter from the Ministry of Planning and Finance: "The minister will go to Washington for Spring Meetings."

"You mean the deputy minister," I say without thinking.

"No, it says the minister," she confirms. Now we have a problem.

The minister, U Tin Oo, was appointed by Aung San Suu Kyi. I am told he is loyal to her and her party, the National League for Democracy. He was a low-level civil servant in the tax administration and then an advisor to foreign investors for twenty years under the military regime. Our Myanmar staff say that he fought for democracy back in the day—was maybe even imprisoned for it—but I am never able to get a clear story.

Business leaders and academics in Myanmar tell me he is loyal but also ill-equipped, indecisive, and even incompetent.[22] I meet with him

---

[22] Thomas Kean, Clare Hammond, and Hein Ko So, "An Overdue Appointment: What Went Wrong at the Ministry of Planning and Finance," *Frontier Myanmar*, June 14, 2018, https://www.frontiermyanmar.net/en/an-overdue-appointment-what-went-wrong-at-the-ministry-of-planning-and-finance/.

regularly, but we get our work done through his two competent deputy ministers.

One of the deputy ministers, U Kyaw Thein, single-handedly drafted the Myanmar Sustainable Development Plan, quelling critics in the international community who complained that the government had no economic vision. It is a pretty good plan, even including a pillar on peace and security that addresses the Rohingya crisis. For the first time in writing, it commits the government to implementing the recommendations of the Annan Commission, including revising the discriminatory 1982 Citizenship Law.

Unfortunately, neither U Kyaw Thein nor his fellow deputy minister will be going to Washington for the World Bank Spring Meetings. Instead, the minister will lead the delegation. Although unfortunate, this kind of thing happens everywhere. A good director just works harder to ensure a successful visit. And I am a good, experienced director.

The minister will meet my boss, the vice president. Delegations from important countries or with globally important issues often meet our Chief Operating Officer (COO) and president as well. The Rohingya crisis is front and center in global newspapers, and World Bank leaders would like to believe that they can influence the situation.

"Given recent progress on the Relief-to-Recovery-to-Development Plan for Rakhine, maybe now is the time for a higher-level meeting?" Charlotte muses.

"Yeah, maybe," I reply, but I am worried about putting such a weak minister in front of my senior management. I need a government representative who can speak to the progress Myanmar is making on economic reforms as well as responding to the Rohingya crisis. A lousy meeting could undermine support at headquarters to implement our strategy of focusing more on inclusion in conflict areas.

We draft talking points for my vice president to meet with the minister. And then I fly to Nay Pyi Taw to ask the minister what he wants to talk about. He has not thought about his agenda—the lure of his first trip to the United States seems to be enough.

"What do you suggest, Madam Director?" asks his chief of staff.

"Progress on economic reforms, finalization of the Myanmar Sustainable Development Plan, progress on the Rakhine crisis for sure, and next steps to prepare the Relief-to-Recovery-to Development plan for Rakhine," I reply, outlining the same points for the minister that I sent my vice president.

It is what all good directors do to ensure productive meetings. We want good connections and a meeting of the minds. His chief of staff scribbles notes and then repeats the issues I have flagged. I repeat the list in an email to her afterward.

Before the meeting, I wait to greet the delegation in the impressive atrium of World Bank headquarters in Washington. The minister looks lost as I shepherd him to the conference room. The room is packed—Myanmar is a hot topic these days—and directors from all technical areas are there: Transport, Social Development, Health, Education, Finance, and on and on. So many World Bank directors that we cannot squeeze in any more chairs. Some stand in the back, hoping for a chance late in the meeting to advocate for their own work.

I usher the delegation to their seats and take my place to the right of my vice president, where I can whisper, write notes, or interject if something unexpected arises. But I am not worried; Charlotte excels at this.

"Minister, it is such a pleasure to see you again," she says. "I would so welcome an update from you on progress in economic reforms and, of course, on the government's response to the crisis in Rakhine."

We wait politely and expectantly.

The minister fumbles around in his briefcase. Finally, he pulls some wrinkled sheets of paper out and lays them on the table, smoothing them with his hand before pushing them toward my vice president.

Bloody bodies. Mutilated torsos. Corpses lying on muddy ground. I am stunned and panicked by the photos he is pushing toward us.

"These are Hindus who have been murdered by Islamic terrorists—by the Arakan Rohingya Solidarity Army in Rakhine State," says the minister through a translator.

I hear a faint "oh my" escape my vice president's lips, but the minister rushes forward with his story.

"The world does not understand Myanmar," he explains. "If you understood the truth, you would not defend the Muslims. It is the Hindus and even Buddhists who have been killed by Muslim terrorists, so Myanmar must protect itself. The Bengalis have used propaganda to tell a false story that they are being killed and driven from Myanmar, but they are the ones responsible for the killing. See? Here is the proof in these photos."

It seems the minister came to Washington to "set us straight" on the story of Myanmar. He continues, finally finishing by asking Charlotte to share this with the World Bank president.

We are too shocked and horrified to interrupt.

My mind is racing. How should we respond? Refute his version of events? Provide other evidence? Call him a liar?

Or maybe we should try to shift him to the issues on the agenda? But it would now be impossible to credibly discuss progress to safeguard the remaining Rohingya and ensure safe, voluntary, and dignified refugee return.

There is simply no going back from his complete denial of violence perpetrated by the military against defenseless Rohingya.

Finally, my boss speaks. I try to focus. She says the right things—good things—and concludes, "We have a quite different interpretation of these events, Minister, and we remain deeply disturbed by the ongoing violence in Rakhine State. We are committed to resolving conflicts and fostering peace among all communities regardless of ethnicity."

The minister smiles and nods through the interpretation. And then time runs out and the meeting ends.

No discussion of economic reforms or development plans or the Rakhine response or refugee return. Aung San Suu Kyi had sent the minister to Washington to shore up international support, but he is failing in the most egregious way.

I stand stiffly from my chair. One of my colleagues passes by and mutters to me, "This is the most interesting World Bank meeting I have ever been to."

I am crushed. A rare opportunity to tell a good story—the one where Myanmar is making slow but significant progress on its most difficult ethnic conflict—is utterly, completely lost. I feel a sense of despair.

As I accompany the delegation out of the conference room, the vice president's assistant pulls me aside. "The COO's office called. She has back-to-back delegation meetings solid for the next few days. They simply cannot open a space to meet the Myanmar delegation."

"Well, that's one bullet dodged," I reply.

News of the bad meeting precedes my return to Yangon. Our Myanmar staff shake their heads sadly when I brief them. I meet one of the deputy ministers for an informal dinner in Nay Pyi Taw. He also heard it went poorly. He also shakes his head but says nothing.

A few weeks later, newspapers—including those aligned with the government—break a story from two years earlier. Minister of Planning and Finance U Tin Oo had padded his resume, adding a master's degree and PhD from a fake university abroad. The ruling party knew it when he was confirmed in 2016 but apparently did not find it disqualifying.

In mid-June, I am scheduled to meet the minister for a regular catch-up in Nay Pyi Taw. It will be our first meeting since the debacle in Washington. A few minutes before it starts, Mya Mya calls from Yangon. "The minister's office just called to cancel your meeting."

"No! Damn it! I got up at dawn for the flight! What a waste of time," I reply angrily. "What's going on? What happened?"

But the minister's office gave her no explanation for the cancellation.

That night a new story emerges in the local press. The minister and his son are being investigated by the government's anti-corruption agency for dealings with certain Chinese and North Korean investors. It seems the ruling party may have known of these dealings earlier, but the minister is now under investigation.

The minister's resignation is accepted the next day by the state counsellor.

So this is how loyalists get fired by The Lady, I think. I will never know for sure, but it seems the debacle in Washington is the final strike against a minister who is clearly in over his head.

Minister U Tin Oo leaves quietly and fades into obscurity.

He is replaced by U Khin Maung, a former managing partner for KPMG in Myanmar. His affiliation with a prominent consulting firm suggests a welcome and unaccustomed level of managerial competence. He resisted the appointment due to his age—he is an old man of eighty years and the product of British Burma's education system before it was destroyed by the military dictatorship. For those old enough to have benefited, education before the 1962 coup encouraged critical thinking and individual initiative in ways that were heavily suppressed during fifty years of military rule.

The new minister proves to be both competent and charming. He holds team meetings on important economic topics like banking reform and fiscal policy. He is balm on an open wound for Myanmar's business community and international partners like us.

He refers to Yangon's streets and parks by their colonial names rather than the Burmese names of the past six decades.

"We would run to Scott's Market to buy sweets in the evening," he tells me about his childhood in colonial Rangoon.

Scott's Market is now the Bogyoke Aung San Market, near my office in modern-day Yangon. Although we now have a better partner at our most important ministry, it is not sufficient to turn around the government's response to the Rohingya crisis.

We are languishing, waiting for a green light from above to move forward on the Relief-to-Recovery-to-Development Plan for Rakhine State.

CHAPTER 27

The United Nations Reasserts Itself

(June 2018)

Kyaw Tint Swe, Minister in the Office of the State Counsellor, is now the right-hand man of Aung San Suu Kyi. It is a curious choice, given The Lady's leadership of the pro-democracy movement, which protested military rule in Burma for decades. Most of her other appointments have been among loyalists who fought with her against military rule. Kyaw Tint Swe is not a military man himself, but he served the military regime as a diplomat from the late 1960s onward. He is erudite and charming, as one might expect from Myanmar's former ambassador to the United Nations.

He poses thoughtful questions about economic reforms. We talk about the broader Myanmar economy before I turn to the subject of Rakhine. This is my best effort to get a green light to move ahead with the R2R2D plan.

"It's very important to bring together relief and repatriation with longer-term development in Rakhine," he agrees after I explain the plan and our need for The Lady's approval.

We agree to stay in touch regularly on economic issues. Afterward, I send him documents with a little note: "With the compliments of Ellen Goldstein, World Bank Director for Myanmar."

I am hopeful we will finally get the green light for which the Ministry of Social Welfare, Relief and Resettlement has been waiting these past three months.

My hopes are dashed. We wait a week, then two. Then three. We never get the green light...but also never get a red light. We get nothing at all. No answer. The R2R2D plan is dead on arrival. Our attempt to push the government to do the right thing has come to naught.

I am disappointed but also relieved that the World Bank will not have to take the lead in areas we are not qualified to handle, such as relief and repatriation, for which we rely on our UN friends.

Soon thereafter, I meet the United Nations resident coordinator.

"We are close to signing a Memorandum of Understanding with the government to work on the Rakhine crisis," he tells me. He seems to be gloating a bit over his success where I have failed.

I have seen this before: United Nations officials who worry about their status relative to the World Bank. At the World Bank, we never worry about our status relative to the United Nations. We have much more money to offer governments, and in most cases, money talks. But here in Myanmar, it does not speak the right language.

The relationship between Myanmar and the United Nations is like an old married couple. They bicker constantly yet are deeply dependent on one another. Some UN agencies were present throughout the military regime and learned to do business within the constraints imposed. Ultimately the Myanmar government—first the military regime and now the civilian government—cannot make good on international promises without falling back on their UN relationship.

On June 6, a Memorandum of Understanding (MOU) is signed between Aung San Suu Kyi's government and UNHCR and UNDP. The UN calls it "a first and necessary step to establish a framework for cooperation between the UN and the Government aimed at creating conducive conditions for the voluntary, safe, dignified and sustainable repatriation of refugees from Bangladesh and for helping to create improved and resilient livelihoods for all communities living in Rakhine State."[23]

No other details are publicly provided.

The government will not allow disclosure of the agreement. UNDP and UNHCR must contort themselves to adhere to UN standards for information sharing. Eventually they circulate a background note to international partners to describe the content of the agreement they cannot share.

But I want more information. So I have tea with two of my favorite people in Myanmar: Rodrigo, the UNHCR representative, and Dennis, the UNDP representative. They both have extensive experience in the worst conflict zones in the world. They are both pragmatic and politically astute. And they both laugh a lot, using humor to alleviate the anxiety of unanswered questions and suboptimal solutions.

"Really, Ellen, there isn't much more to say than what was in the press blurb," Rodrigo confesses.

"The language is vague right now. Much remains to be defined," says Dennis.

"But I consider it a triumph that the MOU addresses both refugees and the remaining Rohingya in Rakhine," continues Rodrigo, "and that the government will take guidance from us on repatriation and resettlement."

"And on recovery and development," adds Dennis. "We consider it a win that the government recognizes the need to do assessments in villages before taking action."

[23] "UNHCR and UNDP Sign a Memorandum of Understanding (MOU) with Myanmar to Support the Creation of Conditions for the Return of Refugees from Bangladesh," press release, United Nations High Commissioner for Refugees and United Nations Development Programme, June 6, 2018, https://www.undp.org/myanmar/press-releases/unhcr-and-undp-sign-memorandum-understanding-mou-myanmar-support-creation-conditions-return-refugees-bangladesh.

"We have already submitted a list of villages in northern Rakhine where we want to do a first round of assessments," concludes Rodrigo. "We are waiting on our travel authorizations from the government."

"Good luck," I say, and I really mean it.

The international community heralds the UN Memorandum of Understanding as a long-awaited step in the right direction nine months after the Rohingya crisis escalated.

At the World Bank office in Yangon, we do not mourn our R2R2D plan for long. Instead, we redesign projects already in the works to focus more on inclusion in conflict areas and start designing new projects to support Myanmar's peace process. We even start designing a project to support the crisis response in Rakhine—assuming UNHCR and UNDP succeed in pushing the government forward in the next year or so.

We stay engaged in Myanmar yet change the way we do business. Just like we said we would.

CHAPTER 28

Meanwhile in Bangladesh

(July-September 2018)

The president of the World Bank, Jim Yong Kim, is scheduled to join the UN Secretary General on a tour of the Kutupalong Refugee Camp in southern Bangladesh. Kutupalong is now billed as "the largest and most densely populated refugee settlement in the world."[24] With the rainy season upon us, concerns are real that a cyclone coming up the Bay of Bengal will turn the camp into a life-threatening mudslide for the Rohingya refugees.

I am a bit depressed. Yangon is a dreary puddle of a place in July, with constant sheets of rain beating down. I am also scared.

My parochial fear is that our careful balancing act in Myanmar, which feels like walking a tightrope, will be blown off course by Jim's visit to Bangladesh. He is prone to reacting emotionally and making sweeping statements to the media as he seeks to "bend the arc of history" and secure his place in it.

---

[24] "World Bank Calls for Global Support to Respond to Rohingya Crisis," press release, World Bank, July 3, 2018, https://www.worldbank.org/en/news/press-release/2018/07/03/world-bank-calls-for-global-support-to-respond-to-rohingya-crisis.

My boss is scared too. She tries to join him on the Bangladesh visit but is rebuffed. She nonetheless plans to visit Myanmar a few days later. Whatever the president says, whatever he does, she can do damage control with the Myanmar government. Beyond that, she also can do damage control with our global shareholders who endorse our strategy to stay engaged in Myanmar, with a greater focus on inclusion in conflict areas.

Jim is moved by what he sees in Kutupalong camp. He is quoted in the global press: "I have spent my entire life in developing countries providing health care [and] education for the poorest people; this is one of the worst situations I have ever seen. Today, we are all Rohingya. We have to stay in solidarity with them so that they can live a life with dignity...we, as the World Bank Group, are committed to doing more and more to make sure that the Rohingya, all of us, can seek justice."[25]

But in their joint press conference, the UN Secretary General wins this publicity round. His remarks are more personal, stirring, and aspirational. He speaks in detail of the atrocities committed in northern Rakhine and calls for international solidarity to end discrimination against the Rohingya and create proper conditions for refugee return.

"Jim is fuming after his visit to the camp," Charlotte informs me soon thereafter. She explains that he is talking about punishing Myanmar by taking away the low-interest loans that we offer from our International Development Association (IDA) and giving them to Bangladesh.

"I get it," I say, "but explicitly punishing Myanmar to favor Bangladesh just exacerbates tension between the two countries. Tension is already running high, and it could jeopardize the bilateral agreement on refugee return that the two countries signed last year."

---

[25] Jim Yong Kim, "Transcript of President Jim Yong Kim's Remarks at a Press Conference in Cox's Bazar, July 2, 2018," World Bank, July 3, 2018, https://www.worldbank.org/en/news/speech/2018/07/03/statement-after-rohingya-camp-visit.

"The bilateral agreement is not brilliant, but at least it's a start," acknowledges my boss. "It would be counterproductive if we undermine trust between the two countries."

"And we've already reallocated that money anyway," I continue. "I already downgraded Myanmar's ratings for social inclusion and rule of law. They've lost hundreds of millions of dollars in IDA as a result."

The World Bank's formula for allocating money to developing countries looks at progress on policy reform and institutional development every year. When the Rohingya crisis exploded, I downgraded ratings in several important areas. This reduced Myanmar's allocation by hundreds of millions of dollars, and that money was released to other developing countries, including Bangladesh.

So without fanfare, the World Bank had shifted money away from Myanmar and toward Bangladesh over the past year. Jim's wish has already been granted.

"That's a good point," Charlotte concludes. "Let me try to talk to Jim."

More money has flowed to Bangladesh over the past year because the government had to be persuaded to maintain the refugee camps rather than force-march the Rohingya back over the border as they have done in the past. Persuasion requires both money and prestige.

Jim's visit to Bangladesh is an occasion to announce nearly half a billion dollars in additional grants from the World Bank that have been negotiated in the past ten months to maintain the refugees and support surrounding Bangladeshi communities. This is the culmination of difficult negotiations with the government of Bangladesh, which has been unwilling to borrow money—even at the lowest interest rates—to support the refugees.

Beyond the refugees, over the past year the World Bank has doubled its annual support for Bangladesh to nearly $3 billion in low-interest financing.[26] Other international partners have done the same with

[26] World Bank, "World Bank Calls for Global Support."

their foreign aid, not only to convince Bangladesh to let the Rohingya stay but to avoid housing the refugees in prison-like situations.

The international community takes care to speak effusively of Bangladesh's decisions. Jim follows suit during his visit: "The Government of Bangladesh has done a great service by keeping its borders open and supporting the refugees...Bangladesh has an inspiring development story: it has emerged as a global leader in reducing poverty and creating opportunities for all...we are firm in our commitment to enhance support to help Bangladesh achieve its aspirations."[27]

This is quite an about-face from five or six years earlier, when I led the World Bank office in Bangladesh. At that time, Prime Minister Sheikh Hasina and her family were accused of wrongdoing in a corruption scandal brought to light by the World Bank. Sheikh Hasina was vilified by the international community for rampant corruption and poor governance—for which the country ranked last on global indicators. She became something of an international pariah, never invited to speak at global conferences, and something of a poster child for corrupt leadership.

Now six years later, to further its persuasion on the Rohingya refugees, the global community appeals directly to Sheikh Hasina's ego. They offer her a platform to speak at the UN General Assembly in September 2018. She cannot resist this.

Sheikh Hasina has said publicly that *she*, not Aung San Suu Kyi, deserves a Nobel Peace Prize. Like Aung San Suu Kyi, Sheikh Hasina is the daughter of an independence hero who was assassinated in her youth. She is locked in a perennial struggle against her political opponent, who herself is the widow of a slain independence hero. Depending on the balance of power, Sheikh Hasina has been periodically jailed by this opponent on corruption charges.

---

[27] World Bank, "World Bank Calls for Global Support."

Now the Rohingya refugees offer her a chance to burnish her reputation as a great humanitarian. Perhaps even win the Nobel Peace Prize!

In the past, her government had starved the Rohingya out of their refugee camps and force-marched them back into Myanmar. Choosing not to do this again is worthy of praise. And the international community obliges. Seemingly, it does not matter if the Rohingya are trapped inside camps in Bangladesh, if their camps wash away in mudslides, or if they cannot put their children in Bangladeshi schools or take a job in the Bangladeshi labor market. It does not even matter if Sheikh Hasina wants to effectively imprison the refugees on a remote and precarious island in the Bay of Bengal.

At the UN General Assembly, Sheikh Hasina tells her personal story:

> When my father and family members had been killed, I was not allowed to return home for six years. My sister and I were compelled to live abroad as refugees. I can feel the misery of losing one's loved ones and of living in a different land as a refugee.

She addresses the Rohingya crisis:

> The Myanmar situation repeatedly reminds us of the genocide committed by the Pakistan occupation forces against our people in 1971...from the outset, we have been trying to find a peaceful solution to the Rohingya crisis...despite their verbal commitment to take back the Rohingya, in reality the Myanmar authorities are yet to accept them back.

And she tells the remarkable story of Bangladesh's development over many decades, giving credit to her time in power:

> All my life, I have been working selflessly to make a difference in the lives of my people. In the last nine years and a half,

> Bangladesh has achieved remarkable success...that Bangladesh the world knew as the land plagued by disasters, floods, droughts, and hunger has done wonders in maintaining international peace, managing disasters, empowering women and consolidating development gains.[28]

Perhaps a Nobel Peace Prize *is* in her future.

Do not get me wrong. I am happy that Bangladesh has welcomed and sustained the refugees. It has become clear that repatriation will be a slow affair, if it's even possible. I know many dedicated Bangladeshi officials in the government who are working hard to improve conditions for the refugees. And the World Bank is doing the right thing to support them with additional resources.

But the international community of diplomats and development partners creates heroes and villains among the leaders of developing countries to fit our needs. The same prime minister vilified for corruption this year will become a great humanitarian a few years later. It is the personalization of it all. We love Sheikh Hasina. We hate Aung San Suu Kyi. Or the reverse, depending on the year. We need a personality to embody our story and carry the weight of our aspirations for a better world.

And we want it to be simple: good versus evil. That way it is easier to do the right thing. Well, not necessarily easier to *do* it, but easier to *know* it.

---

[28] Sheikh Hasina, "73rd Session of the United Nations General Assembly Address by Sheikh Hasina Hon'ble Prime Minister Government of the People's Republic of Bangladesh the United Nations New York, September 27, 2018," Permanent Mission of the People's Republic of Bangladesh to the United Nations, September 27, 2018, https://bdun.org/2018/09/27/73rd-session-of-the-united-nations-general-assembly-address-by-sheikh-hasina-honble-prime-minister-government-of-the-peoples-republic-of-bangladesh-the-united-nations-new-york-27/.

CHAPTER 29

Incentives for Progress in Myanmar

(July 2018)

I am back in Aung San Suu Kyi's reception room. This time I am not on the sofa next to the state counsellor but in a chair on the side, taking notes as my boss talks with The Lady, working off the talking points we prepared about faster and better progress on the Rohingya crisis.

"It's important to accelerate progress in restoring security in Rakhine, removing restrictions and discrimination, and creating the right conditions for refugee return," Charlotte says.

"We're committed to implementing all the recommendations of the Annan Commission," reaffirms the state counsellor. "And we're working to speed our progress with support from international friends like you."

After Jim's visit to the Rohingya refugee camp, we are under more pressure to influence how the Myanmar government responds to the crisis. Much talk occurs inside the World Bank about leveraging our aid money to create positive incentives for the government to do the right things.

"We have heard your request to use World Bank resources to support the country's broader peace process," continues Charlotte. "So we propose a future Peaceful and Prosperous Communities Project for up to $200 million that will reward communities in conflict areas that have chosen peace and intercommunal harmony."

"This is very important," agrees The Lady.

"In this way, peaceful communities will be rewarded with money to invest in small infrastructure and job creation," explains my boss. "It's a kind of peace dividend."

We are responsive to her requests and hope she will be responsive to ours. Especially on making better and faster progress in Rakhine.

Our team sees good prospects for a project starting in southeast Myanmar, where ethnic armed organizations have signed the National Ceasefire Agreement and are willing to talk with the central government. We had initially hoped Rakhine State could be included in the Peaceful and Prosperous Communities Project if the government made progress on security and repatriation there, but it quickly became clear that the complexities of Rakhine would paralyze the entire operation. So we offer a separate project, making the total financial incentives even larger.

"We are also prepared to design a Rakhine Recovery and Development Project for up to $100 million," my boss announces to the state counsellor. "This could be delivered when the government, working with the United Nations, makes real and measurable progress on restoring security; allowing humanitarian access; creating conditions for safe, voluntary, and dignified refugee return to places of origin; and implementing the Annan Commission recommendations on Rakhine."

This is a tall order for the government, but we want to demonstrate that doing the right thing will pay off.

Aung San Suu Kyi nods and says, "These projects are appropriate and will be much appreciated."

The two future projects are announced that evening through our press release and the state counsellor's Facebook page.

To many people, $300 million sounds like a lot of money to incentivize good behavior. But I am afraid that the sound of this money will fall on deaf ears in Myanmar. Following its historic isolation, the Myanmar government—both civilian and military—is not accustomed to responding to financial incentives.

Apart from one or two individuals at the Ministry of Planning and Finance, most government officials, including the state counsellor, have no idea how much aid money the country receives. Nor have they thought about the fiscal and political impact of losing aid flows. In a $70 billion economy that receives billions of dollars a year in aid, trade, and investments from China alone, the sound of our aid may be too muffled to make any difference.

As of July 2018, the World Bank has committed no funds to Myanmar since the onset of the Rohingya crisis nearly a year ago. This represents a loss of more than half a billion dollars for the country.

Now we are turning around and leveraging our money to create incentives for the government to do the right thing for the Rohingya and others affected by conflict. We use the only tool we have to nudge a weak government down a path to which it has sworn commitment.

Preparation of these projects will take at least six months to two years, providing ample time to judge the government's progress.

While Charlotte is in Myanmar, I take her to meet with representatives of the Rohingya community.

"We need your help desperately," they say. "We are afraid our international friends will leave us alone. The Tatmadaw is too strong. We are scared. And the NLD government is too weak."

So we put our shoulders to the wheel and begin preparing these projects as we come up to the first anniversary of the attacks that sparked the crisis.

CHAPTER 30

First Anniversary of a Crisis

(August 2018)

I carefully monitor the international press on the first anniversary of the Rohingya attacks on security posts that launched indiscriminate military reprisals in Rakhine State and forced the displacement of 750,000 Rohingya to Bangladesh. Headlines summarize what we see on the ground: "Year After Rohingya Massacres, Top Generals Unrepentant and Unpunished."[29]

In this year, I have heard stories of murder, rape, torture, arson, and forced displacement by the Tatmadaw and other security forces. The fleeing Rohingya remain confined to refugee camps in Bangladesh—unwanted there, unwanted at home, unwanted anywhere in a world where populist leaders stoke fear of immigrants, especially Muslim ones.

A week later, our communications officer sticks his head into my office. He tells me that Wa Lone and Kyaw Soe Oo, the two Reuters journalists who were entrapped by the military for reporting on the

[29] Hannah Beech, "Year After Rohingya Massacres, Top Generals Unrepentant and Unpunished," *New York Times*, August 25, 2018, https://www.nytimes.com/2018/08/25/world/asia/rohingya-myanmar-ethnic-cleansing-anniversary.html.

massacre at Inn Din, have been found guilty and sentenced to seven years in prison.

"How can that be?" I cry, shaking my head in disbelief.

"It's the Official Secrets Act. It is hard to imagine, but more journalists have been trapped by it since the transition began in 2011 than under the old military regime," he says.

It's frustrating and disappointing. And deeply ironic that the flowering of a freer press since 2011 has resulted in a greater number of journalists being ensnared by the Official Secrets Act. The Act is a 1923 holdover from the colonial era and covers trespassing in prohibited areas, handling government documents considered secret, and communicating with "foreign agents." Its lack of specificity makes possible the prosecution of many journalists covering current events in Myanmar.

This time, Aung San Suu Kyi demurs and defends the arrest of the journalists as necessary to respect the rule of law. But her party has a majority in Parliament that would allow her to modernize obsolete and authoritarian laws if she tried hard enough. Her government is shutting down journalists investigating the Rohingya crisis, and in the meantime, the government's own response has been painfully slow and unsatisfactory.

In contrast, the World Bank has moved quickly to change the way we do business in Myanmar, and I am proud of what we have accomplished. It is my job to explain this to the world, making presentation after presentation to governments in Asia, Europe, and North America.

"Our strategy has changed dramatically from a year ago. We have remained engaged in Myanmar but with a much greater focus on social inclusion and peace-building in conflict areas," I explain. "We have canceled nearly three-quarters of a billion dollars in direct support for Myanmar's budget, and we have committed no new funds to Myanmar since the Rohingya crisis began."

Then I go through my list of changes, noting that we have:

- generated and analyzed important new data on conflict and exclusion in the country,
- trained our teams and developed tools to design more inclusive and conflict-sensitive operations,
- tilted our nationwide operations more toward minority border areas, the most deprived and conflict-affected zones,
- put inclusion and equitable access at the heart of design of new operations for health, education, and social assistance,
- begun designing an operation linked directly to peace in specific conflict zones, and
- taken steps to identify a project to help the remaining Rohingya and all ethnic groups in Rakhine State.

On the proposed Rakhine project, we are coordinating with our colleagues at UNHCR and UNDP to gauge whether the government's progress merits our support. So far, the answer is a disappointing no.

The government, with no explanation, has allowed the UN to do initial assessments in some—but not all—of the requested villages in northern Rakhine. In some of those villages, the UN has launched quick impact projects (QUIPs). These are small, confidence-building exercises among wary communities. Little else has occurred to improve the welfare of remaining Rohingya or create the right conditions for refugee return.

Still, the changes we are making are quite impressive to my audiences. Our shareholders acknowledge that we are changing the way we do business. They seem to recognize that we are trying to operate in a complicated political environment that is immune to much of our persuasion and financial clout. I appreciate their support and wonder why my senior management fails to offer the same. Our president, Jim, and our COO, Birgit, have not taken the time to meet with me and

Charlotte to understand the significant changes we have made to our strategy in Myanmar since the crisis began. Whenever articles critical of Myanmar's response to the Rohingya crisis appear in major newspapers, they apply pressure on us to take a "stronger stance" without really understanding the stance we have already taken.

After the one-year anniversary of the Rohingya crisis, what had been anecdotal evidence of murder, torture, rape, arson, and forced displacement starts turning into hard data and documents. Those of us on the ground in Myanmar once again feel rising pressure from our superiors—and then from our wider constituencies and from all over the world—to push the government to do the right thing.

CHAPTER 31

The United Nations Turns on Itself

(September 2018)

The United Nations has become an ouroboros, a snake eating its own tail.

The UN Secretary General names Christine Schraner Burgener, a former Swiss ambassador, as Special Envoy for Myanmar. Quiet diplomacy is the name of the game, with the ambassador paying three cordial visits to the country before issuing a public statement.

She knows from our experience that if she openly criticizes Aung San Suu Kyi or her government, she will lose access, the ability to get a meeting or even visit the country, and any influence over the government's response to the Rohingya crisis.

So she steps carefully and seizes on bits of good news to highlight progress made by the government. She rehashes old news, mentioning "the agreement with Bangladesh on refugee repatriation," which ignored international standards, as well as "Government's Memorandum of Understanding with UNHCR and UNDP," which remained only vaguely defined, and the "completion of village assessments and launching of quick-impact projects," but only in villages approved by the government. She even reports on "more learning facilities in internally displaced persons camps," even though closing the camps remains an important international goal.[30]

She highlights forward movement, however slow and inadequate. It is always two steps forward and one step back for the ambassador.

In anticipation of the UN General Assembly in late September, the UN Human Rights Council reports on its Independent International Fact-Finding Mission on Myanmar, which was established in 2011 to report on the situation in Rakhine State and in Kachin and Shan States, where conflicts had escalated.[31]

Their report, based on over eight hundred interviews with victims and witnesses, was unsurprising in its findings yet shocking nonetheless in its descriptions of brutality and abuse at the hands of the Tatmadaw.

> The mission established consistent patterns of serious human rights violations and abuses in Kachin, Rakhine and Shan States in addition to serious violations of international humanitarian law. These are principally committed by the Myanmar security forces, particularly the military. Many violations amount to the gravest crimes under international law.

With respect to the Rohingya's long-term plight, the mission reported:

> The extreme vulnerability of the Rohingya is a consequence of State policies and practices implemented over decades, steadily

---

30 "Note to Correspondents: Statement Attributable to the Secretary-General's Special Envoy on Myanmar," United Nations Secretary-General's Office, October 20, 2018, https://www.un.org/sg/en/content/sg/note-correspondents/2018-10-20/note-correspondents-statement-attributable-secretary.

31 UN Human Rights Council, *Report of the Independent International Fact-Finding Mission on Myanmar*, September 12, 2018, https://www.ohchr.org/sites/default/files/Documents/HRBodies/HRCouncil/FFM-Myanmar/A_HRC_39_64.pdf.

> marginalizing them. The result is a continuing situation of severe, systemic and institutionalized oppression from birth to death...for decades, security forces have subjected Rohingya to widespread theft and extortion. Arbitrary arrest, forced labor, ill-treatment and sexual violence have been prevalent.

It is a relief to see the truth written plainly in an official report. In fact, the government of Myanmar refused entry to the fact-finding mission and criticized the UN Human Rights Council as biased. The mission sent official request letters to visit on September 4, 2017, and again on November 17 and January 29, 2018. They received no response.

As a result, interviews with victims and witnesses were conducted remotely or outside Myanmar, especially in refugee camps in Bangladesh. In a long history of violence, discrimination, and abuse against the Rohingya, the scale of the 2017 crisis was unprecedented:

> Mass killings were perpetrated...villagers were gathered together before the men and boys were separated and killed... women and girls were taken to nearby houses, gang raped, then killed or severely injured. Houses were locked and set on fire...bodies were transported in military vehicles, burned and disposed of in mass graves. Rape and other forms of sexual violence were perpetrated on a massive scale...sometimes up to 40 women and girls were raped or gang-raped together...rapes were often in public spaces and in front of families and community, maximizing humiliation and trauma...children were killed in front of their parents...many fled alone after their parents were killed.

As I read about the fate of so many innocents, including women and children, vomit wells up in my throat.

The fact-finding mission also showed that the Tatmadaw had planned well in advance to decimate the Rohingya community in northern Rakhine. This was no spontaneous reprisal against unexpected terrorist attacks. It was a premeditated and carefully calculated campaign to drive the majority of Rohingya out of Myanmar.

The military spent decades portraying the Rohingya as "illegal immigrants" who were an existential threat that might "swallow other races" in Myanmar with their "uncontrollable birth rates." Never mind that the Rohingya numbered only about one million in a country of fifty-four million, largely Buddhist ethnicities. In early August of 2017—well before the border post attacks by Rohingya insurgents on August 25—the Tatmadaw had directed a large buildup of troops and other military equipment across northern Rakhine. Soldiers were airlifted in and took over border posts. Local ethnic Rakhine men were fast-tracked into the local police and armed militias. They positioned themselves purposefully to neutralize what they perceived as the Rohingya threat to a Buddhist-dominated Myanmar.

Time-stamped satellite photos also documented what I had seen from the window of a cargo plane:

> The mass displacement and the burning of Rohingya villages were followed by the systematic appropriation of the vacated land. Bulldozers flattened [the] burned, damaged and even surviving structures and vegetation, erasing every trace of the Rohingya communities, while also destroying criminal evidence.

The Tatmadaw did not take great pains to hide its intent afterward. Commander in Chief Min Aung Hlaing posted on Facebook on September 2, 2018, that "the Bengali problem was a long-standing one which has become an unfinished job despite the efforts of the previous governments to solve it. The government in office is taking great care in solving the problem."

Overall, the report concluded that the Tatmadaw exhibited genocidal intent that warranted an investigation and prosecution of senior military officials for genocide and crimes against humanity, including murder, imprisonment, forced disappearance, torture, rape, sexual slavery, persecution, enslavement, and, in the case of the Rohingya particularly, persecution and apartheid.

I close the fact-finding mission's report feeling nauseated. Yet it comes as no surprise. Its gruesome findings are exactly what I expected after one year of living in Myanmar and learning about the Rohingya's plight.

More surprising is the shade thrown at Myanmar's civilian authorities, whom the UN has thus far sought to support and strengthen in their struggle against the Tatmadaw.

> Nothing indicates that the civilian authorities used their limited powers to influence the situation in Rakhine State...the State Counsellor, Daw Aung San Suu Kyi, has not used her de facto position as Head of Government, nor her moral authority to stem or prevent the unfolding events...On the contrary, the civilian authorities have spread false narratives, denied wrongdoing of the Tatmadaw, blocked independent investigations and overseen the destruction of evidence. Through their acts and omissions, the civilian authorities have contributed to the commission of atrocity crimes.

These are hard-hitting words from the Human Rights Council. Frozen out of Myanmar, the mission wrote a damning document. Rather than mitigate the tragedy, the civilian government has aided and abetted military coverup and denial.

It is the first time I have seen in writing the world's growing doubts about the intent of the civilian government and its leader, Aung San Suu Kyi. However, what is written is no different than the private conversations I have with ambassadors after frustrating meetings with civilian officials.

The fact-finding mission still was not finished. They also took aim at their UN brethren. And the snake began eating its own tail.

> Many United Nations agencies have continued to prioritize development goals, humanitarian access and quiet diplomacy. That approach has demonstrably failed; and the United Nations as a whole has failed adequately to address human rights concerns in Myanmar. Even now, the approach taken displays few signs of any lessons learned, with human rights missing from agreements recently signed with the Government.

This last sentence refers to the Memorandum of Understanding between the government and the UN, with its village assessments and quick-impact projects in Rakhine. It also alludes to the dozen or so UN agencies moving ahead with long-standing development programs in other parts of Myanmar.

This criticism of the United Nations from within the United Nations claims its victims. Suitable scapegoats are found among the aid workers on the ground in Myanmar. This includes the previous UN resident coordinator, who was removed shortly after I arrived, and the acting coordinator who followed her, who was never confirmed in his role. Blaming them obviates the need to question the judgment of those above who approved their actions on the ground.

As I survey the scene, it is starting to feel like an unwinnable position.

The human rights defenders of the United Nations take aim at practitioners on the ground who are responsible for relief, repatriation, recovery, and development in one of the most complicated and frustrating environments in the world.

I feel sorry for my UN colleagues in Myanmar. For the most part, they are good people with strong moral compasses and personal integrity. They see all the warts on the frog they are trying to kiss. They are exhausted from trying to push the civilian government down a better path. They are exhausted from responding to diplomatic pressure to fix intractable problems and help Myanmar emerge as the liberal democracy we all imagined a few years earlier.

It is easy to advocate to do the right things. It is much harder to make them happen in an environment where neither government nor public opinion favors it.

I am in exactly the same position as my UN colleagues as I implement our agreed-upon strategy in Myanmar. It requires hundreds of small compromises to inch Myanmar toward inclusion and equity and rule of law. And it risks becoming death by a thousand cuts for those of us who try.

CHAPTER 32

The US State Department Weighs In

(September 2018)

Late in September, I visit the US Embassy to discuss our mounting frustration with the civilian authorities.

"The problem is that we have no sticks and few carrots," says the ambassador.

He is a career foreign service officer, a seasoned diplomat, and a smart guy. He has worked off his instincts and sense of values since the Trump Administration stopped providing regular guidance to foreign service officers. In previous administrations, they received a daily briefing summarizing the official US government position on foreign policy issues. This ended as the new administration vilified foreign service officers as part of a "deep state" bent on undermining President Trump's agenda. Facing mistrust and neglect, many foreign service officers took early retirement. For those who stayed, in the absence of clear guidance, they based decisions on their own sense of the values that defined the US and its foreign policy. This was true of the US ambassador to Myanmar.

"We can put targeted sanctions on high-ranking military officers. Financial and other stuff. They hate it when their kids can't study in the US. Once we've done that, there is not much else we can do on that side," he says.

"What do you think of using the World Bank's money as incentive for the civilian government to make faster progress on Rakhine and on peace and social inclusion in general?" I ask.

"We need to use the few carrots we have with the civilian government, and that is one of them," he agrees.

Having support from the United States, the World Bank's biggest shareholder, reassures me that I am on the right path. I check in with other ambassadors before heading to Washington for our annual shareholders meeting. I get a consistent message about staying engaged in Myanmar and using whatever incentives we have to move the government forward.

The UN General Assembly is now underway in New York, and I expect it will focus the world's attention on the one-year anniversary of the Rohingya crisis and the minimal progress to date. So I position myself in Washington to await the global reaction.

The data and documents tell a horrific tale of violence and repression. Politicians across the globe are calling for greater action—more action, different action—to address something akin to genocide. Or at least genocidal intent.

I am ready, at least in our own way and within our own mandate. I lay out my thinking to our shareholders: "The World Bank is in Myanmar to support equitable growth and reduce poverty. Ethnic exclusion and conflict are barriers to both," I explain. "So we've adopted a new strategy built around social inclusion and fostering peace, including in Rakhine."

"Government's progress seems negligible. What more can you do?" asks a European executive director.

"Systemic discrimination and baked-in ethnic identities lie at the root of Myanmar's problems. We can work on this within our mandate, but it will take decades—maybe generations—to unwind," I explain, trying to manage their expectations. "We know we can't solve everything. We have neither the mandate nor a magic wand to address today's humanitarian and refugee concerns. And we have neither the mandate nor the geopolitical clout to influence Myanmar's political structures."

"It's a complicated political situation," acknowledges an Asian executive director.

"We are doing the best we can to implement a strategy aimed at equal opportunity, social inclusion, and nondiscrimination everywhere in Myanmar," I reassure them.

But inside I am screaming, *You try it! You try to find a better approach! Try working with a government that seems to lack the will and capacity to do the right things. You find a way to motivate them and build capacity to counteract the military's abuses. You will discover it is exhausting and soul-crushing!*

Toward the end of the day, I am sitting at my borrowed desk in my borrowed office at headquarters when Levon drops a bound printout in front of me.

"Read this," he says.

"Do I have to?" I respond, knowing that any news will be bad news.

I glance down and see a report titled "Documentation of Atrocities in Northern Rakhine State."[32]

It delivers on its promise. Never ones to rely on the United Nations, the US State Department conducted its own assessment of what happened in Rakhine State after August 2017. In 2018, they sent intelligence officers to interview a representative sample of 1,024 Rohingya refugees in Bangladesh.

They found that more than 80 percent of the reported incidents (killings, injuries, rapes, destruction of property) occurred in August and September of 2017.

---

[32] Bureau of Intelligence and Research, *Documentation of Atrocities in Northern Rakhine State*, September 24, 2018, https://www.state.gov/wp-content/uploads/2019/01/Documentation-of-Atrocities-in-Northern-Rakhine-State.pdf.

More than 80 percent of the refugees saw at least one killing as well as village destruction. More than half saw rape or other sexual violence. One in five reported seeing a mass casualty, with more than one hundred victims at a time.

Refugees identified the Myanmar military—army, police, and other security forces—as the perpetrator in 84 percent of the killings and injuries. And the tactics were appalling, including locking people in burning houses, fencing off entire villages before shooting into the crowd, sinking boats full of fleeing Rohingya, throwing infants and children into open fires, slashing the stomachs of pregnant women and ripping out the fetuses, and raping and then shooting women and hanging or hacking their bodies, including cutting off their breasts. It is a sickening story from those who made it out alive. I instinctively curl into a ball as I read, drawing my knees up to protect my own breasts and vital organs.

The question being hotly debated in the corridors of the State Department at this moment is whether the US government will label this as genocide or crimes against humanity. Both designations would have legal implications for US trade, investment, and aid to Myanmar. An official designation would legally obligate the US government to withdraw most of its foreign aid and reduce its presence in Myanmar. The World Bank would certainly follow suit, forcing us to largely disengage from the country. *Are they saying genocide? Are they?* I search the news online. *What did they say in the official press release?*

The answer is *nothing*. Secretary of State Mike Pompeo makes no statement. The Trump Administration is silent. This devastating report is posted online without an official press release. Just a quiet ripple in a still pond.

I feel relieved yet repelled. I am relieved because a designation of genocide would force us to disengage, and this would not help the Rohingya in Myanmar or the refugees in Bangladesh or support the country's economic and political transition. It would do nothing except make headlines.

Yet I am also repelled that the Trump Administration has nothing to say about the egregious human rights violations against the Rohingya. It is sadly consistent with their Islamophobia and attempts to impose a ban on Muslim visitors to the US.

Their silence scares me to death and rekindles the voices of my childhood: *If you do not say something, it could happen again. If you do not do something, it could happen again.*

It could happen again to the distant Rohingya, who are seen by the Trump Administration as suspiciously Muslim. Or it could happen to me, an American and a Jew, sitting just a few blocks away from the White House.

CHAPTER 33

Black Mirror

(September 2018)

By this point in my tenure in Myanmar, the Trump Administration has identified its only true bogeyman: China. The administration lacks coherent foreign policy in many domains, but thwarting China wherever possible is the closest it comes to doctrine.

With China's national income now rivaling that of the United States and China investing aggressively to control natural resources around the world, it is a priority for last century's superpower to push back on this century's superpower. Relentless China-bashing is the preferred way to achieve Trump's campaign slogan to "make America great again."

China's dominance of the world may be new, but its dominance of Southeast Asia is long established in terms of political influence, military might, trade, investment, and foreign aid. Nowhere is this truer than in Myanmar, where China accounts for more than 80 percent of all foreign investment and provides copious—albeit shadowy—amounts of economic and military aid. Throughout the country's five decades of isolation from most of the world, China has remained present and dominant—Burma's big brother.

When I ask in Myanmar who can bring the military commander in chief and Aung San Suu Kyi together around the same table, there is only one answer: China. And now China is investing heavily in Myanmar, with a deep seaport, railway, and pipeline through Rakhine and Chin States to its border. This is China's long-awaited access to the Indian Ocean and, some would argue, to India itself.

In contrast, China does not dominate the World Bank. Despite growing economic might, China's financial contribution to the World Bank—and hence its voting power—remains below that of the United States. This is a carefully negotiated political issue, with the balance of voting shares established by the Western powers at the Bank's creation in 1946 only slowly evolving over time to reflect shifting economic powers. It is not surprising that China decided to start its own global development bank in 2015, the Asian Infrastructure Investment Bank, while continuing to wield as much influence as possible at the World Bank.

To move forward in our work in Myanmar, I need both the United States and China on board with our strategy.

Supporting international institutions like the World Bank is a low priority for the Trump Administration, and they do not rush to appoint their executive director to our board. Instead, they leave us hanging for a year and a half with an acting executive director who is a businessman and a Trump appointee.

We go to see the acting executive director as a multicultural team: an American (me), an Armenian, an Indian, a Latvian, and an Italian. And we are jet-lagged, having arrived from Asia in recent days. But we know what to expect from this type of meeting with executive directors. We typically explain our strategy and answer questions, usually about the Rohingya crisis or Myanmar's progress on economic reforms.

The acting executive director is friendly, with the firm handshake, thick blond hair, and wide smile of an American businessman.

"I visited Burma in 2016!" he says.

I nod enthusiastically, realizing he had joined the World Bank president there after Aung San Suu Kyi took power: a symbolic visit to celebrate the democratic transition.

"You want to know something crazy? The men wear skirts in the streets!" he continues, referring to the traditional wrapped longyis.

I feel my eyes widen and eyebrows start to rise. I force my face muscles to relax, fixing a smile.

"The Chinese are investing heavily there, right? It's good that you are working to counter that. This is the most important thing," he says before I quickly present our strategy.

"Have you seen *Black Mirror*?" he asks after I finish.

I have no idea what he is talking about. My colleagues stare awkwardly at their shoes.

"The Chinese are using phones and screens to monitor citizens. They have a system of social credit scoring for behavior, like spitting in the street or criticizing the government. They give rewards and punishments depending on the score," he explains. "It's just like *Black Mirror* on Netflix."

"Really? That sounds...um...fascinating. I'm not familiar with the show," I say, wondering how to get off this crazy topic and refocus the discussion on Myanmar. But we never go back.

The meeting ends and we spill down the hallway before bursting into gales of laughter. My non-American colleagues find it hilarious: he brought to life all the ignorance and weird conspiracy theories we have come to expect of the Trump Administration. I shake my head sadly. My country has become a laughingstock on the world stage.

Back at my hotel, I parse the conversation and conclude that pushing back on China guarantees that our biggest shareholder will support our work. And later we prove to have strong support from the Trump Administration to stay fully engaged in Myanmar as a counterweight to Chinese influence and ambition.

We need this seal of approval. US support is essential for the World Bank to remain engaged in Myanmar and focus on inclusion in conflict areas.

I'm no fan of the Trump Administration. But I will take what I can get in support of our work.

That evening, I Google "Black Mirror" and "social credit scoring." It turns out he is not wrong about what China is doing.[33]

---

[33] Gabrielle Bruney, "A 'Black Mirror' Episode Is Coming to Life in China," *Esquire*, March 17, 2018, https://www.esquire.com/news-politics/a19467976/black-mirror-social-credit-china/; Mara Hvistendahl, "Inside China's Vast New Experiment in Social Ranking," *WIRED*, December 14, 2017, https://www.wired.com/story/age-of-social-credit/.

CHAPTER 34

On Capitol Hill

(September 2018)

The reports by the UN and US documenting military abuses and atrocities are prominent in the global press. Following the UN General Assembly, political meetings about Myanmar multiply in Washington in late September.

Charlotte and I pay a visit to the US Capitol. We are there to meet Paul Grove, clerk for the Senate Appropriations Committee and long-time staffer of Senate Majority Leader Mitch McConnell. Through his work on the Appropriations Committee, Grove has outsize influence on foreign aid decisions, including financial support for the World Bank, which is why my vice president was willing to meet with a staffer rather than the senator.

We pass security and are led through a warren of small office spaces to Paul Grove's area. I am always surprised by the modest working conditions, the stained carpets, and chock-a-block desks inside legislators' offices, even for the powerful on Capitol Hill.

I am wary of Paul Grove given his conservative pedigree, but I try to keep an open mind. He wants to talk about Cambodia, not Myanmar, one of the other countries where I am responsible for the World Bank program.

He wants us to halt operations in Cambodia due to anti-democratic and authoritarian decisions of the Hun Sen regime prior to elections. His assessment of the Cambodian regime is spot on. His understanding of World Bank policy and legal precedent is flawed. The World Bank is a multilateral organization operating across a range of political systems to promote economic reforms. We cannot halt operations on political grounds alone. Who among our shareholders would decide which governments or political systems were acceptable? Often we are called into decidedly undemocratic environments to promote economic reforms that ultimately bring about a more open society.

We had halted operations in Cambodia some six years earlier due to government violations of World Bank policy. But walking away served no purpose other than to weaken our influence on issues like transparency and voice, which serve the cause of democracy. We reengaged about two years ago and are still fighting to build trust and gain influence. I am determined not to disengage from Cambodia again, just as I am determined to stay engaged in Myanmar.

But Paul Grove has an important influence on appropriations for the World Bank. He drafts amendments and shepherds bills through the legislature that determine foreign aid policy. So we do our best to convince him that we are doing the right things in Cambodia to promote democracy through citizen engagement and government accountability.

Grove is dissatisfied with our answers on Cambodia. And then I notice on the wall behind him is a framed photo of Grove with Aung San Suu Kyi before she took power. It is autographed by The Lady herself. The democracy icon has a place of honor in Grove's office.

Given his concern about democratic backsliding, I cannot help asking, "And how do you feel about the World Bank's engagement in Myanmar since the Rohingya crisis began?"

Paul Grove feels fine about that. "It's vitally important for the World Bank to remain engaged in Myanmar to strengthen Aung San Suu Kyi and her government in fighting against military abuses," he responds. "This is Myanmar's best opportunity for democracy. We must support it."

The past year's events apparently have not dented his conviction that we must remain fully engaged in Myanmar.

I leave the Capitol feeling discouraged about Cambodia but encouraged about Myanmar. Not only the White House and the State Department but key members of Congress appear to support our strategy to remain fully engaged in Myanmar to promote economic transition while focusing on social inclusion in conflict areas.

While I am in Washington shoring up US support, the team is back in Myanmar working hard, redesigning planned projects, and designing new operations focused on inclusion. We are ensuring that ethnic minority children have access to classrooms, minority mothers have basic income and nutrition training, and minority entrepreneurs have access to credit and business advisory services.

Inclusion. Nondiscrimination. Opportunity for all. These are our watchwords. We know there are no shortcuts to creating a tolerant and inclusive society in Myanmar. It will take decades of sustained work by government, civil society, and international partners like us.

The letter from Maxine Waters to the World Bank president arrives a few days later, and it hits hard. The fiery Democratic congresswoman from Los Angeles is the ranking member of the House Financial Services Committee. She has become a symbol of resistance to the Trump Administration since she went viral for assertively reclaiming her time during questioning of Trump's treasury secretary. I love Maxine Waters.

But in her letter, she beats us up.

She points to "credible findings by the UN of ethnic cleansing and genocide...by the Myanmar military and the complicity of the country's civilian government, led by Aung San Suu Kyi."

She goes on to argue that "the fundamental moral case against further World Bank engagement in Myanmar is obvious and unequivocal, and the case against the World Bank's involvement on developmental grounds is equally clear."

She concludes with a threat: "If the World Bank continues to fund activities in Myanmar before the government of Myanmar formally acknowledges the brutal raping, slaughtering, and ethnic cleansing of its Rohingya population, and brings those responsible to justice...it may become increasingly difficult to garner the necessary support in Congress for US contributions to the Bank."[34]

Maxine's letter is a slap in the face for Jim Yong Kim. Appointed by President Obama, Jim runs in distinctly Democratic party circles. The world gave Jim a unanimous thumbs-up for a second term as World Bank president late in the Obama Administration, when fears of a possible Trump presidency arose. This would have meant a Trump appointee as World Bank president, a terrifying idea for many of our global shareholders. They did not love Jim Kim, who seemed overly dismissive of the executive board. In the longer run, they hoped to break the precedent of choosing only American presidents for a global institution, but there was no time to quibble. He was a safe choice with just one job in his second term: protect the World Bank from the worst excesses of the Trump Administration.

Jim took heat for toadying up to the Trumps, but in doing so, he shielded the World Bank from much of the administration's anti-UN and anti-foreign-aid rhetoric. But now, to be accused of ignoring genocide in Myanmar by a heavyweight Democratic lawmaker must really sting. World Bank funding may be at stake, as well as his professional network and future career prospects.

"Jim is livid over the Maxine Waters letter," says my boss. "And he is furious at us!"

"Furious at us?" I ask anxiously. "For what?"

"For continuing to engage with the civilian government," she says.

[34] Maxine Waters to Jim Yong Kim, Washington, DC, September 26, 2018, https://democrats-financialservices.house.gov/uploadedfiles/09.26.2018_cmw_ltr_to_president_kim_wb_support_for_myanmar.pdf.

"For continuing to engage? Isn't that what we all agreed on?" I say, as my stress level rises. "Does Jim know that we've changed our strategy to focus on social inclusion in conflict areas? Does he know that we've not approved any new projects in a year and a half?"

"I've told him, but he is disappointed in Aung San Suu Kyi. He wants to send a stronger message," she says. "We need to do something to respond to Maxine's letter."

"Can we meet with him first to explain what we've done so far?" I suggest.

"Yes, that would be good. I'll try to set it up," she concludes.

In the meantime, I am sent back to Capitol Hill, this time on my own. Charlotte keeps a low profile on Myanmar given Jim's irritation.

Those accused of complicity in genocide do not get to meet the formidable Maxine Waters. I meet her chief of staff and bring out my full arsenal to convince him that staying engaged in Myanmar is the right thing to do—the moral thing to do.

"Walking away from Myanmar leaves the civilian government alone to battle against the abusive military," I explain. "It pushes Myanmar back toward isolation and autocratic rule. It leaves systemic discrimination in place without external pressure to dismantle it and leaves public opinion distorted by decades of ethnic nationalist propaganda with no countervailing forces.

"Walking away deprives ethnic minorities of millions of dollars in financing for social services and infrastructure that we've targeted to border areas, and it undermines the initial dialogue between government and ethnic armed organizations brokered by the World Bank! This is critically important. It also does nothing to help the remaining Rohingya in Rakhine State or create the right conditions for refugee return. Our UN partners want us there to incentivize a better government response.

"We have already taken punitive action against Myanmar—more than any other aid partner. We have eliminated three-quarters of a billion dollars in budget support and stopped approving new operations since the Rohingya crisis began fourteen months ago. We have substantially redesigned our strategy to address discrimination and exclusion, putting a greater focus on social inclusion in conflict areas."

Maxine's chief of staff is unimpressed.

"It doesn't matter. Anything the World Bank does legitimizes a regime engaging in gross human rights abuses, even genocide. How can you justify that?" he says.

He makes no distinction between the military and civilian parts of government, so he does not separate the Tatmadaw's military actions from the response by the civilian government under Aung San Suu Kyi. He may be assuming that the civilian authorities have oversight of the military as in Western democracies, but this is decidedly untrue in Myanmar. And I wonder why Myanmar alone warrants an angry letter from Maxine to the World Bank. What about China's systematic persecution of the Uighurs? Or India's increasing discrimination against its Muslim minorities? Where are the threatening letters asking the World Bank to disengage there?

And why us? Why is the World Bank the only target of criticism in Myanmar? The Asian Development Bank has continued financing projects in Myanmar with only the most cursory analysis of conflict and exclusion. And the UN remains engaged in Myanmar, even financing small projects in Rakhine State, including on land once inhabited by Rohingya and now bulldozed into history!

I feel like the World Bank is being used to assuage the world's conscience.

I am being used to assuage the world's conscience, and I carry this crippling weight on my shoulders all the time.

With the US government, I am caught between a rock and a hard place. We need bipartisan support on Capitol Hill to ensure US contributions to the World Bank. For Jim and our senior management, this question overshadows any concerns for Myanmar and the Rohingya. At the same time, the Trump Administration wants us to stay fully engaged in Myanmar, to continue to support the transition away from China. And they, not Congress, vote on our board.

I am walking a tightrope, and the wind is picking up from all directions.

I am also lonely. I spend more time in hotels in Washington than back home in Myanmar. I work all hours of the night and am increasingly sleep-deprived. I miss my husband, who recently moved from Myanmar to Cambodia for work, and I miss my team in Myanmar who best can understand and share my pain. I miss the peacefulness of my lush garden in Yangon, where I sip tea among the palm fronds and flowering vines.

While in Washington, I also miss the long-awaited birth of a baby girl to my housekeepers, Susie and Nay Moo. It is a joyous event after previous miscarriages. They believe my support of better prenatal care made a difference this time. Upon my return they ask me to name the baby, which surprises and delights me.

I worry that she should have a Karen or Burmese name, but Mya Mya tells me to pick a Western one. Her family will choose a local name. I suggest a few favorites and, after trying them out, they choose Phoebe, meaning *radiant one.*

"It's a good school name, Madam," explains Susie. They want her to have the education they could not.

And now I am in heaven each night, returning home to a sweet and happy baby! I dote on her—I am her American *pipi,* or grandma. I bounce her in my arms and dance with her each evening, skating around the polished marble floors.

Our antics are reflected in a large mirror on the back wall. I begin daily affirmations with her almost as a joke. Holding her tiny round face up to the mirror, I say, "You are strong. You are wise. You will be the future leader of a diverse and tolerant Myanmar!"

And then we dance away. She gurgles appreciatively. I do this every day until I leave the country for good.

CHAPTER 35

Pressure Rising

(October 2018)

In Washington, I visited many of our executive directors to shore up support for our work. All of them favored continued engagement in Myanmar as long as we use our tools—our few carrots—to help resolve the Rohingya crisis and promote peace and inclusion in Myanmar.

My private meetings reflect our shareholders' public statements. The US administration avoided declaring genocide to ensure we could all stay engaged. The Chinese wanted us to promote stability in Rakhine and Myanmar as a whole. The Japanese favored positive encouragement to prevent a turn toward China. The Australians were realistic, expecting only gradual movement toward full democracy. The Europeans wanted to see progress toward democracy and global integration, even as they called out human rights abuses. The Saudis and other Muslim-majority countries wanted us there to protect the interests of the Rohingya and other Muslim minorities. The ASEAN countries of Southeast Asia wanted us to partner with them to influence the Myanmar government.

"So it's everybody?" asks Charlotte.

"Uh-huh. Nobody thinks we should walk away."

All in all, we've done well in carving out a strategy for Myanmar that meets all their expectations.

We eliminated aid to the budget that could be seen as supporting the military. Now we are following the lead of our UN colleagues on relief and repatriation in Rakhine and offering significant financial incentives to do the right thing. We are maintaining our focus on reforms and strengthening institutions to produce a more open society and create economic opportunity for all. We ask ourselves the right questions about conflict and exclusion and then design interventions that promote social inclusion and foster peace. We ensure that everything we do contributes to the long-term development of a multiethnic and tolerant society—a society baby Phoebe could someday lead.

Now, less than a month later, I am back in Washington. My body is aching from the thirty hours of flying between Myanmar and the United States yet again. I feel the pressure of the Rohingya situation like a heavy weight on my shoulders and chest. My heart is palpitating, and I wonder if I will have a heart attack before age sixty like my brother did.

I stay in the hotel a block from headquarters so I can focus on work. I even have the same room as last time. The days are punishingly long on both ends. I start with dawn video conferences with the team in Myanmar, then meetings at headquarters all day, followed by more video conferences in the evening. I take advantage of the time difference to maximize output on both sides of the world. But this takes a toll on my physical and mental health.

I will have a chance to listen to President Kim today at the twice-yearly meeting of World Bank directors from all over the world. For those of us based overseas, especially in smaller or less important countries, this may be the only time we see the president face to face during the year.

In Jim's summary, he recycles perennial messages of support. "You are on the front lines," he says. "You are client-facing, and you know what our clients need better than we do."

This is standard fare, as is his closing line: "Whenever you are at headquarters, come by and see me. Or send me an email if you want to talk. You are closest to our clients. I really value that unique perspective."

And then he hustles off to his next meeting. As he rushes out, a group of directors—all male—push forward to get a little face time with the big boss.

The irony is that I cannot get a meeting with Jim.

It is busy after Annual Meetings, I admit. But given the global attention on the Rohingya crisis after the first anniversary and the interest on Capitol Hill and among our executive directors, I would have thought Jim would have wanted a meeting with those in charge of the Myanmar program—if not with me, at least with Charlotte, my vice president.

But she cannot get a meeting either.

"Some VPs can just pick up the phone and talk to the president anytime," Levon says.

But not Charlotte. She is struggling for access. And it is hurting us. It is not Charlotte's fault that our president favors some vice presidents over others, but it still makes our jobs more difficult.

"Jim read Maxine's letter but was never briefed on what we discussed with the State Department or Treasury," I say.

"He read *New York Times* headlines from the Human Rights Commission but didn't hear from us about actual UN efforts in Rakhine," adds Levon.

"He has no idea how our strategy has changed over the past year in Myanmar," I add wistfully. "Or what other development partners have done."

"I doubt he realizes that we canceled six years' worth of planned budget support," says Levon, "and we haven't approved any new operations since the crisis broke."

"We have changed so much," I conclude. "It's definitely not business as usual."

But Jim does not know this. I imagine that Charlotte and I are just thorns in his side anytime we raise the subject of Myanmar. We complicate his relationship with Capitol Hill. We create reputational risk for the World Bank (complicit in genocide, no less!) without any real reward except the painfully slow and bumpy evolution of Myanmar toward a more tolerant and prosperous society.

Nothing in the short term makes this worthwhile for a World Bank president. There are no headlines praising the World Bank's principled stance. There is no self-congratulatory partnership among the Righteous Doing the Right Thing.

The World Bank does not have the financial or political clout to turn the tide in Myanmar—it is hubris even to think so. And I am just an infuriating reminder to Jim that we are not strong enough to fix this problem.

The UN Secretary General, who is also not strong enough to fix the problem, cautions our president not to overreact, to be patient and stay quietly engaged because *it is complicated* in Myanmar.

I leave for Yangon without a meeting with anyone at the top of the organization. So until I am told otherwise, I will just keep implementing our agreed-upon strategy.

Back in Yangon, I am not alone in feeling the pressure of my inadequacy. Ambassadors, special representatives, and heads of agencies are all facing daily criticism from back home about the lack of progress in Myanmar. The Rohingya have been left hanging for over a year in overcrowded and perilous refugee camps in Bangladesh. Those in Myanmar face severe insecurity and discrimination. The Tatmadaw has not been held accountable. Our authorizing environments—bosses, shareholders, taxpayers—have just one message for us: this simply cannot continue!

"What are you doing differently?" we ask each other frequently.

I see the other heads of development agencies two or three times a day in meetings or on flights to Nay Pyi Taw. They are an impressive group of seasoned professionals who have worked in some of the world's most notorious conflict zones, veterans of relief and development work in places like Afghanistan, South Sudan, Syria, and Timor.

Now we are part of an exclusive but unenviable club: we must defend our organizations' decisions on Myanmar even as we face relentless pressures and unrealistic expectations from above. At our monthly dinner, we self-medicate with a selection of good wines and compare notes on what we're doing differently.

"We are shifting away from the government and working more with nongovernmental organizations," says the head of the UK aid program.

"We are orienting our program more toward democracy and governance, with emphasis on inclusiveness, even in Rakhine," says the head of USAID.

"We are looking to see how we can do more in post-conflict zones," says the head of AusAid.

"We are increasing our focus on social inclusion in conflict zones," I add.

Our terminology is strikingly similar. We are selling roughly the same strategy to our constituencies. It is the only thing that makes sense given persistent ethnic conflict, systemic discrimination, and the incomplete transition to democracy.

It is comforting to see them shift their strategies in the same direction. It is the right thing to do despite the failures, delays, and weaknesses of the civilian government.

I take advantage of a pause in the conversation to ask, "On a scale of one to ten, how stressed are you?"

A split second of awkward silence and then laughter. And a shaking off of tension.

"Are you kidding? It's ten!"

"Easily eleven."

"Off the charts."

"I was a political activist on the run in apartheid South Africa, and this is worse!" says one.

Then we regale each other with *they just do not get it* stories from our respective headquarters.

"Why don't you go talk to Aung San Suu Kyi? Surely you can persuade her to make faster progress. Surely she will see how much foreign aid is at stake," say our superiors in Washington, in London, in Tokyo, in Canberra.

As if we have not tried.

We all feel the weight of our superiors' quizzical looks and slight frowns. *If you were a better director, a better representative, a better ambassador, then certainly you could persuade her. Certainly you could solve this. How hard could it be? What is wrong with you?*

Dinner ends, but the next day we are back at work in what feels like a no-win situation.

If we make bold public statements, we are frozen out of meetings with Aung San Suu Kyi and her government.

If we remain silent, we might eventually get a meeting. But if we are too upbeat in the meeting, then we make no progress and right none of the wrongs.

If we are too critical in the meeting, we are ignored and frozen out of future meetings.

If we manage to strike the right tone and encourage faster progress on sensitive issues, Aung San Suu Kyi commits to doing the right thing. Then she asks for our help. Which we agree to give. Because that is why we are here.

But then progress is glacially slow, if there is progress at all, and we keep glancing around while we do something good over here in case bad things—immoral, criminal things—are happening over there.

If only you were a better director, a better representative, a better ambassador. Surely you could solve this.

CHAPTER 36

Rolling Up the Carpets

(October 2018)

Our sleek new office is on the twenty-first floor of the Sule Square Tower in the heart of Yangon. It is a magnificent space befitting a new era for Myanmar—an era of opening to global markets and to the modern world.

I bask in a flood of light from my floor-to-ceiling windows and smell the new carpets as I take in a magnificent view of Shwedagon Pagoda, Yangon's religious and cultural center.

I did not choose this new office. The decision preceded my arrival in Myanmar. Now that I am seeing it, it seems like too much, too slick for an aid organization like ours. But mostly I do not like the location, which is far from the airport despite our weekly commute to Nay Pyi Taw and my frequent trips to Bangkok, Phnom Penh, Vientiane, and Washington.

We had to do something, though. Our staff of nearly one hundred in Yangon was overflowing our charming but decrepit villa, working split shifts so everyone had a place to sit and relying on noise-canceling headphones to concentrate. The rodent problem was getting worse.

"We had a careful selection process, Ellen. It's too late to fight it," the real estate team in Washington told me.

And I knew if I escalated my concerns and kept pushing back, especially so soon after my arrival in Myanmar, it would just confirm my reputation as a difficult woman, another aggressive and abrasive female leader. Not a team player, for sure. That was the last thing I needed dogging me as I started my new job.

And the earlier decision had a logic. Back in 2016, it made some sense to invest in a large and modern office, capable of absorbing the fastest-growing program in the World Bank. Such an office was needed to upgrade Myanmar from the small local office to a large hub for a multi-country department. My department. I would be the inaugural director of this exciting new department, ushering in a new era for Myanmar!

So I sucked it up. Better to choose my battles wisely.

Besides, we found some lovely connections when first touring the office space. We were gazing down at the small golden Sule Pagoda in front of the river when the building manager said, "Yangon's historic synagogue is visible just a few blocks away."

"Then my office will be on this side!" I joke.

"And on the other side lies the old Armenian Orthodox church," she points out.

"This is my side then," says Levon, who would attend this church with the few remaining families of Armenian origin.

We moved into the new office just after the first anniversary of the Rohingya crisis.

The move was a game changer and morale booster for staff. They felt liberated, appreciated, and energized by the light, airy surroundings, and spectacular views.

And now here I am, sitting in my spacious new director's office in late October after returning from Washington. But I do not feel liberated, appreciated, or energized.

I am beaten down by extreme travel and the constant pressure of urgent briefing notes for headquarters. I produce one-pagers, two-pagers, short policy notes—often in the middle of the night on impossible deadlines—trying to explain what we are doing in Myanmar to help the Rohingya who remain there and the refugees waiting to return home.

"Jim never trusted Aung San Suu Kyi after they met in 2016," says Charlotte in our weekly phone call. "He remains unhappy over the Maxine Waters letter. He thinks we need to send a stronger message about the Rohingya."

"A stronger message?" I ask. "Does he know what we're doing already? I mean, we've sent a lot of briefing notes."

"I don't think he understands," she says. "Can you develop some scenarios, Ellen? Develop some tougher scenarios, things we can do to send a stronger signal on the need for progress."

"I guess so," I say weakly.

"We have to, otherwise he may pull the plug completely," she says ominously and hangs up.

My anxiety skyrockets. My chest tightens. I recall that the symptoms of a heart attack are harder to detect in women.

But I develop a few scenarios to punish Myanmar for its treatment of the Rohingya. This involves withholding some, most, or all our financial support. This is the only stick we have.

I try to make rational choices in defining these scenarios. It is easy for us to stop preparing new projects. It is quite difficult to stop implementing existing projects by overriding legal agreements and breaching contracts that have already been signed. So I focus mostly on scenarios that stop some, most, or all new projects.

On a Friday afternoon in late October, my boss calls me again. It is first thing in the morning in Washington, and she sounds agitated.

"Jim is talking about rolling up the carpets in Myanmar!" she blurts out. "He's unhappy with our response. He wants to pull out. He said he'll make his decision this weekend. I just want to warn you, Ellen."

Bombs are exploding in my head. Could he really kill our whole strategy, our whole program? Would he really pull out of Myanmar entirely?

"Is there no way to have a conversation first?" I splutter.

"He told Birgit that he would make a decision this weekend," she repeats.

So apparently there will be no further conversation.

I hang up, and my mind is racing. *This is nuts. It makes no sense. Our shareholders do not want this. Nobody wants this. It helps nobody. Certainly not the Rohingya.*

Rolling up the carpets. Stopping new projects and canceling existing projects and then shutting down our office and walking away is almost unheard of except in a war zone. I knew that the World Bank had shut down the office in Rwanda in 1994 when the capital city, Kigali, was engulfed in ethnic fighting and staff had to flee for their lives. Nothing like that is happening in Yangon or Nay Pyi Taw.

I have been at the World Bank for nearly thirty-five years, a bit player in some high-profile situations around the globe. Our presidents fret and fume, but their decisions are inevitably tempered by our shareholders, the big countries that shape global affairs, as well as our institution's policies and precedents. None of our shareholders want us to stop engaging with the Myanmar government or pull completely out of the country. And none of our policies and precedents would support this either.

It would give the World Bank a satisfying headline, and a sense of moral righteousness, even moral superiority. Then that sense of moral righteousness would fade away, and we would be left with no influence, no presence, no voice in Myanmar to pursue peace, prosperity, or whatever we believe to be right for the Rohingya.

I do not get it.

I sit in my glass office high above Yangon, feeling panicked. Everything we worked for and fought for over the past fifteen months—all the heavy lifting to change our strategy to respond to the Rohingya crisis—may be wiped away this weekend. Without ever consulting me, my boss, or our shareholders. I am usually a straight talker with my team about how our shareholders and our management see the Myanmar program. But I buffer them from the daily ruminations and emotions of our president. Why raise anxiety among the whole team? Why demoralize them and slow our daily work when no decisions have been made? But now a decision seems imminent. And crushing.

Levon is heading out to start his weekend. He sees me through my glass doorway and steps in. "Something wrong?" he asks.

I hesitate. But I must warn him.

"Yeah, something is wrong," I acknowledge. "Jim is saying he wants to roll up the carpets in Myanmar."

"Roll up the carpets? Shut down everything?" he says, looking alarmed. "That can't be true!"

"I'm afraid it might be," I say glumly. "And if he decides this weekend and makes a public statement on Monday, we need to be ready."

"Oh my god. We'll need to warn the team!" he says.

"We'll also need to warn ambassadors and heads of agencies," I say, knowing that they will be shocked and then turn to our executive directors for an explanation they will not have.

"But we also need to explain to the government!" he says.

"They aren't going to understand," I say.

These government counterparts have come from decades of isolation and do not comprehend the politics of foreign aid.

"Nope, not at all," he says. "The World Bank came in 2012 and mysteriously, we're leaving six years later. That's all they'll understand."

For the moment, we tell nobody.

We sit sadly on the new couch in my new office, gazing out the windows and saying nothing. We watch as boats gently ply the river behind the Sule Pagoda, its golden spire glinting as the sun sets over Yangon.

CHAPTER 37

A Message to the President

(November 2018)

I do not sleep that night. It is partly jet lag from my travel to Washington. Mostly it is my spiking anxiety. I thrash about, tossing and turning until dawn, when I drag myself downstairs, my thoughts still spinning wildly.

What if Jim decides to pull us out of Myanmar? It seems crazy. It is not the right thing to do. Not for development. Not for peace. Not for democracy. Not for human rights. Definitely not for the Rohingya.

"Whenever you're at headquarters, come by and see me. Or send me an email if you want to talk. You are closest to our clients. I really value that unique perspective," Jim told us just a few weeks ago.

Well, that was a bunch of bullshit. Such a farce. I am disgusted by the hypocrisy.

But I could take him up on his invitation. The president's direct email address is a loosely guarded secret within the World Bank. But I know it. After more than thirty years in the organization, I know my way around.

Hell, why not? My boss cannot seem to schedule a meeting with Jim to discuss Myanmar. Maybe those around him are protecting him too much, shielding him from uncomfortable information. Maybe I should try to cut through that.

Dear Jim:

The history of the Holocaust was a constant refrain in my childhood, so I do not take allegations of genocide lightly. I remain appalled by the violence and human rights abuses perpetrated by Myanmar's security forces against the Rohingya in the past year.

The Myanmar team sent a strong message of concern to the Government by canceling our budget support operations and pausing new projects since the Rohingya crisis began fourteen months ago. We are the only development partner to have done so. At the same time, we have made a fundamental shift in our country strategy to focus on social inclusion, non-discrimination, and creating equal opportunities in conflict zones, including Rakhine State.

Government's response to the Rohingya crisis has been slow and unsatisfactory. Nonetheless, my recent discussions with diplomats and development partners here in the field—as well as with our Executive Directors at headquarters—have reaffirmed their desire to see the World Bank remain engaged in Myanmar.

Remaining engaged with a greater focus on social inclusion in conflict areas is seen as critical to continuing Myanmar's historic transition, strengthening a weak civilian government as a counterweight to a powerful military, gradually reinforcing the rule of law and building a multiethnic and tolerant society.

I would welcome a chance to brief you more fully on how we have adjusted our strategy over the past year, as well as examine options to further strengthen our response before additional decisions about the Myanmar program are taken.

Best regards,
Ellen

I contemplate my message. It has a personal hook. A friendly, diplomatic tone. It reminds him that we have already done a lot. It is reasonably short.

And it ends with the kicker: none of our shareholders want us to pull out of Myanmar. I think I have found a diplomatic way to say what must be said: *Not a single one of the board members who voted for your second term thinks rolling up the carpets is a good idea. So why do you?*

It is a good message. It is an unusual step at an unusual time. I hesitate. Then I press send.

Did I just end my career?

Later that day, I get a call from Kathryn, my desk officer in Washington. She has picked up rumors that a cataclysmic Myanmar decision is imminent.

"Wow, very courageous, Ellen!" she says when I tell her about my personal message to the president.

"Or stupid?" I ask.

"Probably both!" we say simultaneously.

The weekend passes in silence. No response from Jim. No decision either.

We work all Monday in Yangon while Washington is asleep.

I meet with the team preparing the new Peaceful and Prosperous Communities Project. They spent a week jolting along unpaved roads and sleeping in rundown guesthouses to meet with ethnic armed organizations in southeast Myanmar. But they are feeling jubilant.

"Some ethnic groups are happy to talk to us," says James, the team leader. "And they are even willing to talk to the government about the proposed project."

"So they are on board to prepare the project?" I ask.

"It depends on what we propose. They are not up for big infrastructure. They say that would only serve the Tatmadaw and their cronies," he explains. "But they are up for smaller stuff: support for microenterprises, basic health and education services, community infrastructure."

"We can do that," I say, pleased that something seems to be going right.

I meet with Jorge, our bright young labor economist. I plucked him from his research on migration in Myanmar and gave him the dubious honor of preparing the proposed Rakhine Recovery and Development Project. He is working in a scorched-earth environment just in case the government eventually makes enough progress on relief and repatriation in Rakhine. Just in case UNHCR and UNDP need us there to further incentivize the government to do the right things.

Jorge is as painstaking in his consultations as he was in his research. He wants to ensure that all voices in Rakhine are heard, all stakeholders are on board, and all communities can participate.

"The UN thinks we should start in central Rakhine until more progress is made in the north," he begins.

"Okay. And what would we finance?" I ask.

"In the short run, we can provide income through cash-for-work programs."

"To everybody, even remaining Rohingya there?"

"Yes, all communities without exception. But work teams would need to be separate," he explains.

"Separate? Is that okay?"

"The communities themselves say it is too explosive to put Rakhine and Rohingya on the same teams."

I grimace. "But could we build in some kind of intercommunal dialogue? Something to break down barriers?"

"Yeah, that's what we'll have to do. That is all we can do."

"Sounds okay as a first step. What else?" I ask.

"Well..." Jorge sounds more hesitant. "Land is a problem."

"No work can be done on land once occupied by Rohingya. That would be completely unacceptable," I say.

In some brighter future, they would be repatriated to that land. We cannot be party to paving over their land and erasing their history.

"So we'll need some kind of prescreening for land issues and a really close monitoring system," continues Jorge.

"Yup," I reply.

"I may need more money to prepare that."

"Yup."

Jorge sighs.

"Whatever you need. This must be done right," I say. "Everybody is watching us."

Sometime that night an email lands in my inbox. It is from the president.

> Thank you for your message on the situation in Myanmar. Rest assured that we will have a full discussion on the situation before any decisions are taken.
>
> Best,
> Jim

Hmmm. It is minimal.

But it does not appear we will be rolling up the carpets in Myanmar this week, and that is huge.

I exhale and slump my head down on my desk. I am relieved but exhausted. I feel like crying, but tears do not come.

Jim says we will have a full discussion. Finally. It is way past due.

CHAPTER 38

Gaslighting Begins

(November 2018)

I'll never know if my email to the president really made any difference but judging from Jim's decision—or lack thereof—my warning was received.

Several ambassadors in Yangon also express concerns to our board members. I am surprised because I have not discussed it with the ambassadors—or anyone, really—in Yangon. Nonetheless, they hear rumors the World Bank may be disengaging from Myanmar.

"That would be a grave mistake," says a Nordic ambassador to me.

"It's extremely complicated," says another European ambassador.

"We need at least a generation for meaningful change," adds an Asian ambassador.

All of them send a message to my headquarters that transforming Myanmar into a peaceful and prosperous country—and a tolerant multiethnic society—is a marathon, not a sprint. Even as we condemn the atrocities perpetrated against the Rohingya.

We never roll up the carpets in Myanmar. But we also never have the promised discussion about Myanmar within the World Bank.

I continue to implement our strategy, and we maintain our fragile relationship with the government. Our team remains dedicated. Our projects deliver results. Households get electricity. Poor children go to school. Women get better health services. Mobile banking reaches rural areas. And ethnic minorities share in these benefits.

We are doing good in most parts of Myanmar.

But my email to the president has repercussions.

"Why did you send that, Ellen?" asks Charlotte in our next phone call. "Birgit is furious!"

"I wanted Jim to know what I was hearing on the ground," I say. "He claims to welcome such personal messages."

"Birgit is angry you didn't copy her," Charlotte explains. "She thinks it's arrogant and shows poor judgment."

"Sorry if it was a mistake," I say, feeling contrite. "You said Jim might shut down the whole program that weekend! I was desperate. It seemed urgent."

I suspect that my boss sees this as an opportunity. She made it clear when I interviewed earlier to become director for Vietnam that I was not her personal choice. She was obligated to take me on as Director for Myanmar, Cambodia, and Laos to compensate for disregarding the normal recruitment process for Vietnam.

Now the person she never wanted working for her has screwed up. This is not something to be wasted.

Soon thereafter, I travel to Washington again. It is the third time in two months, reflecting the political sensitivity of the Rohingya situation. I pack my carry-on automatically and for maximum efficiency: an all-black uniform every day, with a few patterned blazers and colorful scarves to change the look. I travel in jeans, a sweater, and short boots: my only casual look for the rare times I am out of uniform. I stopped carrying a stylish handbag long ago in favor of a sturdy tote big enough for my laptop, tablet, global phone, local phone, power cords, and chargers, as well as some documents and a sheaf of draft memos, letters, and speeches for my clearance. I have twenty-five to thirty hours of travel each way. I can get a lot done.

Truth be told, I love traveling. I like the spaciousness and anonymity of airports, the suspension of everyday life while in the air. Disconnecting from the emails, phone calls, messaging, and texting that follow me everywhere and demand immediate answers. Sometimes a message chirps on my phone as the plane touches down in Dubai or Seoul, where I wait for my connecting flight. I race to the business lounge and drink tiny cans of Diet Coke to stay awake, frantically editing another briefing note or preparing a memo for senior management. I know that Wi-Fi on airplanes is fast becoming a thing, but I resist because it violates the sanctity and serenity that I feel in air space.

Upon arrival at headquarters, I wander over to Charlotte's office to say hello. She is friendly and gracious, and she waves me into her office.

We discuss how our strategy is proceeding in Myanmar. Then we have a different sort of conversation.

"I was in the senior management talent review last week," she says pleasantly. "We reviewed all the directors. I want to share feedback with you that might be helpful."

"Of course," I say, but a warning bell is going off in my brain. It is not normal to share what was said in a confidential talent review meeting. This is not friendly advice; it has some other purpose that I cannot yet discern.

"In your review, a number of vice presidents mentioned your reputation for being...uh...difficult," she says pleasantly. She does not elaborate on who found me difficult or why. Or what conversation led to them revealing this.

"Really?" I respond neutrally. "This was something I heard occasionally earlier in my career. However, I've worked hard to smooth the sharp elbows since then. I didn't think this perception was still there."

"Well, apparently so," she says. "You may want to be a bit careful."

"Thank you," I say and walk out feeling pissed off.

I have heard this before, back in my twenties and early thirties, when I thought that being smart and working hard would be sufficient for professional advancement. Back then, I was labeled with all the A-adjectives thrown at strong women: assertive and aggressive, occasionally even abrupt and abrasive. I was not enough of a team player.

Performance evaluations from thirty years earlier noted that I "did not suffer fools gladly." As if this were a bad thing.

And it hurt me. I cried in frustration and took it all to heart. I vowed to fix it. I volunteered for leadership training. I worked with professional coaches. I worked to neutralize my body language, lower the register of my voice, listen more attentively, display more empathy, and inject more humor into my management style. Gradually I stepped into my power more comfortably. And criticism faded over the years.

But I also took some knocks in more than thirty years at the World Bank. My career suffered in the 1990s when I became a whistleblower. My boss had an affair with his own staff member and then rigged recruitment for a managerial position in her favor. Somehow, I suffered the consequences of their inappropriate relationship. My career also suffered twenty years later as the Director for Bangladesh. I was vilified by the government for pursuing a high-profile corruption case at the ministerial level and above. While wanting me to maintain good access and influence with the government, World Bank senior management urged me to take a strong public stance against corruption and press for government accountability. This nearly impossible balancing act led to rumors at headquarters that I was soft on corruption or had "gone native" until ultimately, I was removed by the World Bank from Bangladesh to take up another assignment.

Despite these bumps, looking back on more than thirty years of my career, I can count myself a successful female leader in a male-dominated organization.

I can accept that some people still think of me as difficult or demanding. I am philosophical about it. You cannot please all the people all the time. But I will keep working to smooth those rough edges and rein in those sharp elbows.

On this trip to Washington, however, I hear more.

"Hey, Ellen, what's going on in Myanmar?" ask friendly colleagues in the corridors. "People are talking about it, saying you may be in trouble."

"Oh yeah?" I reply. "What people? And what are they saying exactly?"

But it is not clear who. Or what. Or why.

It becomes clearer on my last day as I prepare to return to Yangon. It is the end of another exhausting trip of chock-a-block meetings inside the World Bank and outside, with diplomats, members of Congress, and human rights advocates. They all want to know what we are doing in Myanmar and why.

I stop by to check out with Charlotte before heading to the airport. We run down our lists of things to do on the Myanmar program before the conversation turns.

"I spoke with Birgit again," says my boss hesitatingly.

"Oh yeah?" I respond. "What's she thinking?"

"Well, you know...she's not sure you're the right fit for this job," my boss says gently.

"What do you mean?" I stammer.

"It may be better if you had another position," Charlotte continues vaguely.

"What other position is she thinking of?" I ask warily.

"Well, you could leave Myanmar and then compete for other country director positions," she says.

I suppress a snort. "Compete? Compete for other jobs? You know as well as I do that if I'm pulled out for being a 'bad fit,' I'll never get selected as a country director again," I answer vehemently.

She looks at the ground. But as a former country director, she knows.

"You're probably right," she says finally. "Why don't we wait and see what happens?"

Well, that's unsettling.

I stand too fast and get dizzy. My ears are buzzing and my stomach is churning, but I thank my boss for her time and stumble out the door. I wheel my carry-on down the long corridors and out of the World Bank.

My friend is waiting at our favorite sushi spot nearby.

"Hey, how are you?" she asks breezily as I walk up.

"I think I was just fired!" I blurt out.

"What? What do you mean? What happened? *Why*?" My friend looks incredulous.

"I think I was fired for failing to prevent genocide," I say.

CHAPTER 39

A Completely Different Visit to Rakhine

(November 2018)

I fly back to Myanmar feeling stunned—almost paralyzed—by my boss's words. Since the Rohingya crisis exploded, I have sweated blood and pushed my team so hard to do the right thing in Myanmar. I have tried to do the thing that would make a real difference over time, the thing that draws on the strengths of the World Bank for maximum benefit. *Is this really the thanks I get from an organization to which I've devoted my entire adult life?*

I am feeling burned and burned out.

A few days later, I say to myself, *Fuck it all. If I am going to be fired, I want to see as much of Myanmar as possible before I leave.*

That is how I find myself turning a corner in a dim corridor with thick sandstone walls. I have lost track of where I am. A shaft of sunlight stabs me in the eye, blinding me temporarily. I blink rapidly and see them sitting tranquilly, gazing through stony eyes. A row of life-size Buddhas is waiting for me, their carved faces illuminated by the sunlight, soft green moss growing on their shoulders. I am soothed by their presence.

My breathing slows and my mind focuses as I continue to wind through the silent maze of corridors. Buddhas bigger than me. Buddhas the size of my hand. Buddhas the size of my thumbnail. Repeated in an abstract pattern from floor to ceiling. And animals—real and imaginary—slithering and stalking and swooping across the sandstone walls. Then more incarnations of the Buddha. I emerge feeling restored.

This is Shittaung Temple, the Temple of 80,000 Buddhas, in Mrauk-U. And it is beyond anything I had imagined.

Mrauk-U is the ancient capital of the Arakan Kingdom, now Rakhine State. It was founded in the mid-fifteenth century as a fortress city. It was built to repel invaders crossing the Bay of Bengal from the west and armies from the kingdom of Burma to the east. It was a glorious capital and a cosmopolitan commercial center for the Arakan people until the Burmese invaded in 1784, taking the king captive and emptying the city. The British took it in the first Anglo-Burmese War in 1824 and held it through 1948, when it became part of an independent Burma. But the Arakan rulers and Rakhine people were never happily subsumed by the Burmese majority.

The Tatmadaw had declared northern Rakhine off limits for security reasons, but visiting the central part of the state was still possible. Against the odds, I managed to get a travel authorization from them to visit Mrauk-U.

I feel extraordinarily lucky. It takes effort to get here. But I have a legitimate professional reason to visit. The World Bank is carrying out the environmental assessment for Mrauk-U to become a UNESCO World Heritage Site. This was one of the eighty-eight recommendations for Rakhine in the Annan Report. Kofi Annan had called Mrauk-U "the greatest physical manifestation of Rakhine's rich history and culture."[35]

---

[35] Joshua Hammer, "The Hidden City of Myanmar," *Smithsonian Magazine*, December 2019, https://www.smithsonianmag.com/travel/hidden-city-myanmar-180973486/.

Yi Yi is our specialist in Yangon organizing the environmental assessment. She is ethnic Rakhine as well; she speaks the local language and knows the local players. I marvel once again at the talent and diversity we have gathered in our office: we always have the ideal person for the job.

I bring along several friends from America. We are probably the only tourists in Mrauk-U that week. Yi Yi tells us that the rest of the tourists are mostly in Bagan, the country's tourism center, with its thousands of Buddhist temples, pagodas, and stupas spread over fourteen square kilometers.

"Bagan gets two hundred times the daily visitors of Mrauk-U," she explains. "All the flights land there."

What she does not say is that Bagan embodies the triumphant Burmese culture. Mrauk-U reflects the vanquished Arakan Kingdom and culture lost to the world not merely for decades but for centuries.

Yi Yi takes us to Moe Cherry, the only bustling restaurant down the road from the Royal Palace and Shittaung Temple.

"Try the tea leaf salad," I urge my friends, pushing forward a plate of my favorite Myanmar dish. "And this fried tofu is amazing!"

"Why is it yellow?" asks my friend. "Some spice?"

"Because it's made of chickpeas, not soy," I explain. "I had never tasted it before coming to Myanmar, but it's delicious!"

We wash it all down with Myanmar Beer, which is less delicious but mercifully cold.

The next evening, Yi Yi suggests we eat at an expensive resort hotel. We discover that the gates are padlocked; they have no guests. She talks the guards into letting us in anyway, and we walk the beautifully landscaped grounds under the moonlight. She stumbles upon the chef and talks him into opening the restaurant and cooking us a meal. We sit alone in an enormous hallway with soaring cathedral ceilings as dish after dish emerges from the kitchen.

It is all a bit isolated, surreal, and mystical.

Our days are spent visiting unheard-of temples, pagodas, and stupas built of massive sandstone blocks. Not just Shittaung, but KoTaung, Htukkanthein, Andaw Thein, and others.

We also visit unrestored vestiges of the Arakan Kingdom's military defenses: crumbling ramparts, guard posts, and a system of sophisticated canals and reservoirs with built-in sluices and spillways. Irrigate in peacetime. Wash enemies away in wartime.

Standing on these ancient ramparts, I feel saddened—maybe even ashamed—at the shallowness of my understanding. All my reading, all my discussions about ethnic identity in Myanmar have given me a basic understanding. I probably understand more than most foreigners here. But it is only at this moment that I truly feel the Arakan "otherness" and the historic pride of the Rakhine people in an independent kingdom and culture.

Within a month, the window into this extraordinary world closes.

An armed insurgent group representing young, ethnic Rakhine begins attacking police and security posts. They call themselves the Arakan Army. The Tatmadaw vows to crush them.

The military engages in its usual tactics, including torture and indiscriminate attacks on civilians in Rakhine. The victims are mostly ethnic Rakhine, but also some remaining Rohingya, as well as Mro and other small ethnic groups.[36]

The thick stone walls of the ancient fortresses and temples serve the Tatmadaw well. They position artillery and men within the temple complexes of Mrauk-U and fire indiscriminately, sending civilians fleeing. They kill a few innocent souls and damage the cultural heritage of the Arakan kings, including the Temple of 80,000 Buddhas.

Mrauk-U is sealed off. No access is allowed for tourists, diplomats, development partners, or journalists to report on what is happening. Myanmar's most hidden city is hidden once again.

---

[36] "Myanmar: Military Commits War Crimes in Latest Operation in Rakhine State," Amnesty International, May 29, 2019, https://www.amnesty.org.au/642130-2/.

CHAPTER 40

Forced Repatriation

(November 2018)

As the Arakan Army flexes its muscles and the Tatmadaw responds in Rakhine, an improbable scenario for repatriation of the Rohingya refugees unfolds across the Bay of Bengal in Bangladesh.

"Ellen, could you try to persuade Aung San Suu Kyi to stop this? Doesn't she realize how bad this looks to the international community?" my boss asks in an urgent phone call. She cannot hear my eyes roll.

Even now, Birgit and Charlotte still count on my relationship and the inadequate clout of the World Bank to persuade the state counsellor to abandon a lousy plan to repatriate the Rohingya.

Sure. I will get right on that, I muse to myself.

I am back from Mrauk-U. And it is an emergency. China has decided to solve the festering Rohingya problem that creates instability in Rakhine, jeopardizing important investments it has made there. Given their clout, they put unrefusable pressure on both Bangladesh and Myanmar. They have decided that it is time for both countries to make good on the earlier bilateral agreement to repatriate the Rohingya. International standards be damned.

"What are the ambassadors and other heads of agency saying to Aung San Suu Kyi?" my boss persists. "She needs to understand that the conditions are not met for safe, voluntary, and dignified refugee return!"

Not hardly, I think. Basic security and minimal civil liberties for returning Rohingya are not guaranteed. "Nothing has changed on the ground in Rakhine," I say firmly.

Nonetheless, November 15 has been set as the date to begin repatriating a first wave of 2,260 Rohingya from 485 families. Myanmar has a list of 4,355 Rohingya they have approved for return to Rakhine.[37]

Of course, nobody has asked the Rohingya.[38]

"The UN High Commission on Refugees won't support what appears to be forced repatriation," confirms Rodrigo, head of UNHCR in Myanmar. "Our team in Bangladesh will interview those who are on the list to determine if they are willing to go, but we won't support the repatriation given unacceptable conditions in Rakhine."

The plan is to process 150 refugees a day through the reception center that I visited and then transfer them to the transit camp I saw, built on land once occupied by Rohingya families. Both are surrounded by barbed wire and essentially prisons for incoming refugees, much like the internal camps in Rakhine that have housed 120,000 forcibly displaced Rohingya for years.

A spokesperson for the government's UEHRD insists, "Repatriation of refugees will be voluntary, with relocation to their original villages."

---

[37] Human Rights Watch, "Halt Rohingya Repatriation Plan: Conditions Unsafe until Myanmar Ensures Rights, Security," Progressive Voice Myanmar, November 15, 2018, https://progressivevoicemyanmar.org/2018/11/15/halt-rohingya-repatriation-plan-conditions-unsafe-until-myanmar-ensures-rights-security/.

[38] Shaikh Azizur Rahman and Hannah Ellis-Petersen, "Rohingya Fears Grow as Refugees Face Forcible Return to Myanmar," *The Guardian,* November 11, 2018, https://www.theguardian.com/world/2018/nov/11/rohingya-myanmar-bangladesh-genocide-repatriation-un-warning#:~:text=Rohingya%20fears%20grow%20as%20refugees%20face%20forcible%20return%20to%20Myanmar.

This seems impossible. Nothing has been prepared for that to happen.

The diplomatic and development community grows more frantic as the date approaches. The news out of Bangladesh is frightening. The army has surrounded the refugee camps. Refugees are quoted as being terrified. Several commit suicide rather than face repatriation. In one camp, all fifty families on the list "disappeared from their shacks" and went into hiding.[39]

I find myself thinking about my aunts and uncles and the parents of my childhood friends. American Jews who did not live through the Holocaust but would never set foot in modern Germany. I also think of concentration camp survivors who could have returned to their villages in Poland, Austria, or occupied France but went instead to Palestine, Australia, or Mexico. Anywhere rather than relive the horror. Anywhere but next to the neighbors who betrayed them.

If I were Rohingya, I would not return to Myanmar. Probably ever.

As Director for Myanmar, I have the unusual advantage of knowing Bangladesh from my earlier years as director there. They have an election looming. Kicking out unwanted Rohingya is a winning campaign strategy for their Prime Minister, Sheikh Hasina.

"Really, we don't have much leverage in Myanmar. Somebody needs to tell Sheikh Hasina that she'll lose all her money if she goes ahead with the repatriation," I urge Charlotte.

The World Bank has given Bangladesh around half a billion dollars to help the Rohingya refugees and surrounding communities. Other donors have brought this to well over a billion dollars in the past year and brought prestige for Sheikh Hasina. Her future Nobel Peace Prize is at stake.

---

39 Hannah Ellis-Petersen, Shaikh Azizur Rahman, and Michael Safi, "Bangladesh Admits No Rohingya Willing to Take Repatriation Offer," *The Guardian*, November 15, 2018, https://www.theguardian.com/world/2018/nov/15/rohingya-refugee-repatriations-bangladesh-myanmar.

Later the same day, we hear that a first group of 150 frightened refugees have been taken to a transit camp in Cox's Bazar. Buses and trucks are idling, waiting to transport them over the border.

So the World Bank joins the United Nations in urgently telling Bangladesh—not Myanmar—about the dire consequences of forced displacement back to a hostile environment. It is what the UN calls "refoulement," pushing the Rohingya back from whence they came against their will. It would spell the loss of billions of dollars in aid money for Bangladesh. And international condemnation.

A few hours later, Bangladesh blinks. Sheikh Hasina blinks. Moments before the refugees are scheduled to board the buses, the Bangladesh government announces that their departure is delayed. It is then postponed and then quietly abandoned altogether.

The refugee commissioner in Bangladesh acknowledges the dilemma: "Bangladesh has conceded that it will be unable to voluntarily repatriate Rohingya refugees to Myanmar as it had planned because it cannot find anyone willing to go back, though efforts to motivate people to leave will continue."[40]

Sheikh Hasina does the politically expedient thing and says nothing.

Back in Myanmar, diplomats and development partners breathe a sigh of relief. At least for today, the Rohingya have been spared further human rights abuses. Tonight, I can sleep peacefully.

But days later, the soldiers convicted for killing Rohingya in the Inn Din massacre are quietly released from prison. They are less than a year into a ten-year sentence. The Tatmadaw has the authority to reduce their punishment. The two Reuters journalists who were sentenced to seven years for reporting on the massacre remain in prison.

---

[40] Ellis-Petersen et al., "Bangladesh."

CHAPTER 41

Negotiating My Exit

(December 2018-January 2019)

They cannot really fire me.

Like many bureaucracies, the World Bank has difficulty getting rid of people. Even grossly incompetent people. Which I am not.

And this annoys my bosses. They have the right to pull me out of Myanmar, but it would be easier to pull me out if I were *failing somehow.*

Instead, a subtle disinformation campaign continues through the fall of 2018. They rake up past crimes. All those instances of being difficult and a woman. Those times when I was "not a good fit for the job."

And this is what I cannot bear: to be accused of incompetence. I will grudgingly accept "difficult," but I won't accept "incompetent." This goes to the core of my straight-A student self, the smart girl who does not suffer fools gladly. The girl who worries that she is never good enough.

I am not going to let them tear down a thirty-year reputation of competence, delivery, and results just to make it easier for them to pull me out of Myanmar.

"I am not the kind of person who stays in a position where she is not wanted," I say amiably to my boss during my next trip to Washington.

She nods and smiles.

"So if you want me to leave, I am more than happy to do so," I continue.

This is my gift to her. She does not have to justify or defend her actions.

"I will go quietly if it is done without further attacks on me," I conclude, trying to keep the edge out of my voice.

She understands. I will not make a scene. I will not seek lengthy legal remedies from the Internal Justice System. I will not file a claim with the World Bank's Administrative Tribunal. All the painful human resource nightmares available to a disgruntled employee will disappear.

If they shut up. Stop spreading rumors and innuendos that tear me down.

And then I bring it in for the landing.

"So when I leave Myanmar, I will be here for the next four years," I say, waving my arm vaguely around her office.

She looks puzzled.

I remind her that if they pull me out of Myanmar, I am still guaranteed a job on her team at headquarters. It is part of the agreement to go overseas. So if I leave Myanmar, I would end up right here. Right outside this nice corner office. They can pull me out of my current job, but they will have a hard time trying to fire me.

"I'll want to stay until I turn sixty-two, of course," I add, noting the four more years until my pension stops accruing. She knows the rules. She is just a few years shy of her own sixty-second birthday.

"So you may want to give some thought to what I could do for you here."

Her eyes narrow almost imperceptibly. An expensive employee stuck at headquarters with no real job for four years! It does not get much worse for a vice president with a tight budget and expensive, far-flung country offices. And she knows as well as I do that I can be pulled out of Myanmar by the president or the COO at any time but concocting a reason to fire me from the World Bank would be difficult, time-consuming, and likely impossible.

And that is how I find myself negotiating my departure from the World Bank.

"Salut, mon frere!" I say to an old friend from West Africa who is now the Vice President for Human Resources.

"I hear you are leaving us, *ma soeur!*" he replies cheerfully.

"Well yes...but I don't want to leave until the end of the school year," I say.

"Of course. I understand," he says.

And he does. The World Bank pays about two-thirds of my daughter's tuition at a private university only if I stay overseas. Why would I forgo that?

"I'm jumping before they push me off the cliff," I offer.

"Yes, yes, a wise decision," he says reassuringly.

And that is all I am allowed to say about my decision to leave the World Bank.

Of all the sensitive, morally fraught decision-making about the Rohingya crisis during the previous two years, the information deemed by the World Bank to be most sensitive and highly confidential is the story of how they got me out the door.

CHAPTER 42

Bad Mother

(December 2018)

Myanmar remains in the global headlines for failing to progress on the Rohingya crisis. I face urgent deadlines. The eleven and a half hour time difference between Yangon and Washington keeps me up to all hours of the night in back-to-back meetings and preparing endless variations of briefing notes for our president, for the board, for US Congress.

Because of the urgency, I have been flying back to headquarters every month. The thirty-hour flights leave me dazed. My body aches all over. I face criticism from my superiors as well as criticism from government officials with whom I am expected to nurture relationships. I am criticized by members of Congress and by human rights advocates. I am fighting for the Myanmar program and losing my job at the same time.

I want to protect the team in Myanmar from the stress of uncertainty about their future and mine, so I buffer the team from the worst of it. I absorb that stress and keep it to myself.

It is exhausting.

But now I am awake. I am on high alert. It is evening in Yangon, but dawn in New York where my daughter Danielle is at university. She texts me:

"I didn't sleep at all because I can't get the voices in my head to stop screaming."

Oh my-fucking god, is she having some kind of psychotic break? I think in a panic.

I call, and she really is hearing voices. Screaming ones.

"I'm so tired. I wish I were in a hospital now," she says. "At least I could rest and just give up on everything."

I frantically phone the university to get her the help she needs. Now. Immediately.

"I'm sorry, but according to our records she does not have university health insurance, so our mental health services are not available to her," says a cheerful woman in New York City.

"But she needs help right away," I say.

"You said she has a psychiatrist. You should contact that doctor," she adds.

"It's kind of an emergency," I repeat. "She says she is hearing voices."

"If it is an emergency, I can alert the campus police to break down the door. Shall I go ahead and do that?"

"No! I mean, um...that would be kind of insane. I am talking to her on the other line. She is fine. Not fine, but she can open her door," I add limply.

Then I hang up and try to reach her psychiatrist.

"Danielle has not been showing up for appointments for the past few weeks," she says frostily, as if this is the problem right now.

"Why didn't you tell me?" I say, wanting to shout but trying to remain calm.

"Danielle is an adult. She needs to tell you herself," she replies.

I sigh. My adult daughter has been unable to get out of bed most days. Unable to get up, get dressed, eat a meal, or focus on her studies. And now she has voices screaming in her head.

I book the first possible flight to New York, but still I must wait until tomorrow to leave Myanmar.

I pack hastily for a trip to New York and Washington. I will bring Danielle to Washington, where she has her sister and a loving support network of family friends. And where I can continue to work because… I must. I call my husband in Cambodia to place him on high alert too. He will remain in constant contact with Danielle while I fly.

I swing by the office in the morning on the way to the airport to warn Levon that I am leaving urgently, unexpectedly.

"Shit, are they threatening to shut our program down again?" he asks, assuming I am racing to headquarters to avert the most likely disaster.

I wearily shake my head and tell him, in a tumble of words, about my daughter, the voices in her head, and my panic. And the guilt for not realizing it sooner.

I spend thirty hours in airplanes and airports beating myself up. I am filled with shame. *What kind of crappy mother is too busy to notice her daughter having a nervous breakdown?* My child must have voices screaming in her head before I pay attention to her. I am a world away, in fucking Myanmar, attempting to help people, but I cannot even help my own daughter.

The university proves understanding and accommodating. My daughter is apparently not the first or the last student to have a mental breakdown halfway through her senior year. They place her on medical leave and encourage her to return whenever she is able. I take Danielle home to Washington and scramble to find immediate mental healthcare. The voices in her head are quiet now, and the tension has ebbed from her body, leaving her spent. I stay with her for a few weeks, and then I return uneasily to Yangon in mid-December. Both daughters will follow in a few weeks for Christmas and New Year's in Myanmar and Cambodia.

Getting fired from the World Bank is starting to seem like a really good idea.

My daughter needs me, and I am exhausted from the struggle in Myanmar over the Rohingya crisis and overwhelmed with guilt over my failure as a mother. My stress-induced adrenaline rushes have left me spent and wrung out.

The long flight back is dehydrating, and my throat is scratchy. I cough lightly. Between work and family obligations, I simply cannot afford to be sick. Luckily, I can rest on our family holiday.

CHAPTER 43

Sick and Tired

(January and February 2019)

A few weeks later, the family is at Ngapali beach resort in southern Rakhine State. It is lovely and peaceful, yet it is just miles away from the violence and insecurity in northern Rakhine.

I desperately need a few days of rest on a warm and sunny beach, but I am coughing and feverish. Upon return I straggle onward to Cambodia, unwilling to ruin the family's vacation on account of my cold or flu or whatever has me down.

Soon we are in Siem Reap to show the girls around Angkor Wat.

"I'm not feeling well enough for the bicycle tour today," I tell my husband. "You all go ahead. I'll stay here and rest."

But I make a snap decision and hire a local *tuk tuk* to bring me to the Royal Angkor International Hospital. The ramshackle vehicle putters up to an impressive medical facility mixing state-of-the art healthcare with world-class tourism, attracting wealthy patients from across Asia and the Middle East.

Service is shockingly rapid, well organized, and cheap. A thorough exam, chest X-ray, and blood tests reveal nothing unusual. I am prescribed antibiotics anyway and return to my hotel before my family gets back.

I drag through the rest of the vacation and return to Myanmar.

The French doctor at the international clinic near my house prescribes a different antibiotic and waits. I have a deep hacking cough that hurts. Sometimes I feel like I am choking and cannot breathe. I try to go to work—I have so much to do—but halfway there I reverse course back to the clinic.

"I really can't breathe," I wheeze, rushing through the door. "Please, you have to help me."

My doctor rushes out. "Let's nebulize her," he says.

They stretch me out and place a mask over my nose and mouth. I try to calm my panic and breathe the mist that will reduce the inflammation in my lungs. It has been over a month, and I cannot go on like this.

"I'm wondering if it's a mycoplasma infection," my doctor says. "My wife had one last year. It's difficult to diagnose." He tells me about an atypical bacterial and viral mix that does not respond to the usual antibiotics.

I nod through the mask, still trying to breathe calmly.

To know for sure, he decides to evacuate me to Bumrungrad, Bangkok's best international hospital.

It is not an emergency evacuation. I take a commercial flight and wear a face mask, which is not uncommon throughout Asia. But people avoid sitting next to me on the plane once they hear me coughing and hacking uncontrollably. Eric hurriedly flies in from Cambodia to meet me.

I stay overnight at the hospital. They do a bronchoscopy and a biopsy of my lungs. No sign of mycoplasma infection. No evidence of anything more serious either, like lung cancer.

"You are a lifelong asthma sufferer," the pulmonologist says. "You have chronic asthma."

"No, I don't," I reply, thinking he is asking me a question.

"Yes, you do. Your lungs show the evidence," he insists, showing me X-rays and scans.

"But what is wrong with me now?" I ask desperately.

"Probably viral. But we can't really say," he concludes. "Let's try oral steroids for a few months."

I walk out of Bumrungrad on shaky legs in late February 2019, armed with an impressive array of inhalers and steroids.

I check into a hotel near the World Bank's Bangkok office, where colleagues are gathered for a team retreat that I am supposed to attend. Despite the inhalers, I am too congested to breathe and sleep easily. I feel completely drained. I walk slowly down to breakfast the next day, wheezing gently as I scan the crowd for an open spot.

The head of human resources waves me over to a table, and I sink down, exhausted from my walk.

"How are you, Ellen?" he says breezily.

"Not great," I reply, but he does not really want to know.

"Everything set for your departure?" he asks.

"Uh-huh," I reply, taking a drag on my inhaler. "I leave on June 30."

"Good decision," he says, then hurries off as I erupt in a fit of coughing.

That's it. I am officially fired. I am dazed. I gaze around the lush terrace draped in bougainvillea, sun sparkling off the glassware. I hear the clink of cutlery on plates and my colleagues chatting animatedly.

Yes, I jumped before I was pushed off the cliff. But the landing feels the same.

I am bruised and broken. I feel screwed over by an employer to whom I devoted my entire adult life. For whom I traveled round the clock. For whom I worked hundred-hour weeks. For whom I even risked my life in perilous, war-torn places. An employer, a job, and a life that I loved. The life I had dreamed of as a child.

Judaism does not glorify a heavenly afterlife. What matters is what you leave behind. What matters is a life of purpose. I had always held fast to the words of the poet Tagore: "I slept and dreamt that life was joy. I awoke and saw that life was service. I acted and behold, service was joy."

I had that life of service, a life of purpose. But in this moment, I am feeling no joy.

CHAPTER 44

Delivering What I Promised

(February and March 2019)

I have four more months on the job before my departure. To maintain momentum and morale among the Myanmar team, I tell no one that I am leaving.

To be more accurate, I tell one person: my deputy. Levon needs to be ready to serve as acting director when I leave. But we tell no one else—not the government, not diplomats, not development partners, not staff in our office.

We especially do not discuss why I am being forced to leave. I must leave, but everything else stays the same. The strategy I designed with the team for our Myanmar program stays the same. This is the puzzle.

I feel oddly liberated. I know what I want to accomplish before I leave, and I am ruthless about allocating time to these things.

Making sure that my daughter remains stable and makes progress on her recovery is my top priority. To my surprise, she chooses to return to New York for her spring semester. She is adamant about graduating with her class in May regardless of her recent hurdles. But she continues to struggle with depression and anxiety. I flail around, trying from afar to find the right mix of mental healthcare for her in a city where I have no contacts. I yearn for the time—in just four short months—when I can be near her and better support her.

I also give priority to my own recovery from my unknown respiratory illness. I had been warned that it would likely have lasting consequences and would become a chronic illness requiring permanent treatment. Luckily, through four months of inhalers and oral steroids and considerable bedrest, my coughing and choking gradually subside and my strength returns. I never know what caused it or cured it.

While I slowly reemerge from my illness, I make hard choices about the work that remains.

No more pre-dawn flights to Nay Pyi Taw for me. Others can mince along in their longyis and spend nights in dark hotels trying to deepen the relationship with government officials.

I take a step back instead, remaining in Yangon and guiding teams to deliver everything we promised. More focus on social inclusion in conflict areas. Better analysis of poverty and exclusion. Redesign of nationwide operations. New operations in border zones, including Rakhine. I am relentless. I will give them everything. They will fault me for nothing when I leave in June.

I turn my attention to the least controversial project we can do: better nutrition for mothers and babies. Who could object? The Maternal and Child Cash Transfers (MCCT) for Improved Nutrition Project will provide $100 million to a government social protection program. Poor women who are pregnant or mothers will be paid to participate in activities to improve their own and their babies' nutrition. They will learn how to prepare more nutritious meals or prevent diarrheal disease, for example.

It will be difficult to oppose such a program, especially because the pilot in Chin State is already getting results and demonstrably reducing malnutrition.[41] Women are using the money to buy food and medicine, prepare healthier meals, and keep their babies better nourished than those without the program. This is no small feat in a country where one in four children suffers from chronic malnutrition. In the most deprived areas, like Rakhine, nearly half the children are chronically malnourished.

That is why I want this project to include Rakhine State along with other states and regions. It is an excellent way to fulfill our mandate to reduce poverty while also supporting the remaining Rohingya—the most vulnerable community in Myanmar. It seems like something even the most risk-averse bureaucrat could accept.

I discuss the design of the project with Leana, our team leader.

"Government wants a balanced approach, not just focusing on the Rakhine crisis," she says.

"So what are we proposing?" I ask.

"We suggest Ayeyarwady Region in the center and Shan State on the border," she says, astutely choosing to balance Bamar areas and minority areas.

"Tell me why. Be convincing," I say, knowing that headquarters will repeatedly ask this question.

"Ayeyarwady and Shan are among the worst six states and regions in Myanmar for malnutrition and most other deprivations, along with Rakhine State," she explains. "And they have the biggest populations,

[41] World Bank International Development Association, *Project Appraisal Document on a Proposed Credit in the Amount of SDR 72 Million (US$100 Million Equivalent) to the Republic of the Union of Myanmar for a Maternal and Child Cash Transfers for Improved Nutrition Project*, August 30, 2019, https://documents1.worldbank.org/curated/en/359401569808879957/pdf/Myanmar-Maternal-and-Child-Cash-Transfers-for-Improved-Nutrition-Project.pdf.

so the program will reach the largest number of disadvantaged women and children."

"It makes sense to focus limited resources on places where the needs are greatest."

"The government's program is reaching only 200,000 women and children today. Our project will add around 300,000 in Ayeyarwady, Shan, and Rakhine. Women and children of all ethnicities and communities will participate in the program, even in places with conflict. And Shan State has the highest number of conflict deaths over the past decade, not Rakhine."

"It's a good story about social inclusion in conflict zones, just as we promised. Okay, let's go ahead with Ayeyarwady, Shan, and Rakhine," I conclude.

I am hopeful we can use the MCCT project to reach the remaining Rohingya in Rakhine and eventually help returning refugee mothers and children.

I make a quick trip to Rakhine to assess the potential to do some good despite government's failure to progress. At a different transit center than I visited a year earlier, I see familiar white tents erected. Each one has a white square of paper with government's UEHRD logo handwritten in block letters and taped to the door flap. I walk over and unpeel the tape to find the United Nations Office for Project Services (UNOPS) logo hidden underneath. Busted again. Government is using the tents financed by the World Bank for flood recovery in ways that are unacceptable: to house future refugees under conditions that are not safe, voluntary, or dignified.

Technically, the tents are not being used for refugee return because—still one year later—no refugees have returned. But I am angry at this clumsy, childlike deception. By this point, my trust in the government to do the right things in Rakhine State has crumbled.

Clearly, we must build foolproof safeguards into our projects if we are to ensure that government does the right things and adheres to principles of nondiscrimination and equal opportunities for all ethnic communities. I test the possibility through the Inclusive Access and Quality Education Project, which is aimed at getting more children in school and improving their learning. It seems noncontroversial and builds on six years of our earlier experience funding local schools and giving stipends to poor students.

But even this is controversial in Rakhine. I address this by inviting Theresa, the project leader, to join me at the monthly diplomats' meeting in Yangon. I want her to explain to the ambassadors, who represent our shareholders, everything we are doing to reach the Rohingya and safeguard against discrimination. We hope some countries might provide more funding too.

What should have been a simple project is taking much longer than normal to prepare in the wake of the Rohingya crisis. But Theresa is so competent and persistent that she wears out the naysayers and risk-avoiding bureaucrats inside and outside the World Bank. She has an answer for everything the diplomats throw at her.

"The project relies on results-based financing," she starts out. "Money will be released to schools only after they implement a community participation plan that includes all ethnicities and groups."

"How will we know?" asks one ambassador.

"We will be using mobile technology to verify that all children have access to school," she replies.

"And how will you handle northern Rakhine?" asks another.

"All activities for northern Rakhine will be financed separately from the rest of the country. Money will be released based on a separate set of results that ensure that remaining Rohingya children attend school," she explains. "This includes hiring more Muslim teachers and language assistants for non-Burmese-speaking children."

Heads start nodding around the room.

"The formula for school funding also creates a financial incentive to integrate refugee children into schools," she continues. "And to avoid possible appropriation of Rohingya land, schools in northern Rakhine will not be able to do major renovations. They can do minor repairs of existing structures as well as buy school materials and improve teaching quality like everywhere else."

The diplomats are impressed. She knows her project cold.

"Finally, the project includes support to build stronger relationships between government and ethnic-basic education providers," she says.

I am not sure the ambassadors fully understand how important this last bit is, so I jump in.

"Parallel education systems run by ethnic armed organizations are not recognized by the government, so many minority children cannot go to university or qualify for employment in the civil service, military, or state enterprises," I explain. "Getting government and ethnic schools to start talking to each other is the first step in allowing minority children to fully integrate into Myanmar's labor market and economy."

We have had surprisingly good outcomes in the past few years since brokering discussions between government and ethnic education providers. Now we will ramp this up throughout Myanmar.

Theresa is a big hit with the ambassadors. She attracts $80 million in additional financing to combine with our own $100 million: more children in school, more money to local schools, more teachers trained and mentored, more Muslim teachers and language assistants hired, more textbooks available, more displaced children given the opportunity to learn. The team has taken extraordinary measures to ensure equal access and nondiscrimination, especially in Rakhine.

I am hopeful that the team will be able to finish quickly and present this project to our board for approval.

The education and nutrition projects were both planned before the Rohingya crisis emerged. Now as preparations proceed, they are being designed differently to adhere to our new strategy: focusing more on social inclusion in conflict areas, including in Rakhine State.

We have changed our strategy, but we have not officially told anybody. It is time to fix that.

CHAPTER 45

Cementing My Legacy

(February-April 2019)

I have a plan to ensure that our new strategy—my strategy—is carved in stone before I leave Myanmar. I want to ensure continuity and thwart additional attacks from inside the organization. It is the best I can do for my beloved team. They have worked too hard and suffered too much from the uncertainty out of Washington.

"Ever since the Rakhine crisis flared, we've been changing our strategy," I tell them in a staff meeting. "But we haven't officially changed our strategy."

"What do you mean?" they ask.

"We have made fundamental changes," I reply. "Now we need to write a new document and submit it to our board. That will make it official. That will carve it in stone."

Afterward, I tell Levon, "I just want to avoid future threats from presidents, COOs, or vice presidents to shut down the Myanmar program."

"Who's going to push back on bad ideas from headquarters once you're gone, Ellen?" he asks wistfully.

"You mean all those ideas that protect the reputation of the World Bank at the expense of development?" I ask.

"The organization is so risk averse that we never consider the risk of not doing development—of not actually doing anything good for the country," he says.

Maybe I am as difficult as they say, but I am just fighting for a consistent strategy—a strategy that makes sense in the long run. Not one that just makes headlines today.

And the best way to cement in place a consistent strategy is to write a new document before I leave and submit it to our executive board.

So that is what we do. I will not be around to send the actual document to our board. The preparation process and consultations usually take up to a year. But I tell Levon, "Today I have the power of the pen. And after thirty-four years in this institution, I know exactly what's going to happen."

"Oh yeah? What's that?"

"We'll draft our strategy. It'll get reviewed and reviewed again. The team will engage in a flurry of editing, wordsmithing, and nitpicking to address everybody's concerns. But in the end, it'll emerge largely unscathed and become our official policy," I say. "I'm sure of it!"

This will be my parting gift to the Myanmar team.

Before I even have a chance to move forward on my plan, we receive unexpected news from Washington: our president, Jim Yong Kim, is leaving.

"Are you kidding me?" Levon asks, staggering around my office in disbelief.

"Apparently it's true. But holy shit! Who would have imagined?" I say.

"It's true," says Kathryn. "He's going to Wall Street. Everybody here is in shock."

Two years into his five-year term—the second term he was granted to protect the World Bank from a Trump-appointed president—Jim is walking away.

"Wow! I mean, he had one job—just one job: to stay and prevent a Trump appointee! And now he blew it," I say incredulously.

It is February 2019, twenty-one months before the US presidential election, and the timing is terrible. Our board of executive directors feels angry and betrayed. Senior management feels blindsided. Staff are dismayed. Fear that the Trump Administration will undermine the World Bank as it has other international organizations is palpable, as is anger that Jim would expose us to this risk by choosing to leave now.

Jim tries walking the halls to say goodbye to staff but is rebuffed. The mood is sullen.

He does indeed go to Wall Street, to a fancy-title position for which he is not qualified. No farewell parties are held, and no explanation is given for his sudden move.

In the tradition of bureaucracies everywhere, the rumors swirl and swell with every retelling.

"Didn't you hear, Ellen? Jim got caught having an affair with a subordinate," says a colleague. "Staff knew about it. The board knew about it."

"I hear his wife is filing for divorce," says another. "Jim's new girlfriend is pregnant with his child. It'll be expensive. He wants to cash out on Wall Street..."

We never really learn the truth. Jim even manages to insult the World Bank in his farewell remarks, suggesting that the fate of the world lies with the private sector, not with public institutions like ours. He may be right, but he does not have to say so.

And then he is gone.

"So...any chance you will stay now, Ellen?" Levon asks.

My departure offers him a career opportunity, so it's a mixed blessing for him.

"Nah. The paperwork is done. Plus Birgit orchestrated this," I reply.

Birgit is still with us, but she will have to adjust to a new and radically different boss. David Malpass has been nominated by the Trump Administration to serve as World Bank president. He is a conservative US Treasury official, but hardly an enthusiastic *Trumpista*. Word on the street is that Trump's Treasury Secretary butted heads with him enough that he nominated Malpass right out the door. He is seen as the least of all evils by fearful members of the board and is quickly approved. He proves to be a no-nonsense, *realpolitik* kind of guy who makes only incremental changes to the organization. He is conservative where Birgit is progressive, pragmatic where she is idealistic, low-profile where she seeks the limelight on the international stage. Their relationship will be interesting to watch, but I will be out the door before it matters.

I get back to work drafting the new strategy document for Myanmar before I leave.

I have chosen a young, talented writer from the team to help me. Gwyn is smart, strategic, and speedy in her work.

We spend the month of March preparing a first draft and incorporating the new data we have generated on poverty, social welfare, and exclusion in Myanmar.

"This will be easy, Gwyn," I say. "We've told the story so many times in the past eighteen months."

"Yeah, it all boils down to our tagline," she says. "Staying engaged in Myanmar to support the transition with a greater focus on social inclusion in conflict areas."

"Easy to say. Hard to implement," I add.

But we have done so much to make it a reality. We raised awareness about conflict and exclusion, trained the team, eliminated our riskiest programs, and developed new tools like the Inclusion and Peace Lens to help teams design better projects.

We redesigned our planned projects and then designed new projects to reach minorities in border areas.

We also tried to design a project specifically for Rakhine, although we both know that conditions are not right to take that forward now.

Still, we are impressed by our progress over the past year and a half. And we can easily map out a strategy for the next four years focused on social inclusion in conflict areas.

With all these changes, nobody realizes that we have not approved a new project in over two years.

This is extraordinary. We never actually took a decision to halt new projects. But we paused while assessing our support from shareholders and redesigning our strategy, which ultimately had the same effect. And we downgraded Myanmar for backsliding on areas like social inclusion and rule of law, resulting in hundreds of millions of dollars of aid being lost each year.

"At this point, the Rohingya crisis has cost Myanmar well over a billion dollars in forgone assistance from us alone," I point out.

"It will be billions if we count other development partners," she adds.

"With no discernible effect on bringing the refugees home." I sigh. "So much for using foreign aid to send a strong signal and leverage progress on the crisis!"

A month later, we have the first of two review meetings on our new strategy, chaired by Charlotte.

I let Levon and Gwyn present the strategy, and I take a back seat at the meeting. It makes me feel smaller—nearly invisible—but the strategy must be associated with the team that remains, not with me.

At one point, the vice president who handles Bangladesh speaks up: "Given the lack of progress on refugee return, shouldn't we consider taking resources away from Myanmar to enhance our support for Bangladesh?"

She is flogging the same tired idea: using our aid to punish Myanmar and reward Bangladesh. It is a self-interested proposal wrapped up in supposed concern for the refugees. But money has already been taken away from Myanmar, while Bangladesh's aid allocation has skyrocketed. It is the worst thing we could do: explicitly heighten animosity between Bangladesh and Myanmar when the future of the Rohingya refugees depends on this relationship.

My vice president deftly ignores the suggestion. We hear from every other department in the World Bank with minor additions and suggestions. No opposition. No rejection. No alternatives.

Charlotte swiftly wraps up the meeting.

Afterward, I am confident that the strategy is carved in stone. We will stay engaged to sustain Myanmar's economic transition, but with a greater focus on inclusion in conflict areas to reduce poverty without discrimination.

No abrupt changes will occur when I leave. It will be a smooth transition for the team to a post-Ellen era.

No alternatives to our strategy were suggested in the meeting. And no serious debate occurred about whether we should be engaged in Myanmar or not. That option seems to have walked out the door with Jim.

CHAPTER 46

Difficult Women

(April 2019)

I am on my way out. Out of Myanmar. Out of the World Bank. Out of the institution—and even the lifestyle—that has defined my adulthood.

No matter which continent I am working from, my lifestyle has been punctuated by the twice-yearly gatherings of the World Bank, the IMF and their governors, the finance ministers of the world.

Unlike most staff, who are meeting nonstop with government delegations, I spend much of my time at my last Spring Meetings with a new group of colleagues previously hidden from my view: *end-of-employment specialists.*

"You are too young to retire! Not even sixty! Why are you leaving?" cries Maria, my pension officer. Her competence in calculating my lifetime benefits is equaled only by her bluntness.

"I pissed off President Kim," I say, trying to keep a complicated situation as simple as possible.

"Again? Jeezuz. Thank God he's gone now. That guy has cost us a bundle!"

"Oh yeah?"

"Are you kidding? He fired three women at VP level, and each one cost us a small fortune!" she says.

Hmmm. She has a point. I am being eased out for dubious reasons, but I am not alone. And she is suggesting that the corridor talk is true about generous payoffs to go away quietly.

Jim Kim made firing senior women something of a specialty. These three vice presidents lost their jobs from one day to the next over minor disagreements. One dared to suggest that the World Bank was already doing something that the president wanted done. One got fired between accepting a promotion he had offered and starting her new job!

Each time, rumor had it that end-of-employment specialists reached a financial arrangement to get the woman out the door rather than risk her putting up an unpleasant—and possibly more costly—fight.

But none of them can talk about it.

Maria, however, knows the score: it costs the World Bank a bundle to rid itself of women who speak their minds.

While in Washington, I carry out the last part of my plan to carve the Myanmar strategy in stone before I leave: explaining it to our board of executive directors.

The document, consultations, and official review processes will not be finished for a year. But that does not stop me from informally briefing our board.

I have suggested that we brief the board for months now, only to be rebuffed by Charlotte.

"Maybe it's better to keep a low profile given the uncertainty and lack of progress," she replies.

But now she thinks the time is right. Not for a formal meeting of the board, but at least an informal conversation. Without the danger that Jim might shut down the Myanmar program, she is breathing easier. Which is how I find myself in a large conference room with our executive directors telling our oft-repeated story.

"We believe it's critically important to stay engaged in Myanmar to support the historic political and economic transition," I begin. "Yet the Rohingya crisis has underscored the need to adjust our strategy toward a greater focus on social inclusion in conflict areas. In the past eighteen months, we have substantially changed the way we do business to ensure that we reach ethnic minorities and all those who face systemic discrimination in Myanmar."

My presentation is a *tour de force*. I speak confidently and compellingly about how important it is to stay engaged in Myanmar, how fragile the transition remains, how much progress we have made on economic reforms, how important it is to focus on social inclusion in conflict areas, how we have changed everything we do to focus on inclusion of ethnic minorities in conflict-ridden border zones, including in Rakhine State.

The logic is irrefutable. I am riding high as I finish my story.

"It's encouraging to see that we've changed the way we do business in Myanmar in response to the Rohingya crisis," says one executive director.

"The situation is complex, but you appear to be making the right choices in a high-risk environment," says another.

"This is best practice on how to make good decisions in fragile and conflict-affected countries," says a third.

I bask in the glow of this validation after so much criticism from inside the organization. Yes, we are doing the right thing!

Then the dean of the board—the longest-serving executive director—speaks up.

"I am disturbed," he says.

My vice president's head jerks upward. She has coasted through this whole presentation, but she is paying close attention now. My brow furrows.

"I am disturbed," he repeats, "because you have left the board in the dark for a year and a half on a matter of such critical importance."

I force my face to remain neutral, but the corner of my mouth twitches into a tiny smile. I was right about the need to communicate to the board earlier. I am enjoying my petty victories.

"Madam Vice President," he continues.

Anything that starts this way cannot be good.

"Madam Vice President, the board of executive directors wishes to be kept regularly informed on the situation in Myanmar and the progress on the Rohingya crisis. Are we clear on that?"

It is crystal clear: he does not want to wake up to discover that the World Bank has rolled up the carpets in a country like Myanmar without first discussing with the board.

We have been scolded. Sharply.

I feel vindicated that our strategy is accepted and appreciated by the board, but I am sad and empty because I will not be around to implement it.

The board does not know that I have been forced out of my position. They don't know that I am just another difficult woman pressured to go away quietly.

CHAPTER 47

Pressure from INGOs

(April 2019)

Our communications officer writes to me while I am still in Washington to tell me that Wa Lone and Kyaw Soe Oo, the two Reuters journalists sentenced to seven years in prison for seeking the truth about the Inn Din massacre, have been released from prison.

"Finally, some good news," I reply. "Did they successfully appeal?"

"No, they were pardoned by the president. It changes nothing," he adds sadly.

The journalists walk free just eight months after their harsh sentencing—but five months after the soldiers convicted of the massacre were set free.

The presidential pardon is a workaround, a quiet exception made to address steady international pressure and, more importantly, rare criticism of the civilian government from within Myanmar for jailing two of their own. The pardon eases pressure on the civilian authorities without the Tatmadaw losing face.

What the pardon fails to do is provide a ringing endorsement of a free press and independent journalism in a liberal democracy. It also does not change the Official Secrets Act that imprisoned these journalists or outlaw the entrapment techniques used to arrest them.

Amending the Act does not seem to be a priority for Aung San Suu Kyi's government.

A few days later, I am copied on an unexpected letter to the World Bank president from an array of international nongovernmental organizations, or INGOs. To my surprise, they express concern about the proposed $100 million Rakhine Recovery and Development Project, which is expected to include cash-for-work programs and support for small businesses.

"It is difficult to imagine how meaningful recovery and development are possible in Rakhine without addressing the underlying human rights issues that currently impact every aspect of life for communities," they argue.[42]

Soon, the International Commission of Jurists sends a second letter. Their director for Asia is quoted discussing movement restrictions and other discrimination against the Rohingya: "It seems unthinkable that the project could be effectively implemented while these restrictions remain in place."[43]

I am surprised by these letters because we have never publicly discussed the project.

This is how I learn that Jorge, the team leader, has dutifully posted his Public Information Document for the future project. Posting is required soon after beginning project preparation as a requirement of our public disclosure policy. Jorge followed standard procedure by publishing a short and anodyne description for what is usually an uneventful bureaucratic exercise.

This time, publication sparks an explosion of exaggerated claims and sharp criticism from INGOs.

---

[42] Simon Lewis and Poppy McPherson, "World Bank under Fire for Development Plan in Myanmar's Divided Rakhine," Reuters, May 17, 2019, https://www.reuters.com/article/uk-myanmar-rakhine-worldbank-idUKKCN1SN1J7.

[43] Lewis and McPherson, "World Bank under Fire."

Jorge apologizes for the lack of warning, but I do not blame him. And I do not blame the INGOs either.

"They have no information right now that suggests we know what we're doing," I tell Jorge. "They don't know if we understand the ethnic conflicts in Rakhine, if we're addressing human rights concerns, or even if we acknowledge the atrocities committed in Rakhine."

"True, but we can explain to them now," he offers.

"Even if they knew, I doubt they would waste this opportunity to advocate for the Rohingya," I say. "We are a good excuse to mount a well-justified campaign over the plight of the Rohingya, both those remaining in Rakhine and those stuck in Bangladesh."

Eighteen months after the Rohingya crisis flared, progress by the government has been minimal on the things that really matter: guaranteeing security for all communities in Rakhine; eliminating movement restrictions; dismantling other forms of discrimination; defining a clear path to citizenship; granting full civil rights to remaining Rohingya; and creating conditions for safe, voluntary, and dignified refugee return to their places of origin.

Government has measured its progress largely in terms of infrastructure built to process and house returning refugees. But this infrastructure is often on land previously occupied by Rohingya. And it is often with a visible ramping up of Myanmar's security forces in these areas and with alleged land-grabbing by ethnic Rakhine in areas once dominated by the Rohingya community.

All in all, it is a dismal record.

So I am not surprised that INGOs would use our initial project announcement as an opportunity to hammer home the inadequacy of the government's response.

We reply to the INGOs carefully, in writing, to correct misunderstandings. We tell them that the proposed project is an incentive—a dangling carrot—to entice the government to do the right things in Rakhine. It will not happen unless the government makes significant progress on the things that matter. It is being done in close partnership with UNHCR to ensure refugees return according to international norms. The project will not invest in infrastructure or use land at all, especially land owned by Rohingya. All ethnic communities, including the Rohingya, will be consulted on the design and implementation of the project and will participate and benefit from its activities. This will be closely monitored using mobile technology to prevent discrimination and ensure equal access. Finally, all project activities will be accompanied by intercommunal dialogue to begin unwinding decades of rising mistrust and conflict.

It is a good response. But I am in Washington, so I do more than send a reply. I have lunch with one of the main signatories of the original letter.

Josh is a former classmate of mine, part of a vast network of policy wonks unleashed on Washington by Princeton University's School of Public and International Affairs. He advocates for refugees worldwide. His job is to persuade others to do the right thing.

He has been to Cox's Bazar in Bangladesh and knows much more about the situation of the Rohingya there than about the situation they left in Rakhine State.

I tell him about Rakhine State. I explain Myanmar's military-civilian divide, the ethnic Rakhine-Rohingya divide, the Rakhine-Bamar divide, and the Buddhist-Muslim divide. I talk about the decades-long brainwashing of the public: the dominant Burmese view of Rohingya as subhuman. I want him to understand that it will take decades or even generations to fix all this.

"This Rakhine project is at an initial proposal stage," I explain. "We're working closely with UNHCR to ensure the project will be used as an incentive for the government to do the right things."

"But anything you do in Rakhine legitimizes the government's actions there," he sighs.

"Even if we help the remaining Rohingya? Even if the Rohingya themselves want us there?" I ask.

"Yeah, even if," he responds flatly. Then he shrugs and turns his palms toward the heavens as if to say, *So just stop it. Stop it now.*

I shift uncomfortably in my chair.

Afterward, I feel ashamed. Am I wrong? Am I immoral? Amoral?

He is a moral person. Moral people defend human rights. They work for INGOs.

But I do not think it is as simple as he says.

Is it wrong to try to persuade, incentivize, and cajole a weak and uncaring government to do the right thing for the Rohingya?

At what point do we concede that the efforts undertaken—the slow progress and cautious optimism we find in every tiny step forward—are too minimal to warrant our support? Do we continue to dangle the carrot or not?

The limits of our leverage and influence are disappointing but becoming increasingly clear.

Do we finance government schools in Rakhine that enroll and teach Rohingya children? Even if their parents are denied citizenship? Do we provide cash through a government safety net to Rohingya mothers to nourish their children even if security forces continue to restrict their movements?

When our executive directors ask what we are doing to help the remaining Rohingya in Myanmar, which is worse: to say we are doing something or to say we are doing nothing?

"Ellen, what are you doing to help the remaining 500,000 Rohingya who have been terrorized and tortured and who face systemic discrimination in every aspect of their lives?"

I imagine them asking.

"Nothing. We can't do anything helpful because it would legitimize the government's failure to guarantee fundamental and full human rights," I respond.

Is that really it?

I am left feeling that it is much easier to talk about doing the right thing than it is to do it.

And in the end, it is the perception—rather than the reality—of the Rakhine Recovery and Development Project that brings it to a halt.

"The World Bank is Rewarding Ethnic Cleansing in Myanmar," screams an online op-ed in the venerable *Washington Post* a month later.[44] Most of what it claims is untrue.

It says, "The World Bank is pushing ahead." Nope. We are waiting for the government to make progress in Rakhine.

It calls our work a "unilateral move by the World Bank." Nope. We are coordinating closely with the UN Human Rights Commission and UNHCR.

It says our funding "attaches no conditions on Myanmar." Nope. The future project will include many conditions for the government to fulfill to improve the well-being of the Rohingya and other ethnic minorities.

It claims our project is "rewarding the perpetrators and funding their efforts to appropriate lands." Nope. Land will not be purchased, used, or developed.

It is not the inaccuracy and hyperbole that bother me most. It is the final, completely accurate recommendation: "This project could be used by the international community as leverage to push Myanmar toward a sustainable solution to the Rohingya crisis. And it should be used to that end."

But this disastrous media attention and INGO criticism are what prevent the project from being used to that end.

The World Bank runs from negative press. In this case, we never cancel preparation of the Rakhine project. But we stop moving forward. We sit still and do nothing.

It is still officially "under preparation" today, years after my departure from the country. It is there waiting to be approved whenever the government makes satisfactory progress on the Rohingya crisis.

I am not holding my breath.

---

[44] Azeem Ibrahim, "The World Bank Is Rewarding Ethnic Cleansing in Myanmar," *Washington Post,* May 30, 2019, https://www.washingtonpost.com/opinions/2019/05/30/world-bank-is-rewarding-ethnic-cleansing-myanmar/.

CHAPTER 48

Telling the Team

(May 2019)

This is the worst day. Not the day I was fired. The day I tell the Myanmar team that I am leaving. The day I explain why I am leaving, because they will not believe I am leaving by choice.

The large conference room in our new office is packed with staff seated at the table and on the padded benches along the back walls. Our office in Nay Pyi Daw is on video conference, as are our offices in Bangkok, Phnom Penh, and Vientiane. But the story of my leaving is mostly a Myanmar story.

I think of my Myanmar colleagues as a fragile team in a fragile country. New to the world of foreign aid, donor partners, economic transition, and democracy. Even relatively new to cell phones, social media, and international travel. Requiring more than the usual explanations about the ways of the world and the sometimes-murky decisions of the international community and our own headquarters.

I want to reassure them that everything will be fine.

So I explain. Sort of.

"Hey, everybody. I have some news. I am sad to say that I have decided to retire from the World Bank at the end of June," I begin.

"What? No! What? What did she say?" I hear a buzz of astonishment rise from the team.

My ears are buzzing too, and I feel I might faint.

I push on. "As you know, I arrived just before the Rakhine crisis began and in many respects, I got off on the wrong foot with the government."

They look puzzled. They think my relationship with the government is as good as any diplomat or development partner trying to persuade the government to pursue economic reforms and address fundamental human rights abuses. But I am thinking of my decision to freeze the budget support as well as the embarrassing, aborted phone call between Aung San Suu Kyi and Jim Kim.

I persist.

"I have steered through a crisis when our program was nearly shut down. Things are more stable now, so Washington believes that it might be a good time for new leadership here."

The buzz is becoming overwhelming.

"You know, somebody who could be more effective...turn the page... start a fresh chapter..." I am speaking in cliches now. I trail off.

Faces look shocked. With tears welling in my own eyes, I see tears streaming down the cheeks of many Myanmar staff. Goodbyes feel permanent and catastrophic in a country that just began welcoming foreigners. Especially unexpected goodbyes like this one.

So I maximize my reassurances.

"The good news is that everything will continue as planned. Levon will serve as acting director for a while, and we will continue to implement our strategy of staying engaged with a greater focus on social inclusion in conflict areas. Our work will continue just as it is today. No worries there. Our strategy is clear and accepted by everybody," I add just for good measure.

Crying faces are nodding in agreement.

And then Kyi Sin asks, "If everything will stay the same, then I am sorry, but why do you have to leave?"

I smile weakly and leave it there.

Afterward, we cry and hug, and everybody drifts back to work looking shell-shocked. I feel drained but glad to share a secret I have held for the past six months.

And now is the flurry of impending departure.

"Take whatever you want," I tell Susie and Nay Moo as we begin the familiar process of packing out.

"Yes, Madam," Susie answers, looking sad.

They want a few pots and pans, my bicycle, and a wooden table and chairs. I try to press more furniture on them, but they have no place to put it and do not know where they will be living next. It is a scary time for them.

Whenever my family leaves an assignment, we go through the ritual of selling furniture and appliances, usually to incoming internationals. We mostly sell to aid workers and diplomats rotating to Yangon, Ouagadougou, or Skopje who need a car, a refrigerator, or an ice-cream maker. I always offer our stuff to staff at the office before advertising to the wider community.

This is how I discover that flatpack furniture from IKEA is a highly prized commodity in Myanmar. Our local staff go into a frenzy.

"THE WARDROBES ARE MINE!" answers one colleague seconds after I push "send" on the sales list.

"I will take ANY wooden dressers you have!" messages another. "As MANY as you have."

And on and on it goes until everything is gone.

They are so excited that I surrender furniture I had planned on keeping. I can always buy more back in America.

And then the movers come and wrap everything remaining in cardboard. Clever chair-shaped boxes and sofa-shaped boxes and table-shaped boxes stacked from floor to ceiling in my glass-box house.

For a few days, Susie, Nay Moo, and I are back where we started: in an echoing glass house with mattresses on the floor, a set of mismatched sheets, one table, and a few patio chairs.

Except this time, we have baby Phoebe. She spends much of her day suspended in a round walker with wheels—the kind prohibited in America years ago when babies began rolling into the streets.

Phoebe uses her chubby legs to propel herself around the checkerboard of marble tiles. When she runs into the cardboard boxes, she bounces off and erupts in peals of laughter. It is the most joyous game of pinball ever played.

She remains my daily stress reliever and my hope for Myanmar's future. Our daily affirmations continue even as I pack out.

"You are strong! You are smart! You will be the future leader of a diverse and tolerant Myanmar!"

She gurgles and giggles in return.

Part of the evolving story told in Washington about why I must leave Myanmar is to send a signal to the government that they do not deserve a World Bank director in the country.

Two years earlier, at a time of unbridled hope and optimism, the decision to send me to Myanmar was a signal of how seriously the international community took the country's political and economic transition. Government officials glowed with pride when I explained that my arrival, as head of a regional office based in Yangon, demonstrated the growing significance of Myanmar on the world stage. Their country was moving from an isolated pariah state earlier to a regional hub for a respected international organization in just a few short years!

Pulling me out two years later expresses our displeasure and frustration at the lack of action in Rakhine.

The problem with this story is that we never actually tell the government.

World Bank leadership wishes to maintain a strong relationship with the government even as they try to appease those who call for tougher action on the Rohingya crisis. So, the symbolism of my leaving is entirely lost on the government. I am just another foreigner, like so many since the transition began, who comes, works a few years, leaves, and is replaced by another well-meaning foreigner.

For diplomacy's sake, Mya Mya requests a courtesy visit for me with Aung San Suu Kyi before leaving. But the beleaguered state counsellor is avoiding meetings with diplomats and development partners, knowing that they will urge her to do more on the Rohingya crisis. We get no reply.

A few days before I am scheduled to leave, Mya Mya tells me that some of the ladies from the office want to take me to dinner. The ladies extending the invitation are not the most vocal and demonstrative. These are a few of the quieter ladies. San San is our local macroeconomist, and Khin Ohn Kyi is our education specialist. Others, like Cho Cho, work off the front lines supporting our teams in areas like procurement and financial management. I nickname them "wallflowers" because no matter how much I wave them forward to sit at the table in our staff meetings, they choose to sit on the back benches along the walls. Not attracting attention. Quietly present.

I have always made a special effort to get the wallflowers to speak up. When we have decisions to make, I start with the back benches and go down the line, asking each person for their opinion. At least one word. One feeling. One observation.

Now the wallflowers are inviting me to dinner at a villa on the edge of Inya Lake.

I feel a bit guilty. They are treating me to an expensive restaurant. I know they want to do it, but it is unnecessary. I am grateful to them all for their support in the past two years.

We eat and chat, followed by tea as the evening winds down.

Khin Ohn Kyi clears her throat. "We bought you this," she says, handing me a small gift box. It contains a small sapphire pendant set in gold.

Now my guilt is complete. "This is beautiful. I love it, but you didn't need to do this!"

"We wanted to have this evening," San San explains, "because you are a woman director. This is important to us."

"And you always asked us to say something in the meetings. This is important to us too," adds Khin Ohn Kyi.

"You encouraged us to speak up. But we didn't speak up for you. You defended us in Washington, but we didn't defend you. We should have spoken up," San San says firmly.

"We feel guilty," they say, nodding solemnly.

I am stunned. Then I smile because my heart is melting. These quiet ladies thought they could use their voices to change the World Bank's decision. And they thought they should try.

Progress comes in small gift boxes.

CHAPTER 49

Visiting a Development Warrior

(June 2019)

Before my final farewell from Myanmar, I take time to attend a wedding in the UK with my family. I also use the opportunity to spend a mother-daughter week with Danielle as my husband and older daughter return quickly to their work.

"Where do you wanna go?" I ask Danielle.

"How about Ireland?" she says. "I've always wanted to go there."

This is how I end up spending a night in a castle outside Dublin.

Cara, another international development warrior like me, lives in the castle. She was the head of another aid agency in Myanmar while I was head of the World Bank office. We were too busy addressing the Rohingya crisis to become close friends, but I always liked and admired her moral conviction and common sense. She felt like a kindred spirit.

Her partner remained back in Ireland while she worked in Myanmar.

A few months earlier, she had suddenly vanished from Myanmar, and her assistant had told me she would not be returning, leaving me with more questions than answers.

I did some research and discovered that her partner was in an accident and had likely been permanently disabled. Cara left, and we never got to say goodbye. Her successor arrived two weeks later. Some guy rotating in from Singapore or Thailand.

When we planned our trip to Ireland, I thought perhaps I could still say goodbye to Cara.

I reached out, and she invited us to spend the night at the castle, although her partner was still in the hospital.

So now I am getting a tour of the castle with its huge stone doors and extensive gardens.

After a cozy dinner, I sit by the fire sharing a bottle of wine with her. She tells me the story of the accident and how she rushed back to Ireland immediately.

"And when did you decide that you needed to leave Myanmar permanently?" I ask gently.

"I didn't," she says.

"What do you mean?" I ask. "You're gone. Your replacement has arrived."

"I didn't," she repeats. "I mean, it's logical, I guess. Obviously I need to be here..."

I nod, feeling something rising in her.

"But I would have liked to be asked, at least," she says vehemently.

And then her words rush out.

"They didn't ask me if I wanted to leave. They just terminated me and brought somebody else in. It felt like...it felt like a punishment."

"A punishment? For what?"

"For not doing a good enough job on the Rakhine crisis!" she cries. "Like if I were more effective, if I were better at my job, somehow things would be different in Myanmar, different in Rakhine, different for the Rohingya!"

And I feel her pain deep in my soul. The pain of the accusation. A woman warrior called out for being ineffective. For being incompetent. For failing to resolve the systemic discrimination and human rights abuses in Rakhine.

"Welcome to my sad club." I sigh and pour another glass of wine.

CHAPTER 50

Farewell to Myanmar

(July 2019)

Just before I leave, we host a blow-out farewell bash. It is the long-awaited opening reception for our new office. We could not have this party earlier because it would have sent the wrong signal at a time when we were threatening to leave Myanmar. Now my departure offers an acceptable excuse to throw a party.

We have a jazz quartet in the lobby, a disco in the main conference room, and a copious buffet in the cafeteria. Videos run on loop to show our guests our strong development results throughout Myanmar. And, of course, we offer those views.

"It's spectacular!" guests say, walking our hallways with drinks in hand to get the 360-degree views. Golden pagodas, tree-lined parks, and boats sparkling on the dark river from every side of our high-rise office tower.

I am sparkly too. I wear our team longyi, the equivalent of the matching longyi uniforms worn in the ministries. Our team longyi is a shimmering gold and pink confection from head to toe. Pretty but scratchy. I would never choose it for myself but happily join the ladies of our office in this matching show of loyalty and belonging.

Colleagues, diplomats, and development partners all say embarrassingly nice things about me, and funny things too. How I wave my hands around when I talk. How my heels make an insistent clack as I stride through the hallways. How I zealously mark up the most scrupulously edited memos. We laugh together, and I feel warm inside at this outpouring of love. I return it fully to them when I speak.

But I also reflect on the roller coaster I have ridden since arriving at a moment when the confidence that the international community had placed in Myanmar to transition away from conflict and toward peace and tolerance was shaken to the core.

"As many of my fellow diplomats and development agency heads can attest, we often feel that we have been called upon in Myanmar to bring forth our highest skills as leaders, to weigh the forces of history, to make the right ethical choices, to balance competing priorities, to define better strategies and keep our teams motivated to help the country move forward in all aspects of its transition—toward a vibrant market economy, toward strong civilian rule, and toward a tolerant and peaceful society."

I continue with the one message I want to leave with government:

"Having missed out on the Asian Miracle that propelled its neighbors to prosperity in the past fifty years, Myanmar must now play catchup. But if 30 to 40 percent of Myanmar's people can't contribute to growth because of persistent conflict and exclusion, the country will never be able to grow rapidly for decades at a time. If not everybody is allowed to play, the team will never be able to win the game. And everybody loses out, not just those who are excluded."

Finally, I reflect on my own evolution, "The more I learned about Myanmar, the more I had to adjust my own thinking to recognize that social inclusion must be an *economic imperative,* not only a human rights issue."

I suspect that the government does not really understand this message.

The World Bank did not really understand it either when we first engaged with Myanmar in 2012. We approached this economic transition as we approached the fall of the Berlin Wall decades earlier. We applied the lessons learned from Eastern Europe and the former Soviet Union about first-generation economic reforms. We supported the liberalization of prices and markets, opening the country to the wider world. It was good stuff. Important stuff. It successfully increased economic growth, which was essential. But it reduced poverty much less than expected because we failed to factor in high levels of conflict and exclusion in Myanmar.

Now, seven years and many atrocities later, we are starting to understand.

A few days later, my tenure as World Bank Director in Myanmar comes to an end.

But the farewell does not end at the going away parties. It continues right into the airport and up to the security gate, the point of no return.

That is how I find myself crammed into laminated booths at a fast-food joint in the airport with twenty-five or so of my local colleagues. And Susie, Nay Moo, and baby Phoebe.

"KFC on me!" I cry, trying to create an upbeat mood.

"But really, Ellen, what is KFC?" someone asks.

"Kentucky. Fried. Chicken," I respond.

They look impressed by the vast repository of my knowledge.

Soon we have nothing more to say. We move as a group toward the escalator beneath the "DEPARTURES" sign, and I hug everybody one last time. I take my beloved Phoebe in my arms for a hug and a last round of affirmations.

"You are strong. You are smart. You are the future leader of a diverse and tolerant Myanmar!" I say triumphantly.

She giggles at her silly *pipi*. My colleagues laugh too.

I take photos of the group growing smaller as I rise on the escalator, waving goodbye as I pass through security, board the plane, and settle into my seat.

"It's a pleasure to have you back with us, Ms. Goldstein," says an impeccably groomed flight attendant, proffering juice and sparkling wine.

And I smile, realizing that she recognizes me from my monthly flights to Washington to discuss the Rohingya crisis.

"Yes, it's good to be back," I say and settle in for thirty hours of flight time back home. Back to a new life. A different life.

CHAPTER 51

Second Anniversary of the Crisis

(August 2019)

I am cut loose from Myanmar. Cut loose from the World Bank. No more debates about whether I am doing the right thing. No more questions about whether the good things are good enough.

For the first time in nearly forty years, I have no daily to-do list. No ranking of items from panic-urgent to quite-urgent to important-but-not-as-urgent.

It is a jarring adjustment to stop work and return to my homeland, but I am determined to go rather than join my husband in Cambodia. I was not there when my daughter needed me most—maybe I can atone for that sin by being there now.

Danielle had returned to New York in a less fragile state but was still unable to complete her coursework in time to graduate. Now she is moving home to Washington, DC, where perhaps I can find more effective care and provide real-time support.

So my first task upon arrival is to hustle to find better mental healthcare for her, discovering that in the high-income, high-anxiety world of Washington, DC, supply falls far short of demand.

"Try this number," says a friend. "I know she is not taking anybody now, but if she likes you, she may have a connection for you."

It starts to feel like a back alley, black market deal. I follow leads who give me other leads. I drop names.

"Please, if I could just speak to the doctor for a minute?" I plead. "I know she is not taking new patients, but I just want to talk to her briefly."

I am rebuffed at least a dozen times before finding a psychiatrist willing to talk to my daughter, a psychiatrist who specializes in helping young adults navigate through college and beyond.

I cry when I get the confirmation: a sense of relief. And maybe a slight lessening of my guilt? She needed me, and I was not there physically or emotionally. I did not see it—I did not see her—until she crashed.

In the months that follow, my daughter feels better. Less anxious, more capable. She reaches out to her friends near and far. She defines her own plan to complete school in Washington and negotiates the arrangements with her university herself. I feel relieved at how well she is coping and proud of how she has taken responsibility for moving forward.

The drumbeat of lousy mother starts to ease in my head. I think I am supporting her enough. Not too much. Not smothering. Letting her be the adult that she is.

This is where I am when the second anniversary of the Rohingya crisis rolls around in late August 2019.

The second anniversary is a more muted version of the first. Especially for me. I have no urgent briefings to prepare for the UN General Assembly, no uncomfortable visits to Capitol Hill, no cordial but unpersuasive meetings with human rights advocates. I am merely a bystander now.

Several weeks before the anniversary, the UN High Commission on Refugees and the Bangladesh government try to relaunch discussions on repatriation of refugees. The Myanmar government announces August 22 as the beginning of repatriation. But the attempt is abandoned when the UN once again finds no volunteers.[45]

---

[45] Tofayel Ahmad and Julhas Alam, "Rohingya Refugees Rally to Mark 2nd Anniversary of Exodus," Associated Press, August 25, 2019, https://apnews.com/article/d43f0d79347d48c9b245f2687b3cd582.

Bangladesh is worried. Terrorist groups are recruiting in the refugee camps, where bored and angry young men are plentiful. And talk of repatriation leads thousands of refugees to rally to mark the second anniversary of their flight from Myanmar.

"We want to tell the world that we want our rights back, we want citizenship, we want our homes and land back. Myanmar is our country. We are Rohingya," says Muhib Ullah, one of the rally organizers.[46]

A handful of human rights advocates write blogs and opinion editorials to mark the second anniversary. The titles say it all:

"Two Years On: No Home for the Rohingya."[47]

"It's Been Two Years Since 730,000 Rohingya Were Forced to Flee. There's No End in Sight to the Crisis."[48]

"The Rohingya's Right of No Return: Why the Refugees Still Aren't Going Back to Myanmar."[49]

Two years on and nothing has changed for the Rohingya—whether imprisoned in crowded refugee camps in Bangladesh or facing violence and systemic discrimination in Myanmar. They are caught in a landless limbo with no resolution in sight.

I see that David Mathieson, a human rights advocate in Yangon who led our human rights training for staff a year earlier, has an op-ed in the *New York Times*. He is blunt about why so little progress has been

---

[46] Ahmad and Alam, "Rohingya Refugees Rally."

[47] Phil Robertson, "Two Years On: No Home for the Rohingya," Human Rights Watch, August 28, 2019, https://www.hrw.org/news/2019/08/28/two-years-no-home-rohingya.

[48] Tun Khin, "It's Been Two Years Since 730,000 Rohingya Were Forced to Flee. There's No End in Sight to the Crisis," *Time*, August 25, 2019, https://time.com/5660088/rohingya-crisis-myanmar/.

[49] David Scott Mathieson, "The Rohingya's Right of No Return: Why the Refugees Still Aren't Going Back to Myanmar," *New York Times*, September 24, 2019, https://www.nytimes.com/2019/09/24/opinion/rohingya-refugees-myanmar-return-bangladesh.html.

made on refugee repatriation: "Because many refugees don't want to return. Because Myanmar does not want them back. And because foreign governments don't much care."

He goes on to explain how China and Russia have defended Myanmar out of self-interest and how Japan appeases Myanmar to contain China's influence, concluding: "Western countries, including the United States and Britain, have been sidelined. After Washington and London stung Aung San Suu Kyi with copious criticism for the Rohingya crisis, Western nations lost much of their political influence with her."[50]

And the UN has continued its contradictory behavior: extraordinary condemnation of Myanmar through human rights channels, paralysis at the UN Security Council (where China and Russia would veto any action), frustrated attempts by refugee agencies on the ground to make progress in Rakhine, and business as usual for other agencies working in the rest of Myanmar.

An independent assessment led by Gert Rosenthal, a former foreign minister of Guatemala, concludes that "the United Nation's dysfunctional performance" in Myanmar from 2010 to 2018 was a "systematic failure."[51] His assessment leads to much finger-pointing, but little else changes.

And now, to mark the two-year anniversary of the Rohingya crisis, the Independent Fact-Finding Mission submits its final report to the UN Human Rights Commission, detailing violence in Rakhine over the past year.[52]

---

[50] Mathieson, "The Rohingya's Right of No Return."

[51] Gert Rosenthal, *A Brief and Independent Inquiry into the Involvement of the United Nations in Myanmar from 2010 to 2018*, United Nations, May 29, 2019, https://www.un.org/sg/sites/www.un.org.sg/files/atoms/files/Myanmar%20Report%20-%20May%202019.pdf.

[52] United Nations Human Rights Council, *Detailed Findings of the Independent International Fact-Finding Mission on Myanmar*, September 16, 2019, https://www.ohchr.org/en/hr-bodies/hrc/myanmar-ffm/index.

> Citing the lack of accountability for the perpetrators of these alleged crimes, as well as the failure by Myanmar "to investigate genocide and to enact effective legislation criminalizing and punishing genocide," the UN-appointed independent panel concludes "that evidence that infers genocidal intent on the part of the State...has strengthened, that there is a serious risk that genocidal actions may occur or recur."[53]

In his comments to the Human Rights Commission, the chairman of the Independent Fact-Finding Mission, Marzuki Darusman, also underscores that the threat of genocide persists for the remaining Rohingya.

In other words, it could happen again. If we say nothing, if we do nothing, it could happen again. The lesson of my childhood.

And finally, the report concludes that "accountability can only be advanced by the international community."[54]

So here we are, two years on, and nobody expects the military to hold itself accountable or Aung San Suu Kyi's government to demonstrate the power or political will to demand accountability. If there is to be any accountability for the crimes committed against the Rohingya, it will need to be demanded by the international community.

"Not bloody likely," I scoff, reflecting on my two tumultuous years in Myanmar as part of that community.

---

[53] "Genocidal Threat for Myanmar's Rohingya Greater than Ever, Investigators Warn Human Rights Council," United Nations, September 16, 2019, https://news.un.org/en/story/2019/09/1046442.

[54] "Myanmar's Rohingya Persecuted, Living under Threat of Genocide, UN Experts Say," press release, United Nations Office of the High Commissioner for Human Rights, September 16, 2019, https://www.ohchr.org/en/press-releases/2019/09/myanmars-rohingya-persecuted-living-under-threat-genocide-un-experts-say.

CHAPTER 52

Approving the First Project

(September 2019)

A few months into my new life in Washington, Levon visits from Yangon. He is here to attend the board meeting for approval of the first Myanmar project since the Rakhine crisis began two years earlier.

"So what's the deal with Rakhine?" I ask while scanning the menu at an upscale Indian restaurant in downtown DC.

"We took it out," says Levon.

"Completely out?" I ask in disbelief.

"Yeah. In the end, management thought the risks were too high," he says, snapping his menu shut. "And the government will cover Rakhine on its own."

"So in the end we're not doing anything to help the Rohingya?" I say weakly.

"No, we're not," he says.

For two years we had debated the right response to the crisis and adjusted our strategy to strengthen our focus on inclusion in the conflict areas of Myanmar.

But I have still underestimated the risk aversion of our bureaucrats. After two years of handwringing on behalf of the Rohingya, our first approved project will do nothing to help them. We will do nothing, by design.

Normally our funds would flow directly into the government's program, which was already rolling out in Rakhine State. But this project has been legally circumscribed to cover only two areas: the Bamar-dominated Ayeyarwady Region and the minority-dominated Shan State. Legally circumscribed to ensure that our money does not under any circumstances flow into Rakhine State.

I know that it is not wrong to cover Ayeyarwady and Shan, where the greatest number of poor people reside. And Shan State is the most conflict-affected place in Myanmar despite the headlines about Rakhine. In fact, the project perfectly captures our new strategy to focus on social inclusion in conflict areas—the strategy that I defended until I was removed from Myanmar.

It is not the worst thing to focus on these two areas. It feels right to celebrate the approval of the first project in over two years under our new strategy. It is a well-designed project that will reduce poverty and malnutrition, with a strong focus on ethnic inclusion in conflict areas. It is an excellent step forward.

"Remember that the ministry is already rolling out the program in Rakhine State, using its own resources," adds Levon. "They have made a similar commitment to reach all ethnic communities, working with civil society organizations."

It all sounds plausible—even persuasive—but I am thinking of all the ways this can go wrong without us monitoring the government's efforts in Rakhine.

Plus we had promised our executive board to act in Rakhine State to help the remaining Rohingya and pave the way for refugee return. So far, not so good. We have cut Rakhine out of this project as well as shelving the proposed Rakhine Recovery and Development Project.

It does not seem to matter what these projects would actually do, what kinds of safeguards would be included, or whether humanitarian agencies asked us to be there. It does not matter. In the eyes of human rights advocates and risk-averse bureaucrats, these projects would legitimize government abuses in Rakhine and undermine the reputation of the World Bank.

It does not matter how much good we could do. We are damned if we do and damned if we don't.

It is proving nearly impossible to directly help remaining Rohingya in Myanmar or assist refugee organizations in paving the way for refugee return.

Two years have passed since the world's attention was yanked to Rakhine by gruesome atrocities aimed at a stateless community who suffered decades of systemic discrimination. Two years have passed, and we still do not have any way to help those who survived and stayed, much less nudge a recalcitrant government toward fundamental changes that would allow refugees to return.

CHAPTER 53

A Step Up

(September and October 2019)

Although I left Myanmar in July, I don't formally retire from the World Bank until September 2019.

Several weeks before I retire, I get a phone call.

"You're not going to believe it, Ellen," says my former desk officer, Kathryn. "Birgit's leaving!"

The COO who decided I was "not a good fit for the job" in Myanmar is leaving the World Bank. She will become the executive director of a prominent UN agency. A step up.

Talk in the corridors is that the new World Bank president is relieved to see this strong-willed woman out the door. She was brought in by the board to handle day-to-day operations of the World Bank for Jim Kim, who shied away from hands-on management. But David Malpass is a completely different kettle of fish. He does not want or need Birgit, with her more progressive agenda, wielding too much power inside the organization. He wants to choose his own deputy.

The irony of Birgit leaving the World Bank now is not lost on me or my former colleagues.

"Who would have thought that both Jim and Birgit would leave before you?" asks Kathryn, incredulously.

They pushed me out of a job I loved because I fought to remain engaged in Myanmar throughout the Rohingya crisis. But before I can make it out the door, both are gone. And the World Bank remains engaged in Myanmar.

I am angry but resigned. I feel used and discarded.

A month later I am enjoying one of the small pleasures of retirement: lingering over the morning newspapers and social media updates. That's when I see it: Aung San Suu Kyi's Facebook page is reporting on her meeting with Birgit in Bangkok.

"What the fuck? Can this be real?" I sputter.

But it is real.

As one of her first acts as executive director, Birgit has a high-visibility meeting with a leader she has consistently vilified for the past two years! She is meeting with the failed democracy icon herself!

She had forbidden me to meet with Aung San Suu Kyi for months on end because it would send the wrong signal about lack of progress on the Rohingya crisis. She argued that such a meeting would legitimize the government's lack of action and Aung San Suu Kyi's own lack of moral courage in solving a fundamental human rights problem.

But Birgit's meeting with The Lady is confirmed by the international press. It seems her agency is angling to have a program in Myanmar for the first time.

A day later, when I visit the World Bank headquarters to pick up my mail, I pass Charlotte in the hallway.

"Hello! Hey, check this out!" I say. "Pretty unbelievable, no?"

I show her a photograph of Birgit and Aung San Suu Kyi shaking hands and smiling for the cameras.

"I saw!" cries my former boss. "I couldn't believe it either!" She shakes her head and laughs.

"Funny how things change," she says before moving on.

CHAPTER 54

At the International Court of Justice

(December 2019)

As 2019 draws to a close, Myanmar is taken to court. To the International Court of Justice (ICJ), to be precise, on charges of genocide against the Rohingya.

By whom? I wonder. By human rights–defending Nordic countries? By rule of law–defending Western European nations? Certainly not by Trump's Muslim-banning America. I scan the newspapers for more details.

Myanmar is being taken to court by...

The Gambia.

The Gambia is a tiny sliver of a country slicing through Senegal on the west coast of Africa. A former British colony, once little more than a military outpost, it is surrounded by francophone nations. The Gambia has only around two million people, and weak institutions and rule of law.

It is not typically a cradle of international justice.

I had visited The Gambia years earlier as a State Department intern in Senegal. I traveled through in a bush taxi, stopping for lunch in the capital of Banjul en route to the beaches of Senegal's Casamance region.

It seems inconceivable that the Gambia would take Myanmar to court at the ICJ.

Any member state of the Convention to Prevent Genocide can file a case with the ICJ. Gambia is a signatory of the 1948 Convention, as is Myanmar. But this is the first time that a country completely unconnected to the alleged crimes has taken another country to court.

I discover that the Gambian justice minister was a former prosecutor at the International Criminal Tribunal for Rwanda. He prosecuted crimes related to the 1994 genocide there. When he was in Bangladesh for a meeting of the Organization of Islamic States, he ventured down to meet with Rohingya refugees. After hearing the refugees' stories, he felt a moral obligation to file the case against Myanmar for genocide, a harder charge to prove than crimes against humanity.

And this is how it comes about that Aung San Suu Kyi finds herself in the Hague on December 10, 2019, defending her country against charges of genocide.

"Why would she defend the military for their crimes?" ask my American friends. "After everything they did to her!"

She is not obligated to go. Most heads of government would send their foreign minister or justice minister. Aung San Suu Kyi is both the de facto head of government and foreign minister.

But her decision is not a matter of protocol or hierarchy.

"I know her. This is about her honor and destiny," I reply to my friends. "It's her sense of duty to defend her country no matter the charge. She must be the defender of an independent and sovereign Burma, just as her father was."

Her father, revered today as a founder of the nation, was assassinated just a year before the country signed the Convention on the Prevention of Genocide.

And now, with her beloved country under attack, what else could she do? Who else could speak for the nation?

Inside Myanmar, mainstream public opinion is staunchly with The Lady. My friends there explain the prevailing mood: the world is attacking Myanmar. The world does not understand Myanmar. As their leader, she must rise to defend them no matter the charge.

My former staff in Yangon—warned against political displays that undermine our neutral status—nonetheless update their Facebook profiles. "We stand with Aung San Suu Kyi," they proudly proclaim as her day in court approaches.

As a newly minted bystander, I find myself at home, settled into a comfortable chair, sipping tea and listening to Aung San Suu Kyi defend her country at the International Court of Justice.

She is gracious and lawyerly in her remarks, pointing out helpfully to the court that legal precedents in the Balkans failed to rule on genocide because "the requisite specific intent to physically destroy the targeted group in whole or in part was not present."

In other words, nobody *planned* to kill the Rohingya, and certainly not *all* of them.

She indicates that the case presents "an incomplete and misleading factual picture of the situation in Rakhine State in Myanmar," which is "complex and not easy to fathom."

Now she becomes the university lecturer she once was, explaining the history of Rakhine State and the alliances of its various ethnic communities through World War II.

Now she becomes a savvy diplomat, heightening alarm in the West by raising the specter of Islamic terrorists recruiting among the Rohingya.

And on the charge of genocide itself, she becomes defender of a sovereign Burma:

"It can't be ruled out that disproportionate force was used by members of the Defense Services in some cases in disregard of international humanitarian law, or that they did not distinguish clearly enough between ARSA fighters and civilians...but these are determinations to be made in the due course of the criminal justice process, not by any individual in the Myanmar government."

Furthermore, she adds, "I should refrain from any action or statement that could undermine the integrity of these ongoing criminal justice processes in Myanmar. They must be allowed to run their course."

She could not be clearer. If there is anything to investigate, it is Myanmar's business, to be handled by Myanmar's own systems of justice. It is not for her to judge or to hold anyone accountable.

Nonetheless, she reiterates her two-year-old intention to bring back the refugees.

"Myanmar is also committed to voluntary, safe, dignified repatriation of displaced persons from Rakhine under the framework agreement reached between Bangladesh and Myanmar."

And finally, as she winds down, I hear the democracy icon reassert herself.

"There will be no tolerance of human rights violations in Rakhine, or elsewhere in Myanmar. We shall adhere steadfastly to our commitment to nonviolence, human rights, national reconciliation, and rule of law as we go forward."

It is an impressive performance, hailed as a victory by many of my former colleagues in Myanmar.

"Our nation's mother, Daw Aung San Suu Kyi," they post proudly.

But I am more focused on what she did not say. Her remarks did not acknowledge the crimes committed and the mountain of evidence gathered in the aftermath. They did not assign blame or censure the military in any way. They did not express any sympathy for the plight of the Rohingya or acknowledge the continuing systemic discrimination against them. And they did not use her moral authority within Myanmar to call for a more tolerant society or faster progress in Rakhine.

For me, it is her nadir. I feel heavy with grief. I have been brought from extraordinary optimism and hope for a peaceful and democratic Myanmar to cynicism and despair over continuing crimes against humanity.

I think back to when I was sent out to Myanmar as the vanguard of the international community to ensure that the improbable ascendency of a democracy icon to the helm of government would become a triumph for liberal democracy and global integration. We were ready with money, with knowledge, and with political support to bring a long repressed and isolated society into the fold of peaceful, tolerant multiethnic societies committed to human rights and the rule of law. Excitement was so high and expectations so elevated that Myanmar became the fastest-growing World Bank program in the world.

I have never been a starry-eyed idealist, yet the extent to which these aspirations have not been met is crushing. We have been blinded by our hope and have stumbled into an abyss.

And we have prevaricated mightily. The World Bank did not approve a single new project for two years after the Rohingya crisis escalated. Not by design, but through indecision. And when we finally did approve a project, it did nothing to help the Rohingya.

What is the right thing to do? Which way are the international winds blowing?

World Bank leadership laid low and hung back to avoid having to make or defend difficult decisions.

I am not alone in seeing Aung San Suu Kyi's testimony in the bleakest of terms. For the international community and media, it scarcely matters what she said. It is appalling that she went at all. How could she defend the actions of the Tatmadaw? Defend those who had jailed her? Those who had kept her under house arrest for decades?

It is a dramatic fall from grace.

A fall from grace that "obliterated what little remained of her international reputation."[55]

A fall from grace that accuses her of leadership that "always bordered on authoritarian."[56]

---

[55] "Aung San Suu Kyi: Myanmar Democracy Icon Who Fell from Grace," *BBC News*, November 6, 2019, https://www.bbc.com/news/world-asia-pacific-11685977.

[56] Hannah Ellis-Petersen, "From Peace Icon to Pariah: Aung San Suu Kyi's Fall from Grace," *The Guardian*, November 23, 2018, https://www.theguardian.com/world/2018/nov/23/aung-san-suu-kyi-fall-from-grace-myanmar.

"A spectacular fall from grace," echoes my former dinner companion Bill Richardson. "She has gone from Nobel Prize champion of democracy to just another dictator wanting to maintain her power by defending military repression, genocide, and banishment of the Rohingya."[57]

Ben Rhodes, who was President Obama's Deputy National Security Advisor and personally oversaw reengagement in Myanmar after 2012, writes a long piece for *The Atlantic* entitled, "What Happened to Aung San Suu Kyi?"[58] In it, he notes that first and foremost, "she is her father's daughter."

And he captures my deepest frustration as part of the international community in Myanmar:

> Suu Kyi's fall from grace offers a lesson about resting all our hopes in one individual—the weight of a country is too heavy to place on one person's shoulders...it speaks to a failure by many of us in the West, who are guilty of sometimes viewing political dilemmas in complicated countries as simple morality plays with a single star at the center.

Myanmar's star has been snuffed out. What do we do now?

---

[57] Grant Peck, "International Rohingya Ruling Spotlights Suu Kyi's Fall from Grace," *The Diplomat*, January 28, 2000, https://thediplomat.com/2020/01/international-rohingya-ruling-spotlights-suu-kyis-fall-from-grace/.

[58] Ben Rhodes, "What Happened to Aung San Suu Kyi? A Human-Rights Icon's Fall from Grace in Myanmar," *The Atlantic*, September 26, 2019, https://www.theatlantic.com/magazine/archive/2019/09/what-happened-to-aung-san-suu-kyi/594781/.

CHAPTER 55

The Court Ruling

(January 2020)

Five weeks later, the International Court of Justice makes a preliminary ruling on Myanmar. It is hailed by many as an extraordinary human rights victory. On January 23, 2020, the court's seventeen judges unanimously adopt provisional measures that require Myanmar to take concrete steps to prevent genocide against the Rohingya, to preserve evidence of past atrocities, and to report back regularly on measures taken. In a legally binding ruling, the court orders Myanmar to take all measures within its power to prevent killing the Rohingya, causing them serious bodily or mental harm, deliberately inflicting conditions of life calculated to bring about their physical destruction, or imposing measures intended to prevent Rohingya births.[59]

"I didn't know that the international community had this ace up its sleeve," I tell my husband. "I mean, it's not a ruling of genocide—that will take years to wind through the court—but it's something."

---

[59] International Court of Justice, *Application of the Convention on the Prevention and Punishment of the Crime of Genocide: The Gambia v. Myanmar, Request for the Indication of Provisional Measures, International Court of Justice*, January 23, 2020, https://www.icj-cij.org/sites/default/files/case-related/178/178-20200123-ORD-02-00-EN.pdf.

It is at least some attempt by the international community to enforce accountability for unconscionable crimes. Yes, it will be sent to the Security Council and, yes, the Security Council will remain paralyzed, but at least it will increase global visibility and pressure to act.

Some point out that the ruling is nothing more than a restatement of principles from the 1948 Convention to which Myanmar has already agreed. The new ruling basically says, "Do not commit genocide."

Nonetheless, human rights advocates are quick to hail the victory and denounce their fallen star:

> This court order is a first—but huge—step to hold Myanmar accountable for atrocities against the Rohingya...the fact that [Suu Kyi] went to the Hague and personally spoke in defense of the military's actions against a minority community means she has owned the military's atrocities in court before the entire world. She has aligned herself with the perpetrators rather than the victims.[60]

"Aligned herself with the perpetrators." She cannot sink lower than that.

But in Myanmar it is quite a different story. Thousands line the streets to cheer her return from the Hague. As I watch videos of the glorious return, I am inclined to agree with observers who say, "Whatever the outcome of the trial, Aung San Suu Kyi, Myanmar's de facto leader, looks set to emerge as the biggest winner."[61]

---

[60] Param-Preet Singh and Amy Braunschweiger, "Landmark World Court Order Protects Rohingya from Genocide: How a Small African Nation Took on Myanmar's Crisis—and Won," Human Rights Watch, January 27, 2020, https://www.hrw.org/news/2020/01/27/interview-landmark-world-court-order-protects-rohingya-genocide.

[61] Yun Sun, "Aung San Suu Kyi Comes Out on Top in ICJ Rohingya Ruling," *Nikkei Asia*, February 8, 2020, https://asia.nikkei.com/Opinion/Aung-San-Suu-Kyi-comes-out-on-top-in-ICJ-Rohingya-ruling.

Dominant public opinion in Myanmar sees her as the defender of the nation, heir to her father's mantle.

And now she is also a defender of the infamous Tatmadaw.

"I don't get it," I say to a former colleague. "How does this help her?"

"It gives her leverage over the Tatmadaw," he says. "It will strengthen her efforts to change the 2008 Constitution. By changing the Constitution, she can rein in the military to create a more representative democracy and more powerful civilian rule."

I am dubious.

"It will reduce popular support for the military-backed USDP (Union Solidarity and Development Party) and boost her and her party in advance of the general election," he explains.

The military has been excoriated globally and domestically for the Rohingya mess, which has brought shame on the nation just as it stepped onto the international stage. Indeed, this could affect USDP's performance in the general election coming up later this year.

And Aung San Suu Kyi is grabbing whatever will raise her profile given her lackluster track record on economic reforms and the erosion of her international reputation since the last election in 2015. Her star turn at the ICJ will energize and excite her Burmese Buddhist base.

In their telling, Aung San Suu Kyi is a brilliant political strategist playing the long game for the good of a truly democratic Myanmar. She is a graceful and diminutive figure with a backbone of steel trading today's indignities on the global stage for tomorrow's democratic victory at home.

What difference does the ICJ case make to the world of foreign aid? How does it change things for people like me working inside the system to influence and persuade flawed, fragmented, and sometimes feckless governments to do good things? To do the right things?

From my vantage point, it does not seem to be making much of a difference.

Aid workers still face the same array of competing and contradictory international forces that make it almost impossible to use foreign aid to leverage more progress in Rakhine. If anything, the ICJ case strengthens the view of those working on the ground that building a tolerant society in Myanmar with respect for the rule of law will be the work of decades—maybe even generations.

We can focus on ensuring inclusion for all communities, including the Rohingya, in the economic opportunities we create and the services we deliver. We can slowly build up transparent and accountable institutions. We can slowly influence hearts and minds. None of this will fix the Rohingya tragedy anytime soon.

As I read about Myanmar from the comfort of my new home several miles from the US Capitol, I see illiberal forces gaining ground all around me—right here in America, once considered the bastion of liberal democracy.

As populist nationalism, with its racism and xenophobia, gains strength at home and around the world, I become more convinced that what I tried to do in Myanmar, and what my team continues to do there without me, is probably the best we can do given the circumstances.

CHAPTER 56

Illiberal America

(January 2020)

When I left Myanmar in mid-2019, I left my husband in Southeast Asia to complete his work and returned home to be with my younger daughter.

In the months that followed, Danielle recovered. No more voices screaming in her head. She became less anxious and more hopeful. I was relieved at how well she was coping and proud of how she took responsibility for moving forward. By the end of 2019, she finished school and started looking for a job.

And my lungs slowly recovered too. After four months on inhalers and oral steroids to treat an unknown condition, I weaned myself off medications and resumed life as a mildly asthmatic but otherwise healthy individual. I finally had enough breathing room to turn my attention to other things.

Although I came home to America for a daughter who needed me, I also came home when my country needed me most. It sounds corny, perhaps, or arrogant, to think that I could do something to change the path of my country. But I felt like I must try.

Is that not what I have been doing for the past forty years all over the world? I was sent to countries with deep problems of poverty, joblessness, and social instability to try to do some good. Why not here in America?

This is what I conclude after three years of watching the Trump Administration from afar. I watch with mounting horror the squandering of our democratic foundations. I see my country being ripped off its post-World War II pedestal as a beacon of liberal democracy. It is becoming an intolerant and illiberal America.

I'm aghast at the...

...lying.

...corruption.

...human rights abuses.

...white supremacy.

...xenophobia.

...Muslim-bashing.

...systemic racism.

...misogyny.

...anti-Semitism.

It is not only—or even mostly—about Trump. He is just a buffoonish symptom of a diseased system. We suffer from an excessively individualistic system with an increasingly frayed social contract, a society that is riddled with historic and systemic discrimination and exclusion. It now threatens to overwhelm us.

And now, true to my path, or perhaps my pathologies, I feel I must do what is good and what is right in my own country.

I am here, in the epicenter of our imperfect democracy, focusing on our upcoming election. I go door to door and make phone calls to raise money, get out the vote, and persuade the unconvinced. It is January 2020, and the world is watching as we gear up for the election on November 6, eleven months away.

Fewer eyes are on Myanmar as the country also moves toward a general election on November 8, just two days after the US election. Unlike the highly polarized and hotly contested battle in the US, conventional wisdom has Aung San Suu Kyi and her National League for

Democracy sailing easily, but less decisively, to victory. It will be less decisive than in 2015 because of expected loss of support among ethnic minority parties over broken promises on peace and federalism. Minority parties now sense that Aung San Suu Kyi's democracy may not include them as much as they had assumed earlier.

For their part, the Rohingya—both those who fled and those who stayed—remain disenfranchised. They will not affect the vote tally. Their voices will not be heard.

CHAPTER 57

Reaping the Fruits

(February-April 2020)

By early 2020, more projects begun under my watch in Myanmar are coming to fruition without me. And finally, two and a half years after the Rohingya crisis exploded, we succeed in designing something that will directly help remaining Rohingya as well as support eventual refugee return to Rakhine. It feels like a huge victory.

The board approves the Inclusive Access and Quality Education Project aimed at getting more children in school and improving their learning. It seems noncontroversial and builds on six years of our earlier experience funding local schools and giving stipends to poor students.

Now, a year later, I read the project document after board approval and feel a burst of pride. As I expected, the team has taken extraordinary measures to ensure equal access and nondiscrimination, especially in Rakhine.

The project has more legal covenants than I have ever seen in a single document, including some I have never seen before:

> The recipient shall: (a) not take any action within its control to restrict movement of Project Beneficiaries so as to adversely affect their ability to access and benefit from Project activities

> and facilities; and (b) take all actions within its control to remove restrictions on movement that adversely affect Project Beneficiaries' ability to access and benefit from Project activities and facilities.[62]

It is legalese, but it gives us the right to halt payments and exert pressure if children, parents, or teaching staff in the project are restricted in their movements. We may not be able to solve Myanmar's broader movement restrictions against the Rohingya and other ethnic minorities, but we can enforce freedom of movement within this project.

> The Recipient shall ensure that [the World Bank], including its staff, consultants, or any other representatives, are provided prompt, safe and unimpeded access to Buthidaung, Maungdaw and Yathedaung and any other parts of the Recipient's territory for purposes related to the supervision of Project activities...

Humanitarian and development agencies continue to struggle for access to Rakhine and other conflict zones. With this covenant, we can suspend the entire project if we are not given access to areas where the project is active—especially areas with remaining Rohingya.

And on and on it goes, with many legal covenants to enforce good behavior, ensure nondiscrimination, and prevent appropriation of land. They are not foolproof, but they aim to ensure that we are not only doing good things but doing them in the right way.

---

[62] World Bank International Development Association, *Project Appraisal Document on a Proposed Credit in the Amount of SDR72.4 Million (US$100 Million Equivalent) and Proposed Grants in the Amount of US$70 Million from Global Partnership for Education and US$10 Million from the European Union to the Republic of the Union of Myanmar for an Inclusive Access and Quality Education Project,* February 5, 2020, https://documents1.worldbank.org/curated/en/242701583550119111/pdf/Myanmar-Inclusive-Access-and-Quality-Education-Project.pdf.

I have never seen such specific and detailed covenants. The document is twice as long as usual. But after two and a half years of asking ourselves what more we could do to help the suffering Rohingya in Myanmar—after two and a half years of avoiding risks and backing away—we finally have a project that does something good for the Rohingya.

CHAPTER 58

The World Moves On

(March-September 2020)

Suddenly, in the first half of 2020, the world moves on.

Democracies and authoritarian regimes alike are in varying degrees of lockdown to fight the COVID-19 pandemic. Borders close. Economies falter. Global development stalls. And the life I lead and love, the life of a development warrior gliding through airport hubs the world over, screeches to a halt.

On March 25, Myanmar reports its first cases of COVID-19, and I brace for worse news.[63] The country has a long, porous border with China, the initial epicenter of the virus. Hundreds of thousands of Chinese visitors cross into Myanmar each year. Cramped living conditions and poor hygiene in the poorer areas of Myanmar, coupled with a severely underdeveloped health system, spell potential disaster for the country.

[63] Reuters Staff, "Myanmar Reports First Cases of Coronavirus," Reuters, March 25, 2020, https://www.reuters.com/article/us-health-coronavirus-myanmar-idUSKBN21B0HB.

If the pandemic rages out of control, the country has only seven intensive care beds and five ventilators for every million people.[64] Millions could die unnecessary deaths. Those with money, foreigners and locals alike, would fly routinely to Bangkok or Singapore for acceptable healthcare. Now those countries are sealed off, and the potential is high for things to spiral out of control inside Myanmar.

Authoritarian regimes and even circumscribed democracies like Myanmar have an advantage in pandemic response. People obey government orders. I watch videos coming out of Myanmar:

Aung San Suu Kyi, flush from defending the nation at the International Court of Justice, is inspecting health facilities as they prepare for the COVID-19 crisis.

Here she is as Mother of the Nation—or rather, beloved grandmother of the nation, demonstrating how to wear a mask and wash hands properly.

Here she is encouraging everyone to stay home as ordered and remain in isolation—a subject on which she is an indisputable expert.

The aid community—my global tribe—rushes to support the world's pandemic response despite travel restrictions. The World Bank is on the front lines, with the burden falling heaviest on local staff. I call our local health specialist in Yangon to get more information.

"What are we doing to respond?" I ask Aung Soe Aye, my former staff who trained as a physician.

"The board just approved a $50 million COVID-19 Emergency Response Project," he explains. "We prepared it in less than a month! It was intense. I am exhausted."

---

[64] Republic of the Union of Myanmar Ministry of Health and Sports Department of Medical Services, *Myanmar COVID-19 Emergency Response Project (P173902) Draft Stakeholder Engagement Plan*, March 30, 2020, https://documents1.worldbank.org/curated/en/412241586965653264/text/Stakeholder-Engagement-Plan-SEP-Myanmar-COVID-19-Emergency-Response-Project-P173902.txt.

I marvel at the ability of the World Bank to move fast when it wants to. The project will pump vital resources into Myanmar's woefully underdeveloped health system and social welfare programs. Like all World Bank projects, it rests on the principle of nondiscrimination. But gone is the two-year debate within the organization about how to respond to the Rohingya crisis. Gone are the parsing of language and the endless redesign aimed at enhancing social inclusion and peace, reaching ethnic minorities, and sending the right signals to speed progress in Rakhine State.

This is a bigger crisis. First things first.

But then Aung Soe Aye says, "It's curious, Ellen, but people are not dying in villages."

"It's not just a reporting problem?" I ask.

This is the most common reason diseases are not recorded in poorer countries.

"Many people think the government may be covering up cases and downplaying the pandemic. What do you think?" I persist.

"My friends in hospitals would know. I would know," he answers firmly. "We would hear about people sick, people dying in droves, on Facebook. We would see the bodies piling up. It would be impossible to hide."

I know he is right.

For the rest of 2020, we discover that not just Myanmar but other Southeast Asian countries are seemingly less affected by the first wave of COVID-19. Theories abound: Stricter measures. Better compliance. Younger populations. Genetic protection. Prior exposure and immunity.

I speculate on whether the undiagnosed respiratory illness that left me weak and wheezing for months afterward could have been an early case of COVID-19 in a place where the local population was largely immune or unaffected.

As variants of the virus start to mutate around the globe, Myanmar remains sealed off and under strict lockdown much of the time. I chat online regularly with friends and former colleagues, something that would have been impossible—even inconceivable—ten years earlier.

Through it all, I wonder about the long-suffering Rohingya.

In May 2020, the first COVID-19 cases are confirmed in the refugee camps in Bangladesh. Humanitarian workers sound the alarm that crowded conditions, poor sanitation, and inadequate health facilities heighten the risks of massive disease and death among the refugees.

With the world preoccupied by the pandemic and the economic collapse that follows, the third anniversary of the Rohingya's flight to Bangladesh passes with little notice. The contrast with earlier years is stark. The few articles I see are subdued, using words like "commemorate" and "continued concern" as the Rohingya refugees "quietly mark" their third anniversary.[65]

In Rakhine State, the United Nations' Memorandum of Understanding with the government has been extended to undertake more assessments and to launch more quick-impact projects at the village level. Even this small progress is largely halted now due to the pandemic and the security situation in Rakhine State.

The Tatmadaw has sealed off much of Rakhine State as they battle insurgency by the Arakan Army. The Arakan Army is made up of ethnic Rakhine fighters. They are the majority ethnic group inside Rakhine State but a minority—a Buddhist minority—within Myanmar. The military's techniques remain the same for all those who threaten the nation: the Tatmadaw now commits crimes against humanity targeted at ethnic Rakhine civilians rather than the Rohingya. But they indiscriminately hurt others as well, including remaining Rohingya.

---

[65] "Myanmar Mechanism Commemorates Anniversary of the Rohingya Refugee Crisis," press release, United Nations, August 25, 2020, https://iimm.un.org/myanmar-mechanism-commemorates-anniversary-of-the-rohingya-refugee-crisis/; "Rohingya Refugees Quietly Mark Third Anniversary of Rakhine Crackdown," *Radio Free Asia*, August 25, 2020, https://www.rfa.org/english/news/myanmar/anniversary-08252020192646.html.

For the Rohingya who remain, no substantive progress has been made on underlying injustices: insecurity, movement restrictions, forced displacement, systemic discrimination, and biased citizenship laws. Deep mistrust remains among ethnic communities, and between ethnic communities and the military.

Negligible progress is being made on Rakhine, but now is not the time.

It is not only the pandemic. The general election is approaching in early November. This will be Aung San Suu Kyi's chance to consolidate and strengthen her power. Public opinion within Myanmar staunchly believes that this is the best—perhaps only—way to strengthen civilian rule and rein in the Tatmadaw.

The stakes could not be higher for Myanmar's fledgling and faltering democracy.

CHAPTER 59

Two Elections

(October and November 2020)

"Hello. My name is Ellen, and I'm calling from the Democratic party." *Click.*

"Hi! How are you today? I'm Ellen, and I'm calling on behalf of the Democratic party." *Click.*

"Hello! This is Ellen with the Democratic party." *Click.*

It is October, and I am obsessed with the impending US presidential election. I am doing whatever I can. Giving money, mostly. Making soul-sucking phone calls, sending texts, working at polling stations. I am doing whatever I can to turn out the vote in the middle of a pandemic.

I am exhausted by the past four years. I cannot bear the thought of another four.

We cannot afford to legitimize white supremacy and ignore systemic racism. We cannot afford a weakening of democratic institutions and an erosion of checks and balances within our branches of government. We cannot afford to be an international laughingstock with no moral authority.

So I endlessly dial voters. "Hi! I'm Ellen with Democrats of Virginia. Would you have a minute to discuss the upcoming election?"

Only one in twenty-five callers is willing to talk, but the data shows it makes a difference in whether people vote, so I plug away.

I scarcely pay attention to Myanmar's upcoming election just days after the US's. The outcome is a foregone conclusion: Aung San Suu Kyi and her NLD party will win, albeit with a smaller margin than last time due to discontent among ethnic parties. Her testimony at the International Court of Justice—a disgrace in the eyes of the international community—will serve her well with the home crowd. This is the conventional wisdom.

"They have canceled voting in fifty-six townships," texts a former colleague from Myanmar.

"How can they do that?" I ask.

"On security grounds," he says. "But the canceled polls are in minority areas—mostly in Rakhine and Shan States, where ethnic parties have strong majorities against the NLD."

This is disturbing. The Union Election Commission (UEC) is appointed by Aung San Suu Kyi's government. They have now canceled voting in one of every six townships in Myanmar.[66] This disenfranchises around one and a half million voters, or about four percent of the total. And this does not include groups like the Rohingya who are disenfranchised by their lack of citizenship.

Ethnic minorities and international human rights advocates protest yet another example of the increasingly illiberal tendencies of Aung San Suu Kyi and the NLD. Their concerns are drowned out in Myanmar and on the global stage as all eyes turn to the US election.

I am on pins and needles as election day dawns in the US.

I obsessively check national news even though results will trickle in all day and night—and possibly for days afterward.

---

[66] Sai Wansai, "Strangulation of Political Space, UEC Cancelled Voting in Five Ethnic States and a Division," *Shan Herald Agency for News*, October 19, 2020, https://english.shannews.org/archives/21973.

I do not notice when the Commander in Chief, Senior General Min Aung Hlaing, makes a rare media appearance in Myanmar that same day.

He accuses the Union Election Commission of "widespread violation of the laws and procedures of the pre-voting process" and raises eyebrows in Myanmar by stating, "We told the election commission we want a free and fair election."

He then continues, "I said in 2015...that we would accept the results by the election commission as long as it was free and fair. However, for now, we are in a situation where we need to be cautious."[67]

I only read about this two days later. And I wonder, *Is he seriously casting doubt on whether the military will accept the election results?* This is not good. It is never good. But it is especially not good in a country having only its second election in modern history.

I do not dwell on this. Nobody really does because the outcome of the US presidential race is hanging in the balance.

I stare morosely into my tea the day after the US election. The Democratic party failed narrowly to take a majority in the Senate and lost ground in its control of the House. *How can this be?*

Four days after the election my phone pings.

"They called it!" I yell out to my family. "We did it! We won!"

Trump has been defeated. Given our losses elsewhere, the policy wonk in me has a measured response. But as a child raised on Holocaust history and now seeing its echoes, I must dance in this moment. The worst has been avoided.

I race outside and grab a campaign sign, leaping and raising it skyward.

"Biden! Biden!" I chant.

[67] Reuters Staff, "Myanmar Army Chief Accuses Government of 'Unacceptable Mistakes' Ahead of Election," Reuters, November 3, 2020, https://www.reuters.com/article/us-myanmar-election-idUSKBN27J2EE.

My daughters crank up music and dance in the backyard in their pandemic pajamas.

"Biden-Harris!" they shout as we run up and down our street.

But my neighborhood stays quiet despite its liberal tendencies. Mine is an unseemly display of partisan fervor in this neighborhood, home to other policy wonks and senior civil servants. I do not care.

I spend the weekend celebrating with the rest of blue America while in Myanmar, my friends and colleagues go to the polls on Sunday, November 8.

They post photos on Facebook waving their purple pinkies at the camera: indelible ink to mark their participation in the election and prevent voter fraud. Turnout remains high at 70 percent despite the pandemic.

I click "love" on all their photos. Democracy in action. For only the second time in their lives.

CHAPTER 60

Democracy Prevails?

(January 2021)

Joe Biden will be inaugurated as president of the United States in just a few weeks.

It is January 6, 2021, and my knees are drawn up tight to my chest as I rock back and forth on my couch, transfixed by the television screen. I must remind myself to breathe. *How long will it take? Where are they?*

It is midafternoon as a horde of protestors—wielding truncheons and knives—become insurrectionists, storming the US Capitol just several miles away from me. They have been goaded into insurrection by a sitting US president claiming election fraud. They want to halt the certification of the presidential election and prevent the peaceful transfer of power.

Prevent the peaceful transfer of power! In America!

Where are they? I am dizzy as I hyperventilate. I am counting the minutes, waiting for the National Guard to arrive to defend the Capitol. They have been called in, says my television screen, but uncertainty remains about who is really calling the shots in America today.

With every minute of delay, my fear mounts. I wonder whether the Trump Administration, in its final days, will be able to subvert the National Guard's response to an insurrection. *Is it possible? Is this how democracy dies in a country long synonymous with the word? Is America finished as a bastion of democracy throughout the world?*

Hours later, too terrified to move, I watch as the tide slowly turns. Police and the National Guard clear the Capitol. My breathing slows. Tears finally flow.

The presidential election is certified that night by a Congress too afraid to wait.

A few weeks later President Biden is sworn in.

"Democracy has prevailed," he says reassuringly.

Yet I am not reassured. The internal forces arrayed against our democracy remain strong and armed. I remain hypervigilant. I am on a knife's edge.

I am less concerned about Myanmar. The country has successfully conducted its second election since the political transition began in 2011, despite the pandemic. Many are declaring it a victory for democracy.

And Aung San Suu Kyi has shown herself to be a shrewd political strategist.

She won in a landslide, even bigger than her 2015 victory that brought her to power. Her defense of the nation at the ICJ and her pandemic reassurances have reinforced her status as a national icon.

Her NLD party has captured more than 80 percent of all available seats in parliament. The military-backed USDP crumbled, winning only 7 percent. Remaining seats went to various ethnic parties. Although the military retains its 25 percent statutory share of total parliamentary seats, their political clout has been significantly undercut by this election outcome.

Political observers are quick to comment. Richard Horsey, the former head of the International Labor Organization in Myanmar and now an expert on Myanmar's ethnic conflicts, is quick to dissect the USDP cadaver:

"The further erosion of USDP's support does not come as much of a surprise. The party has failed to reinvent itself as a credible alternative to the NLD," he writes.

"The party has not been effective at putting forward any policies to show how it would do things differently. The upshot is that most Myanmar voters see it as a party of the past," he continues.[68]

Surprisingly, the NLD did better than expected in ethnic strongholds where elections were held.

Richard assesses that "the commander-in-chief alarmed many Myanmar people by criticizing the quality of electoral preparations and hinting that he might not accept the result. Ironically, the commander-in-chief's comment may have actually amplified the NLD's success."

Shwe Kyar says as much the next time we chat.

Proud of her ethnic heritage, she has provided funds and advice to young minority candidates throughout the campaign. But in the end, she felt the need to bolster the NLD to block the possibility of political gains by the military.

"I even thought maybe not to vote," she says glumly. "But I could not. I fought my whole life for democracy! I felt guilty voting for NLD. But I voted for NLD, without even reading the names. What else could I do?"

"What will happen now?" I ask, thinking of our painstaking work on social inclusion for ethnic minorities in conflict areas.

"All those words we say—diversity, inclusion—sound like such baloney now!" she answers vehemently. "The NLD got a blank check to behave as they wish! Who will serve as internal opposition? The voice of ethnic diversity has been completely lost now."

I sigh. The struggle will indeed get harder. Fewer internal voices of diversity. And Aung San Suu Kyi's NLD party will be even more immune to pressure from the international community on all aspects of diversity, social inclusion, and human rights.

Any chance of doing the right thing for the Rohingya in Myanmar and Bangladesh now seems hopelessly lost.

---

[68] Richard Horsey, "Another Landslide Victory for Aung San Suu Kyi's Party in Myanmar—but at What Cost?" International Crisis Group, November 12, 2020, https://www.crisisgroup.org/asia/south-east-asia/myanmar/another-landslide-victory-aung-san-suu-kyis-party-myanmar-what-cost.

CHAPTER 61

Tensions in Myanmar

(January 2021)

"I will accept an election result that reflects the people's will," says the military commander in chief, Min Aung Hlaing, on election day in Myanmar.[69]

This reassurance is widely circulated under a photo of the smiling commander, waving his purple pinkie at the camera after casting his ballot.

Nonetheless, military grumbling continues after the election and into the new year. Taking a page from Donald Trump's playbook, the Tatmadaw alleges massive voter fraud without evidence. The military-backed USDP lodges six hundred post-election complaints, claiming almost nine million irregularities in the voter lists in nearly every township of Myanmar.[70] The Union Election Commission refutes the charges.

---

[69] "Myanmar's Military Chief Agrees to Accept Election Result," *Irrawaddy*, November 8, 2020, https://www.irrawaddy.com/elections/myanmars-military-chief-agrees-accept-election-result.html.

[70] Aung Shine Oo, "Myanmar Military Denies Coup Threats over Vote Fraud Claims," Associated Press, January 30, 2021, https://apnews.com/article/constitutions-myanmar-elections-asia-min-aung-hlaing-1d8af462424d818f96e88dc6ed115dc1.

Constant sparring between the USDP and the NLD party is the norm in Myanmar, so I am unruffled by these post-election tensions. I experienced it through the first mandate of Aung San Suu Kyi's government and expect it to persist through the second.

In January, I guest lecture at a US university about Myanmar's transition.

"Why do people keep voting for Aung San Suu Kyi?" asks a young man with tortoiseshell glasses.

"She is the daughter of a revered founding father of independent Burma," I explain. "And a renowned democracy icon in her own right."

I see eyes rolling among the students at this description of the now-disgraced Nobel Peace Prize winner.

"Following her landslide win in this election, many in Myanmar see her as a clever political strategist," I say. "They think she is playing a long game. She came to power vowing to change the 2008 Constitution. She sees dominating parliament as the only way to do this, bringing the military under civilian control."

Heads begin to nod.

"By this logic, changing the Constitution is the key to true democracy in Myanmar," I continue. "And by crushing the military-backed opposition party, she might now be able to forge a coalition with ethnic parties to change the Constitution."

"Is that likely to happen?" asks a woman, chewing anxiously on a pen.

"It's possible. Perhaps not likely. But since the election, Aung San Suu Kyi has made overtures to some ethnic parties," I acknowledge. "Even if the Constitution is changed, the question remains whether and how this democracy is going to serve all of Myanmar's people. So far, the track record of her government has been quite dismal."

And now my students find themselves in more familiar territory: all the ways that Aung San Suu Kyi has disappointed the Western world as a would-be democracy icon.

Their disappointment in her leadership echoes my own. While I did not expect a great deal of economic vision on her part, I expected more inspired political leadership in defense of democracy and human rights. This is true even within the constraints of her power imposed by the current Constitution. The goal of forging a truly democratic and federal system among all ethnic minorities has remained on the back burner. And fundamental reform for the Rohingya has been no more than a distant prospect.

With a second NLD government looking much like the first, I expect Myanmar to continue moving haltingly and erratically forward on its path toward democracy.

In the meantime, I am reveling in what feels like a return to normalcy in the United States.

On January 20, I curl up on the same couch where I anxiously watched an insurrection at the US Capitol two weeks earlier to watch the presidential inauguration on television. I sip a glass of Malbec and feel a tad more sanguine about the future of my country.

Long before the pandemic and before I moved overseas, I would bundle up in warm clothes and ride the metro downtown to attend the presidential inauguration on the National Mall. Now I am watching on the small screen. Nonetheless it is a joyous, uplifting day. It is a peaceful transfer of power, the hallmark of democracy.

I can feel the reverberations and hear the booming of fireworks exploding on the mall just a few miles away. The reverberations are running through my body, bringing me a sense of hope—hope for our democracy and hope for human decency and tolerance. *Is that too much to ask?*

A week later, on a Wednesday in Myanmar, Commander in Chief Min Aung Hlaing gives a speech to a group of senior military officer trainees:

"The Constitution could be revoked if the laws are not being properly enforced," he says at one point.[71]

[71] Aung Shine Oo, "Myanmar Military Denies Coup Threats."

A flurry of concern follows his vague yet ominous remarks. Revoking the Constitution would mean destroying the foundation of Myanmar's path toward democracy. What would it even mean if the military "revoked" the Constitution? It sounds like nothing short of a military *coup d'état.*

The next day, diplomats on the ground in Myanmar issue a joint statement calling on the military to respect the outcome of the election. I feel useless, far away from the action. Sidelined.

On Friday, my friend Dave, a former researcher in Myanmar, reaches out. "So what's your take on the Myanmar coup fears?"

"Tatmadaw just pounding their chests because they suffered such a humiliating defeat at the polls. I doubt very much a coup will be attempted (watch me be wrong!)" I reply.

I am breezy in my response, but then I elaborate, "I don't think the NLD genie can go back in the bottle—at the same time I don't think NLD can overcome the structural impediments to changing the Constitution in their favor. So the Tatmadaw will retain their firm grip on many aspects of society and the economy. If they want more influence politically, they will need to learn to play that game too..." I trail off.

"Do you know if Japan joined that declaration with the other countries?" Dave asks.

"I would guess not," I answer and then rush to check.

Turns out I am right. Japan's preference for quiet diplomacy remains intact. I am pleased at my continued political savvy even if I am not there.

The next day—Saturday—the military puts out a clarifying statement.

"Some organizations and the media wrote without foundation that the military threatened to revoke the Constitution."[72]

---

[72] Aung Shine Oo, "Myanmar Military Denies Coup Threats."

The statement claims that Min Aung Hlaing's speech was taken out of context—he was just explaining the nature of the Constitution to trainees.

Political analyst Richard Horsey tweets from Yangon, "It appears that the Myanmar military has stepped back from its coup threat and will 'follow the Constitution'...any imminent putsch seems unlikely."

Like I said. Not going to happen.

My political instincts remain sharp. Nothing gets past me.

CHAPTER 62

Crashing Down

(January 2021)

Sunday, January 31, dawns in Washington, DC, with a rare dusting of snow.

It is a sleepy day. I stay in my pandemic pajamas, snuggling into blankets to read some historical fiction. By evening I am puttering around my kitchen perusing the leftovers for dinner when my phone vibrates.

I glance over and see a news flash from the *New York Times*:

"Myanmar Leader Daw Aung San Suu Kyi is Detained Amid Coup Fears."

I blink rapidly, but it is still there, screaming at me.

I grab at the phone, frantically scrolling for confirmation. My brain is racing. My ears are buzzing. *No, no, no, no! This cannot be happening! This cannot be happening!*

But it is.

Breaking news tells me that the president and Aung San Suu Kyi, as well as most of her ministers and even the chief ministers in the regions and states, have been rounded up in a series of dawn raids.

I immediately forward the news to Dave.

"Guess I was wrong about that coup thing," I joke, but I feel gut-punched.

I turn to Facebook, the go-to platform for information in Myanmar. I usually see a steady stream of posts from Myanmar, but now it is a dead space. An eerie silence. The Tatmadaw has shut down the internet and phone service during its morning raids.

Or at least they are trying to. But unaccustomed to the free market they welcomed to Myanmar in recent years, they are unable to fully choke off the flow of information.

I am still standing, dumbstruck, in my kitchen, when an old friend of mine, Thant Myint-U, Myanmar's renowned historian and grandson of the country's most accomplished diplomat, UN Secretary General U-Thant, manages a tweet from Yangon to the world:

"The doors just opened to a very different future. I have a sinking feeling that no one will really be able to control what comes next."

And then in rapid succession, my friends and former colleagues in Yangon wake up to shocking news.

Mya Mya, who helped pry open the doors to Myanmar back in 2008 working for Doctors without Borders, blacks out her Facebook profile in a gesture of mourning and anger.

Kyi Sin, who spent four years in prison for defending democracy, stopped posting on Facebook a week earlier. An abundance of caution, perhaps? I pray the Tatmadaw does not sweep up him or any of my colleagues in its morning raids.

Thein Lwin, one of our IT specialists, who posts weekly videos of himself singing and playing the piano during the pandemic, now posts, "We need to keep going whatever it takes," along with a video of a bear cub clumsily climbing an icy cliff, backsliding repeatedly until he claws his way to the top. Cute. Hopeful.

And then Thein Lwin falls silent. Facebook is too easily monitored. And his technology skills are needed now more than ever to maintain communications. He migrates to more secure applications.

Wai Htun, our jack-of-all-trades and part of our security team, immediately starts gathering and posting intelligence. First, he posts the announcement from the army's television channel, rarely watched by the general public:

> By National President's Office Order No. 1/2021: The state has transferred the three branches, judiciary, legislative and executive to the Commander-in-Chief, as the state is facing a political crisis by refusing to investigate electoral fraud. Acting President U Myint Swe has announced a state of emergency for a one-year period.

Classic gaslighting by the Tatmadaw. The coup is necessary to protect the Constitution and defend a democracy threatened by a fraudulent election. The military is the ultimate defender of democracy in Myanmar.

They claim that they will return the country to democracy and hold new elections within a year, but will they? Last time they said this, it took twenty-seven years to hold another election.

My evening passes in a frenzy of scrolling and texting. I send a message to Susie, my housekeeper: "Very worried about you all. Sad day for Myanmar."

She replies instantly. "Yes, madam. Now we can't go out. Now I can't call my mother."

She sends a picture of Phoebe—now a big girl of two and a half—riding a scooter. Beaming with happiness in the garden of my successor's house. Unaware of the heartbreaking events outside her gate.

We have all been caught unaware. We saw the signs but dismissed them. Ten years into an experiment in democracy, and we forgot how easily it can be snatched away. The Tatmadaw allowed Aung San Suu Kyi to come to power. They gave it to her. And now they have taken it away.

A video is posted to Facebook late in the night and then goes viral.[73]

In it, a young woman is leading an online aerobics class from Nay Pyi Taw. She is taking advantage of the broad, empty streets in the early morning to film and stream her class. She is next to the massive parliamentary complex I visited many times.

She bounces rhythmically to the latest K-pop tunes. Her movements are hypnotic and energizing.

Everything about her speaks to Myanmar's transition to a more open and connected society. The latest tunes. Her modern fitness routine. Her stylish workout clothes. Her freedom to dance on the streets of Nay Pyi Taw. Her ability to stream online to thousands of followers throughout Myanmar. None of this could have happened ten years earlier. It is a bouncing and boisterous testament to progress.

As she steps and stretches, a phalanx of black SUVs with tinted windows rush behind her to the doors of the parliament complex. It is filled with parliamentarians waiting for a swearing-in ceremony later in the day. Armed soldiers in black balaclavas pour out of the vehicles and burst through the doors to round up parliamentarians from the NLD party at gunpoint.

For now, aerobics woman dances on unaware, the sounds of military repression drowned out by her music.

I watch her several times, squinting to see the soldiers behind her, as if my scrutiny alone could stop them in their tracks.

There is nothing else for me to do. I cannot sleep. It all seems impossible. This cannot be the next step in Myanmar's ten-year journey toward democracy.

---

[73] "Watch: Woman Films Exercise Video as Myanmar's Coup Unfolds behind Her," *NBC News*, February 4, 2021, video, 2:03, www.nbcnews.com/video/pe-teacher-leads-workout-as-myanmar-s-coup-unfolds-behind-her-10051898756. We later learn that the young woman is a physical education teacher named Khing Hnin Wai who had been offering outside aerobics classes online from Nay Pyi Taw for eleven months prior to the coup.

My friends and former colleagues in Yangon are afraid. Not afraid for their safety—although maybe it will come to that—but afraid of backsliding. Afraid of losing it all. *Can it really go back, all the way back, to the bad old days of authoritarianism and extreme penury and total isolation? Is this a return to the days of censorship and government informants in every tea shop?*

I am not ready to accept this, and neither are they.

I wake after a few hours of fitful sleep on February 1 and begin scrolling immediately.

Shwe Kyar, of iron will, impeccable integrity, and flawless English, posts a pure cry from the heart:

> The day that I never want to see again—not for myself but for the next generation and young people like my own niece—has arrived. I thought I was having a bad dream when I woke up in the early hours of the morning with all the notices coming in on my social media and emails. The nightmare continues with one news update after another since then.
>
> I am overwhelmed with anger, frustration, sadness, and acute feelings of my own impotence. I have never felt the urge of afflicting physical pain—either to another human being or to myself—but this morning, as I stood standing there in my room, unable and unwilling to process the news, I was overcome by a well of anger so dark and consuming that it could only be assuaged by a physical pain—of mine or others.

Reading her words, I finally burst into tears.

CHAPTER 63

International Reaction

(February 2021)

It is the view out my office window in Yangon. It is the view that looks down on the golden Sule Pagoda, surrounded by traffic and street vendors selling *Ah-Boh*, the Burmese crepes that I love.

Except now it is drone footage, capturing the swelling ranks of protesters. They are resisting the military coup, insisting on the release of Aung San Suu Kyi and confirmation of the November election results. It is not only at Sule Pagoda. As soon as the military's nightly internet blackout is lifted, protesters in every city in Myanmar post images and live stream their resistance on Facebook.

Like me, the international community seems shell-shocked by the sudden, unexpected turn of events. But then, Western leaders voice their outrage. They call for the release of Aung San Suu Kyi and other detainees, respect for the outcome of the election, and a return to the fragile democratic path of the past ten years. The UN Secretary General, the UN Human Rights Commission, and the Group of Seven countries all condemn the coup. They caution the military to refrain from violence against democracy protesters.

The new Biden administration in America vocally defends Burma's democracy and ratchets up targeted sanctions on military leaders and their conglomerates. The US is constrained in its ability to maneuver because many military leaders are already under sanctions for crimes against the Rohingya. It scarcely matters: the Tatmadaw generals have decades of experience working in isolation. It just feeds their narrative of a hostile world aligned against Myanmar.

In the days following the coup, I wonder if we are heading down the same path as before. *Is this just a repeat of 1988, when the Tatmadaw refused to accept election results, unleashing a democracy movement that brought Aung San Suu Kyi to the fore? Will the Tatmadaw once again crush the protests and neutralize the country's beloved democracy icon?* Back then, the military destroyed the democracy movement and pushed the country back into another two decades of isolation, repression, and widespread poverty.

Back then, the West imposed broad economic sanctions that remained in place until 2012. This kind of sanction served only to hurt poor families and further isolate Myanmar's people, while playing into the hands of corrupt military leaders and their cronies. Today, human rights advocates are calling for broad economic sanctions again. *Will the Western world make this same mistake twice?*

To no one's surprise, the UN Security Council fails to condemn the military coup. Members China and Russia are loathe to take a strong position. China unabashedly refers to the coup as a "major cabinet reshuffle" and calls on all parties to "uphold political and social stability."[74]

"What do you think the World Bank will do now?" asks a friend.

"I know exactly what they'll do! They will issue a statement of deep concern and suspend disbursements," I say. "We have policies to halt financing when a country lacks a legitimate government. And the Tatmadaw is not a legitimate government."

Within twenty-four hours of the coup, the World Bank issues a statement titled "Developments in Myanmar," as though if we don't

---

[74] "US Calls Myanmar Military's Takeover a Coup, While China Labels It a 'Cabinet Reshuffle,'" *CBS News*, February 2, 2021, https://www.cbsnews.com/news/myanmar-coup-united-nations-biden-china-russia/.

name it, the coup might still fail. The World Bank shows itself to be "gravely concerned" by the developments in Myanmar. A week or two later, the statement is amended:

"Effective February 1, we have temporarily put a hold on disbursements on our operations in Myanmar. The World Bank Group's internal policies and procedures lay out processes in these situations which we are following carefully."[75]

Unlike economic sanctions, which affect consumers directly, halting foreign aid that goes straight to the military government is the right thing to do.

But I am ineffably sad. Everything the World Bank worked for in the previous decade grinds to an abrupt halt. Expanding rural electrification, training teachers, increasing funding to health clinics, opening markets, modernizing telecommunications, upgrading the banking system. It all stops.

Everything we struggled for in the past few years no longer matters: the exhausting efforts to stay engaged to support the civilian government, the difficult moral decisions around the Rohingya crisis, the endless negotiations with the government to advance ethnic inclusion, my career-ending efforts to strike the right balance. All for naught, it seems.

The question of whether we support a flawed civilian government to counterbalance the Tatmadaw or condemn them for complicity is no longer relevant. We no longer have the choice. And so my whole story of Myanmar—the story of trying to do good and do right in complex moral circumstances—seems smaller now. Swallowed by a new-old reality: no democracy, flawed or otherwise, and the military clamping down with egregious disregard for civil liberties and human rights.

---

[75] "Developments in Myanmar," World Bank, last modified February 19, 2021, https://www.worldbank.org/en/news/statement/2021/02/01/developments-in-myanmar.

CHAPTER 64

Protest Movement

(February and March 2021)

The president, state counsellor, and hundreds of government officials and parliamentarians remain in detention. Aung San Suu Kyi is detained on absurd charges of improperly importing walkie-talkies. After decades of acting with impunity, the Tatmadaw feels no need to concoct a better lie to justify its actions.

Within days of the coup, the protest movement begins to swell. Photos are posted juxtaposing protests in 1988 against today's swelling crowds.

But it soon becomes apparent that this is not 1988. It is not even 2010, the year before the political transition began and the country opened to the outside world. Protests are being organized not by Aung San Suu Kyi or the NLD party but by informal networks of young people who have come of age in a more democratic and open Myanmar. They are technologically savvy, doing an end run around the older Tatmadaw leaders to remain connected despite the military's efforts to disrupt communications. They have lived with freedoms unimaginable to their parents, and they are unafraid. And so the protests grow.

I obsessively check Facebook and other social media sites many times a day, thankful that they are serving as platforms for Myanmar's resistance. I see a clever, colorful, and creative explosion of civil disobedience. Young protesters are breakdancing and singing at major intersections. Cars are conveniently breaking down en masse to block the military's access to protest sites.

Protesters hold signs in English: "Democracy Yes! Military No!" and "Respect our Election!"

A bride protests in her wedding dress. Bodybuilders pose shirtless to attract media attention.

Young women hold bawdy signs in English: "I want to fuck my boyfriend, but the military fucks me every day!"

They flash the three-fingered Hunger Games salute used by young protesters throughout Asia.

As the protests grow, the streets themselves are painted with huge signs in English: "Reject the coup" and "Democracy for Myanmar." It is messaging best seen from the sky. Messaging for the outside world. They will not be pushed back into isolation.

Generation Z is animating protests unlike anything ever seen before in Myanmar, and they are streaming it live on social media.

The military is taken aback by the ingenuity and scale of the youth protest movement.

And now, doctors, teachers, and engineers are joining in the newly christened Civil Disobedience Movement. They wear traditional straw hats—flat and round—with "Reject the Military" emblazoned on top. More messaging for the outside world.

It gives me life to see the Civil Disobedience Movement grow, especially when civil servants from the government join in. Phalanxes of women from the ministries protest military rule. They wear the matching silk longyis they are required to wear each day: green for the Ministry of Agriculture, blue and white for the Ministry of Planning and Finance, and so on. I remember these ladies kneeling in a row in front of their seated male colleagues for obligatory photos when I spoke at government conferences. I remember cringing inwardly at the submissive pose. Now the ladies are not kneeling. They are protesting.

A week after the coup, I grab my phone while still in bed one morning to see the overnight news. But I am locked out of Myanmar. I have been booted out of a private Facebook group—my main lifeline to friends and former colleagues. I panic. *Is this how it happens? Is this how the country closes back on itself? Isolated and unreachable to the modern world?*

I send frantic messages to Thein Lwin, our technology specialist. I am desperate for connection. He answers immediately.

"It wasn't me, Ellen," he texts, telling me the one thing I already knew. He reinstates my access, and I breathe a sigh of relief.

"Was it just a technical glitch?" I ask him. "Or somehow related to the broader internet shutdowns? Or is it possible that the Tatmadaw is trying to cut off voices like me who might speak out?"

"Impossible to say," he says.

Protests continue unabated day after day. The streets around my former office are a main battleground. Aerial photos show swelling crowds, not only in large cities like Yangon and Mandalay but in smaller towns like Hpa-An and Bago. As I watch live streams of crowds surging forward, I breathe, "Go, go, go!" to the protesters like a mantra. I feel inspired and hopeful.

It is definitely not 1988.

I am quite sure that the Tatmadaw will never accept the recent election results, release Aung San Suu Kyi, or restore her to power. And with no grooming of political successors within the NLD, the future of the party is uncertain. My friends in Myanmar do not want to hear this. The Lady remains untarnished in their eyes.

But I am also sure that the military will not be able to crush these protests as they did in 1988. They will not be able to push the country back to the depths of isolation and despair. Ten years of democracy—or at least a path toward democracy—have been good for Myanmar. The country has been transformed in ways that sustain these youthful protesters.

And I feel proud that my work contributed to this—even if just a little. Everything we worked for in Myanmar—freedom of information, modern telecommunications, higher quality education, rural electrification, a budding private sector—has given rise to a new generation accustomed to the freedoms and rights of an open and democratic society.

Democracy has been good for Myanmar, but not everybody has benefitted. Ethnic and religious minorities, facing systemic discrimination and repression, have been denied many of the gains, and the Rohingya are devastatingly worse off.

I realize that returning the country to some form of democratic government will depend on the strength of these young protestors and their commitment not only to democracy, but to a liberal and tolerant democracy. They will need to draw strength from Myanmar's ethnic and religious diversity. This asks a lot of Myanmar's youth. Not only to fight but to join across ethnic and religious lines to fight the true enemy, the Tatmadaw.

Yet the Tatmadaw courts ethnic leaders to join them—even those like the Arakan Army whom they have been chasing down and killing. Most ethnic groups have spent decades in the struggle for democracy and self-determination. They are more inclined to align with the protesters. But they are wary.

By their rapacious standards, the Tatmadaw has been patient with the protesters. For the first few weeks at least, no mass casualties have occurred. But arrests happen every night.

Khin Maung Than, a former staff member in our Yangon office, was named Deputy Minister for Employment a year earlier. Now he's been arrested.

Two of our closest government partners, the Deputy Minister for Planning and the economic advisor to Aung San Suu Kyi, were also arrested. One is an Australian citizen, but the Tatmadaw does not care.

"We don't even know where they are," Levon tells me when I text him. "And if we try to help them, we could make things worse."

Being seen as a collaborator with, or agent of, Western powers would be harmful for the prisoners.

"We have nothing to offer," he concludes.

I think back on the casual dinners and drinks I shared with these close partners. I shudder to imagine where they are now, locked in dank jail cells, alone, afraid, and possibly tortured.

Protesters, democracy and human rights activists, and popular authors and artists continue to be arrested on the streets. Or they receive a knock on the door at night and are taken away to unknown locations. Families gather outside In-Sein prison, searching for answers. During the day, police and military use water cannons, tear gas, and rubber bullets to control protesters. One casualty is announced: a seventeen-year-old girl struck in the head by a rubber bullet.

After one month, the Tatmadaw reverts to form, cracking down on protesters and killing dozens of civilians in cities and towns across Myanmar. We get reports of live ammunition and truncheons being used. One by one, civilians are killed, including a sixteen-year-old boy running down the street below my old office window. More than a thousand people are arrested and nearly thirty murdered. Then the Tatmadaw reverts to a time-honored technique: paying supporters to attack protesters. They beat and maul protestors, kicking them on the ground. Protest organizers and the journalists who stream them are on the run. They sleep at different houses each night to evade arrest. They become democracy nomads.

Especially at night, under curfew and cut off from social media, my Myanmar friends and colleagues suffer through an unfathomable return to the dark days of military dictatorship. The weight of the past falls heavily on them, and they feel the world moving on, leaving them alone in the darkness of their country's uncertain future.

And in the middle of it all, a baby is born to the World Bank family. Our security officer, Wai Htun, who has been carefully documenting the protests and spurring the Muslim community to action, announces the birth of his first child, a little girl.

I imagine him navigating Yangon's narrow streets clogged with protesters and police to bring his wife to the hospital for the delivery.

I wonder what it feels like to bring a Muslim child into the dangerous and uncertain world that is Myanmar today.

"Congratulations on the birth of a future female leader!" I tell him, but it makes me pine for my goddaughter Phoebe. My girl who is strong and smart and a future leader of a tolerant and democratic Myanmar.

Since the coup, I keep wondering if I should try to bring Susie, Nay Moo, and Phoebe to America. *Would it even be possible? Would they want to come?*

I send a text to Susie to check if they are okay. She answers by sending a voice message in her usual cheerful voice.

"We are all okay!" she sings out. "For food, Nay Moo goes to the market in the morning when it is quiet. We stay home in the afternoon and night because of many people in the street. We are good."

And she attaches a video to calm my worries.

Phoebe playing in the garden. The lawn is green and lush. Nay Moo has been watering. Phoebe is twirling slowly in a princess dress—the blue one from *Frozen* I sent for her birthday. She twirls and softly sings the only words she knows from the song "Let It Go." But it sounds like one word, and I smile. I watch her twirl slowly away until I cannot hear her anymore. Then she twirls out of the camera's frame and the video stops.

CHAPTER 65

Protesting in Washington

(June 2021)

"We should have worn our longyis!" I shout to my friend.

"Appropriate but too hot!" she shouts back.

We are swimming in a sea of traditional Myanmar garb, brightly colored silks in many hues, but mostly red, the color of Aung San Suu Kyi's NLD party.

We are protesting the coup outside the Chinese and Myanmar embassies in Washington. People from Myanmar, of Myanmar descent, or with a Myanmar history have traveled from all over the United States to raise the visibility of the country's plight. Because what else can we do? Nobody expects military intervention from abroad to topple the Tatmadaw. Myanmar is not that important in the world, and the risk of irritating China is too great to imagine external intervention. But we can at least raise diplomatic pressure and try to turn off the flow of funds directly to the military regime from global corporations. It is a tricky exercise to choke off funds to the military while trying to cushion the blow to ordinary people, including brave protestors.

"Let's try to move higher so we can take some pictures," I shout through the crowd.

We struggle up the steps of a nearby embassy. I pull out my phone to snap some photos and focus on the crowd below.

Initially, I see an indistinguishable mass of protestors. Then I realize.

"Look! That group there! Chin!" I say.

"Oh, yeah! Look over there! Karen! And Kachin!" my friend says.

"And Mon!" I reply. "Even the Bamar have a sign!"

Each group carries a sign announcing its ethnic affiliation. And I see the differences in dress now: some with woven vests, some with winged headpieces, some with silk longyis. Not all the same.

"If any good can come of the coup, it is helping the Bamar understand who the real enemy is," I say.

I inhale and stand taller to see ethnic groups coming together to defend democracy in Myanmar. It seems the majority Bamar are accepting the other groups as equals for the first time! They finally get it! It feels like a dam has burst, and the water is flowing freely in the same direction toward a truly representative democracy.

In Myanmar, the vestiges of Aung San Suu Kyi's government—those who have not been arrested and hauled away to prison—have encouraged ethnic groups to join with them in a National Unity Government. They *need* the other ethnic groups.

The National Unity Government is bidding for international recognition as a shadow government—a legitimate government to counter the Tatmadaw's illegitimate coup. Some of Aung San Suu Kyi's diplomats, in places like New York and London, have rejected the military coup and joined the National Unity Government, only to find themselves locked out of their embassies and residences. They are unexpected refugees from an unexpected dictatorship.

And then, the National Unity Government issues a statement saying that the Rohingya are "entitled to citizenship by laws that will accord with fundamental human rights and democratic federal principles."

I am stunned. The National Unity Government is offering citizenship to the Rohingya. It helps them gain legitimacy in the eyes of the international community and reflects how desperately they need all ethnic minorities to counter the force of the Tatmadaw.

The National Unity Government's statement promises to repeal the 1982 Citizenship Law that reinforces Myanmar's systemic discrimination. It will be replaced with a law that will "base citizenship on birth in Myanmar or birth anywhere as a child of Myanmar citizens."

Furthermore, the statement commits to "voluntary, safe and dignified repatriation" of the Rohingya refugees and to "actively seek justice and accountability for all crimes committed by the military against the Rohingya and all other people of Myanmar throughout our history."[76]

The Rohingya remain wary. After all, the National Unity Government arose from the remnants of Aung San Suu Kyi's government. They were a government that abjectly failed the Rohingya. Why believe them now?

Still, it is an extraordinary development. It seems only with the destruction of Myanmar's fledgling democracy that a vision of a truly representative democracy—and a tolerant and multiethnic society—begins to emerge. And it is only when the democracy icon is missing, imprisoned, not visible, that the Burmese begin to understand the democracy they need and the real enemy they must fight.

And in Myanmar, minority ethnic groups find themselves suddenly in demand. Their ethnic armed organizations, small armies, and militias are called upon to train young protestors in armed struggle. Young people are now on the run from the Tatmadaw, hiding in remote villages and deep in the hills. They join those who have been defending themselves against the military for decades.

I think of the Burmese youths hanging out in the shopping mall below my office, preening in the shop windows, sipping lattes, and posing for selfies. So *prosperous*. So *modern*. It is difficult to imagine them on the run in a remote jungle, disheveled and hungry, training for insurgency with an ethnic army. But many are. They are blending

[76] Sebastian Strangio, "Myanmar Shadow Government Pledges Citizenship for Rohingya," *The Diplomat*, June 4, 2021, https://thediplomat.com/2021/06/myanmar-shadow-government-pledges-citizenship-for-rohingya/.

warfare tactics honed through the 1980s and 1990s with the advantages of modern technology.

And as the center of the country descends into chaos, the more powerful ethnic armed organizations draw strength.[77] Historic conflict zones become more stable as groups like the United Wa State Army, the Kachin Independence Army, and the Arakan Army organize themselves for this new phase in the struggle for greater autonomy.

Back in Yangon, my professional friends are too old, too settled, too jaded to join the insurgency themselves. Perhaps they donate money to transport, feed, and arm young protestors as they hide, run, and train with ethnic armed organizations. But to say so could be used as evidence of treason.

So I ask no questions. I don't know who is monitoring our communications.

---

[77] Jason Tower, "In Myanmar, the State the Generals Seized Is Coming Apart," United States Institute for Peace, August 19, 2021, https://www.usip.org/publications/2021/08/myanmar-state-generals-seized-coming-apart.

CHAPTER 66

A Perfect Storm

(June and July 2021)

Five months after the coup, my husband has returned home to the US. Both my daughters have moved back home to weather the pandemic. Both are in good spirits. We are safe and together as a family.

I reach out to a friend in Yangon. She looks exhausted.

"So what's happening?" I ask, wanting to go beyond what I read in the newspapers.

"They are still arresting people every night," she says. "Not just protestors. Journalists, artists, anybody really. It's terrifying."

"Is anything working?"

"Government is barely functioning," she continues. "Doctors, teachers, administrators—nobody is going to work, so nothing gets done."

"And what about the banks?"

"They say the banking system may collapse," she responds. "I don't know. People queue up every day at dawn—hundreds of people, waiting for hours in the sun for cash. But the ATMs are empty most of the time. And when they have cash, they give only a little."

I have read this. Only dispensing dribs of cash. Not enough to feed a family. Or support a resistance movement. Tatmadaw techniques to control the population.

"And how are you *doing*?" I finally ask.

She rolls her eyes hopelessly. "Still here," she says tersely.

Then, in a rush, what sounds like a confession, a shameful truth: "For the first month after the coup, I took tranquilizers every night. I had to. I couldn't accept that everything I worked for was gone. All the changes to our country. Down the drain."

Her pain cuts at me.

"But it's not all gone," I respond. "What you did made a difference. Don't you see it in the young people? Their resistance? Their freedom?"

"Yes, I know you're right. They're amazing. They're not afraid," she replies. "But it's not enough. The Tatmadaw will crush them. They've done it before."

Her resignation weighs heavily on me in the weeks to come. And when I think things cannot get any worse in Myanmar, the country plummets to the bottom of the abyss.

As the coup approaches its sixth month, a third wave of COVID-19, the delta variant, ravages India and then sweeps across much of South and Southeast Asia. Whatever protection the population of Southeast Asia enjoyed in the first and second waves has been mutated away.

And now Myanmar faces a perfect storm of COVID-19 and *coup d'état*.

Initially the Tatmadaw abandoned Aung San Suu Kyi's efforts to vaccinate the elderly. Then they arrested the officials who led the pandemic response. The Lady herself, in her early seventies, received her first shot right before the coup. It was a high-profile media event to encourage the population to get vaccinated. Only 3.5 million doses had been secured, far short of what would be needed for the whole population, but more were expected from the international community, especially via COVAX, the global partnership for vaccine distribution.

Soon after the coup, the Tatmadaw claimed these doses had been distributed, but they stood accused of hoarding for their own use. China then donated another half million doses, of which 200,000 were earmarked for the military. More worryingly, with the military junta failing to outline an equitable process for vaccine distribution, COVAX indefinitely postponed delivery of additional doses for Myanmar.[78]

And then within a few months, the situation on the ground spirals out of control.

By July 2021, Myanmar is a hellscape. As always, I see it first on Facebook. My former colleagues begin posting in Burmese, posts I cannot understand. Except they are interspersed with English phrases like "oxygen canister," "concentrator," and "blood oximeter."

I use digital translation to find a population frantically seeking oxygen to save their loved ones. Loved ones who are being turned away from Myanmar's health facilities. Loved ones who are lucky if they can breathe from a rented oxygen tank for an hour or so. Loved ones who are dying at home, in makeshift field hospitals, and in the streets in front of public hospitals, waiting for care.

I see photos of former colleagues shaving their heads in traditional Buddhist mourning for the loved ones they have lost.

"It's desperate. Thousands of doctors and health workers who joined the Civil Disobedience Movement are now volunteering," says Aung Soe Aye. As a physician and health specialist, he is my go-to source for information.

"They are offering telemedicine or trying to work through nongovernmental organizations," he explains.

"Sounds risky," I say.

"I hear that the Tatmadaw is even faking medical emergencies and then arresting resistance doctors when they respond," he says.

"Sadly, I believe that," I reply.

"Bodies are piling up everywhere," he continues. "Families are queuing at crematoriums and cemeteries. The morgues are full. Bodies are piled outside hospitals, lying outside in the heat."

---

[78] Richard C. Paddock, "Virus Surges in Myanmar, Where Generals Control Vaccines," *New York Times*, last modified August 1, 2021, https://www.nytimes.com/2021/07/01/world/asia/covid-myanmar-coup.html.

He concludes ruefully, "The Tatmadaw authorized construction of new crematoriums. Rather than addressing the disease, they are addressing the dead bodies! Can you believe that?"

"Yes, I can."

My former assistant, Mya Mya, posts pleading messages, and I call her on Zoom. She looks exhausted, her eyes puffy with dark circles underneath.

"Have you been vaccinated?" I ask.

"My mother had two shots because she is old. I had one shot, but my brother couldn't get it yet," she says.

"How are they doing?"

"My brother tested positive. He's very sick. His lungs," she replies. "I moved to a hotel with my mother to try to protect her, but she tested positive anyway."

"I'm so sorry, Mya Mya." That is all I can say.

"So far her symptoms are milder," she says.

"Thank god. That's the vaccine," I reply. "Who is caring for your brother?"

"I managed to hire a nurse—somebody from the Civil Disobedience Movement. But I spend most of my time online, looking for oxygen and medicine for him."

"Medicine?"

"Everything is scarce. And expensive. Not just oxygen canisters and concentrators. Even basic paracetamol is five times the normal price," she says.

"What can I do to help, Mya Mya?"

"Your call makes me happy," she says. "Otherwise there is nothing you can do. We are fighting on our own."

I send money to a fund organized by colleagues for World Bank consultants who lack the better salaries and health insurance offered to our local staff. It seems the only thing I can do.

I check back on Mya Mya several weeks later. She sends me a message:

"My mother recovered well. My brother got symptoms which turned out to be serious and needed an oxygen concentrator. With the help of friends, colleagues, and my sister, I got an oxygen concentrator, nurse, medication, home blood tests, and an online medical consultation. He finally is in stable condition, but his liver and lungs need follow-up consultations with specialists."

I shake my head in dismay. The specialists he needs are not in Myanmar.

"Due to the high prices and limited access to essential items for Covid, it cost me around 7,000 US dollars for my brother and mother. I am very happy that I could save my brother's life with my savings. Most of my friends lost their family members."

Tears well in my eyes, but I brush them away. By American standards, seven thousand dollars does not sound like much. But in Myanmar, this is an astounding sum to pay for basic healthcare. And it is most of Mya Mya's life savings—everything she was saving to buy a bigger apartment for herself and her mother.

But as she says, she is one of the lucky ones. Vaccinated. Without deaths in her immediate family.

Deaths from COVID-19 in Myanmar now exceed the horrific toll of Cyclone Nargis, the storm that pried open the doors to an isolated Myanmar back in 2008.

I decide to send more money but wonder if my small contribution makes any difference in the absence of sufficient vaccines, a functioning healthcare system, and high-tech emergency interventions.

I don't know, but I will continue to send cash. It might make the difference between who lives and who dies this month.

And that is all that matters now. Staying alive. Not upgrading the school curriculum. Not modernizing the banking system. Not empowering rural communities. Not any of the development projects we designed with peace and prosperity in mind. Just staying alive.

Surviving today means that tomorrow, or the day after tomorrow, or even next year, one more body will rejoin the fight. The fight for a health system that functions, for an economy that provides jobs, for a government that cares about its people, and for a society that values all its members. It is a future worth fighting for beyond today's despair and disillusionment.

Still, I worry how my colleagues will receive the money I send. It seems they must spend hours lined up outside banks in defiance of the military's stay-at-home orders, hoping to receive dribs of cash.

Aung Soe Aye reassures me on this, "What we're doing is paying an extra percentage to a middleman—six and a half percent of the amount we want to withdraw—to get the cash."

And I nod, remembering how black-market solutions spring up spontaneously to meet the most pressing demands in a failed state. Every time.

For a fee, anything can be arranged. Lives can be saved.

EPILOGUE

Whither Aung San Suu Kyi?

(August 2021 and Beyond)

Six months of military rule. Six months of civil disobedience. Six months of youthful resistance. Six months of indiscriminate arrests and extrajudicial killings. Six months of nighttime terror and isolation. Six months of economic collapse. Six months of ineffectual international response.

Hundreds of thousands of young adults going underground to support the resistance. Hundreds of thousands of innocent people forcibly displaced by the military. Thousands of activists, artists, and others still imprisoned. More than a thousand civilians murdered by the Tatmadaw.

And as the four-year anniversary of their exodus approaches, the return of the Rohingya refugees to Myanmar is as distant a dream as ever. Meeting international standards for safe, voluntary, and dignified return is outside the realm of possibility now. As is any improvement in the welfare and status of the Rohingya remaining in Myanmar. And the international community has largely moved on, preoccupied by the global pandemic and more recent demonstrations of their collective failure in Afghanistan.

Nearing the six-month anniversary of the coup, the Tatmadaw makes it official by voiding the 2020 election on grounds of rampant corruption, for which no evidence is presented. Aung San Suu Kyi's landslide victory is swept aside.[79]

Commander in Chief Min Aung Hlaing will serve as caretaker prime minister until at least 2023, it is announced. This seems straight from the Tatmadaw's earlier playbook. The 1990 election results were also voided in favor of a "temporary" military caretaker government. Temporary became twenty-five years, until the 2015 election that brought Aung San Suu Kyi into office, if not into power.

I think about her often from the comfort of my American life. She is imprisoned once again by the military. Her Faustian bargain with the Tatmadaw has been brought full circle. They brought her to power, and they took it away when their own power was threatened. *Why did we ever think it would be different?*

Now she stands accused of crimes by the military junta. Not only the absurd charge of illegal import of walkie-talkies, but also two instances of violating pandemic restrictions—imposed by her own civilian government—during last year's election campaign.

And then more serious but predictable charges used to stamp out political dissent. A sedition charge for "causing fear that disrupts public tranquility."[80] The military prosecutors cite as evidence her party's Facebook posts after the coup, calling the military junta illegitimate and their orders illegal. There is no way to win that argument.

She also stands accused of accepting bribes and violating the Official Secrets Act—the act that her government failed to amend and that led to the conviction of the Reuters journalists.

---

[79] Khine Lin Kyaw, "Myanmar Poll Results Annulled as Election Body Claims Fraud," Bloomberg News, July 26, 2021, https://www.bnnbloomberg.ca/myanmar-poll-results-annulled-as-election-body-claims-fraud-1.1633197.

[80] Grant Peck, "Suu Kyi's Lawyers Fight over Evidence in Myanmar Trial," Associated Press, July 6, 2021, https://apnews.com/article/myanmar-trials-government-and-politics-c98d240b904b3a615bb2c8adb75b9681.

All told, Aung San Suu Kyi faces a maximum of seventy-five years in prison if convicted of all charges against her.

Of course, seventy-five years will not be necessary. If she is convicted of any of these charges, she is banned from running for office. And that is probably all the Tatmadaw wants. They just need to retain enough power to preserve a Constitution that is statutorily tilted in their favor.

Once, watching the world news, I catch a glimpse of Aung San Suu Kyi in a brief court appearance from Nay Pyi Taw. Her earlier imprisonment seems almost cozy now: house arrest in Yangon on the shores of Inya Lake, in the comfortable home I spied through metal gates back in 2012.

Now it is 2021, and she is in the Tatmadaw's town, imprisoned somewhere in a capital built to serve the military's needs and feed their grandiose vision. She is locked away there, invisible to her people.

I wonder what she thinks about during her long hours alone, knowing she will never hold power again. Does she wonder if she did the right thing? Does she ask whether the many compromises with the military were worth it? Whether she did some good in advancing progress toward democracy? Does she count the many good things that happened under her watch and tell herself that they were enough? That she is enough? That she lived up to her father's legacy?

And what about me? Do I also count the good things and tell myself that they are enough? The children educated, the babies vaccinated, the villages electrified in Myanmar and everywhere else I lived and worked around the globe.

Is it enough to do some good somewhere? Is it the most we can expect from one human being? Is it enough to change the trajectory of some lives but leave others hopelessly unchanged? To leave some moral wrongs un-righted because our powers are just too weak?

Or is it devastatingly too little? Crushingly too little? Unforgivably too little?

The weight of it suffocates me.

I thought the Holocaust lessons of my childhood had prepared me. I thought I would be able to navigate the moral dilemmas I faced in Myanmar. I thought I would be certain. I thought it would be clear how to do right and do good.

Now I am not so certain. I want to do the right thing, but do I really know what it is? Should I take up arms like Myanmar's youth? Or feed displaced children? Or educate the youth for a better future? Or write articles today that bear witness to the struggle?

Will I know the right thing to do, not just for today but for tomorrow and this year and years to come? To battle injustice. To vanquish evil. To change the world.

I remember those who spoke to me with moral certainty while I was in Myanmar, telling me what the international community could have—should have—done differently. What I should have done differently. I envy their certainty. I do not share it.

Because change creeps forward. It is incremental and unpredictable and nonlinear. It is slow and generational. Until the moment it isn't. The moment the flame is lit, the wall falls, and the revolution is sparked.

Acknowledgments

The list of those who encouraged and supported me in writing this memoir is long, and I am grateful to all of you for your unique contributions to the story and the book.

Given the challenges I faced during my tenure in Myanmar, it may seem odd to begin by acknowledging my former employer, the World Bank. I owe a great deal to the institution, which for thirty-five years gave me the professional life of my choice: a life of purpose, social value, and, yes, the life of global adventure I dreamed of as a child. Like all such organizations, the institution has its flawed processes, internal politics, hidden agendas, bureaucratic inertia, and risk aversion. Nonetheless, after thirty-five years on the inside, I can attest that the World Bank has been among the most effective development institutions in the post-WWII period. If its leadership acts boldly, the World Bank can continue to play an important role in solving our planet's most pressing problems.

Within the World Bank, I must acknowledge my former colleagues in Myanmar, without whom this book could not exist. I am particularly grateful to Mya Mya, Kyi Sin, Shwe Kyar, and Aung Soe Aye (names changed), who figured most prominently and shared their stories most freely. A special thanks to Shwe Kyar and Levon, whose reactions as beta readers convinced me to publish for a wider audience.

I also wish to thank my political advisors in Yangon for helping demystify Myanmar's story of ethnic identity, citizenship, and nationhood, as well as the civilian-military balance of power. Despite their best efforts, they gave those of us who rotated in and out as diplomats and aid workers only a tip-of-the-iceberg understanding of this complex country. Any errors in this regard remain my own.

My fellow diplomats and heads of agencies also deserve thanks for candidly sharing their frustrations and fears as we weighed moral dilemmas and made difficult decisions in Myanmar. My appreciation to former US Ambassador to Myanmar Scot Marciel for encouraging and endorsing my efforts to tell this story.

I am fortunate that the talented Thant Myint-U, the most renowned Burmese author and historian, encouraged me to tell a story about Myanmar from my unique perspective. Dr. Mary Callahan also offered keen insights into the politics of foreign aid as well as strong support for my endeavor.

After decades of bureaucratic report writing, I was daunted by the prospect of writing a personal story. I am grateful to those who helped me complete my manuscript and prepare for publication, including Emily Gindlesparger, Hussein Al-Baiaty, AJ Hendrickson, Bianca Pahl, Katherine Shady, Ami Hendrickson, and Mikey Kershisnik. My appreciation also extends to the team at Ballast Books who brought this book into the world.

Beyond the official support team, I owe a debt of gratitude to my fellow memoirists, Melanie Thomas Armstrong and Susan Quinn, for their infectious enthusiasm for shared adventures and daily writing. My lifelong friend and fellow author Wendy Goldstein Rubinyi provided thoughtful advice and moral support at every stage.

This story is drawn from a much longer career and life overseas, a life made possible and enriched by my extraordinary family. My husband made career sacrifices to follow me around the globe. He has been my strongest supporter and emotional bedrock in grappling with difficult development issues and political circumstances worldwide. My daughters came along on a crazy ride for much of their childhoods and, to their credit, have not held it against me. They are my biggest cheerleaders, my greatest source of pride, and the reason I write.

Finally, let me acknowledge my late, loving parents, Bernard and Rosalie Goldstein. They told a shy, Jewish girl that she could be anything she wanted to be. More importantly, they modeled a moral code built on justice and integrity that served me well throughout my career, including wading into the moral complexities of Myanmar.

Printed in the USA
CPSIA information can be obtained
at www.ICGtesting.com
LVHW041332101123
763530LV00022B/32/J

9 781955 026970